Date: 11/8/11

949.2 STA
State, Paul F.,
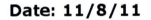
A brief history of the
Netherlands /

A BRIEF HISTORY
OF THE NETHERLANDS

PAUL F. STATE

Facts On File
An imprint of Infobase Publishing

A Brief History of the Netherlands

Facts On File, Inc.
An imprint of Infobase Publishing
132 West 31st Street
New York NY 10001

Library of Congress Cataloging-in-Publication Data

State, Paul F.
  A brief history of the Netherlands / Paul F. State
    p. cm. — (Brief history)
  Includes bibliographical references and index.
  ISBN-13: 978-0-8160-7107-4
  ISBN-10: 0-8160-7107-1
  1. Netherlands—History. I. Title.
  DJ109.S737 2008
  949.2.—dc22   2007014151

Text design by Joan M. McEvoy
Cover design by Semadar Megged/Jooyoung An
Maps by Jeremy Eagle and Dale Williams

Printed in the United States of America

MP Hermitage 10 9 8 7 6 5 4 3 2 1

This book is printed on acid-free paper.

This book is dedicated in fond remembrance to my uncle Ronald James Dehlinger (1932–2005), a visitor who loved the land and the people of the Netherlands.

CONTENTS

LIST OF ILLUSTRATIONS

LIST OF MAPS

LIST OF TABLES

ACKNOWLEDGMENTS

I would like to thank the individuals and the staff of the following institutions for their kind assistance: Esther de Graaf, the Rijksmuseum, Amsterdam; Ellen Jansen, the Van Gogh Museum, Amsterdam; Trudi Hulscher, the Netherlands Government Information Service; Jojan van Boven, the Netherlands Board of Tourism and Conventions; the National Library of the Netherlands; Drents Museum, Assen; Mike Le Tourneau and Yvette Reyes at AP Images; the International Institute of Social History; the Library of Congress; the New York State Archives; the Museum of the City of New York; and the New York Public Library.

I thank also my editor at Facts On File, Claudia Schaab, whose direction and wise suggestions merit much appreciation.

INTRODUCTION

The Kingdom of the Netherlands (in Dutch, Koninkrijk der Nederlanden) is a constitutional monarchy located in northwestern Europe. It comprises a total land area, including inland waters, of 41,526 square kilometers (16,033 sq. miles), and it borders Germany to the east, Belgium to the south, and the North Sea to the west and north. The names *Netherlands* and *Holland* are often used interchangeably to designate the country, even sometimes by the Dutch themselves, although, in fact, the latter identifies only North and South Holland, the two provinces that form the nucleus of the modern nation. The seacoast is longer than the land frontiers, and the country's location abutting the sea has profoundly shaped its historical development. One of the world's great maritime powers in the 17th century, the Netherlands is today a small country with few natural resources, but it remains an important commercial entrepôt and international crossroads, a status that has made the modern nation one of the world's wealthiest.

Geographically low-lying (*Nederland* means literally "low land") and densely populated, the Netherlands's central position between three of Europe's major nations—Germany, France, and Great Britain—has meant that much of its history is that of the history of western Europe in general. Drawn sometimes by design and sometimes by circumstances into the affairs of the wider world, the country has been shaped by, and at times been the shaper of, global political and economic events. The Dutch, few in number and living in a small territory, have played a relatively large part in the history of commerce, government, art, and religion, and they have left their imprint on all the world's continents.

The element that defines the country is, and always has been, water. The same element that carries the potential to destroy the land has been the source of its wealth and the means by which the nation has projected its presence across the globe. That presence survives today. Curaçao, Aruba, and several other small islands in the Caribbean Sea remain Dutch possessions, the remnants of a once vast empire.

The struggle of its people to keep the sea at bay, a constant since earliest times, is matched by a tenacious determination to remain independent from, while at the same time staying open to, foreign influences. That duality is equally evident in society. Idealism and pragmatism are

Provinces of the Netherlands

balanced equitably in the Netherlands—the preacher and the merchant having long held positions of respect—and both the practice of charity and the pursuit of profit remain defining characteristics of Dutch identity.

The Dutch have made their living through trade, which has earned for them a reputation as a remarkably tolerant people. An early haven for dissenters of all sorts, no other western European nation counts more diverse political, social, and spiritual movements today. And because commerce has been their economic cornerstone, the Dutch have nurtured liberty throughout their history. The first country in western Europe to develop genuine democratic institutions of government, the Netherlands is one of the world's preeminent places where freedoms have flourished.

The Land

The Netherlands is a flat country: About 27 percent of its territory lies below sea level and the average elevation for the entire nation is only 11 meters, or 37 feet, above sea level. The lowest portions are situated in the provinces of Zeeland, Flevoland, North Holland, and South Holland. The lowest point measures 6.7 meters (22 feet) below sea level and is found northeast of Rotterdam in the Prince Alexander Polder—*polder* refers to land reclaimed from the sea. The ground in these areas stretches away in an unbroken line to the far horizon, ideal terrain for the bicycle-loving Dutch. It is in places heavily urbanized and intensely cultivated.

Moorlands (*geest*) of sandy dunes and hills line the coast from Zeeland to the Frisian Islands, covered with various grasses, and, in some places, pinewoods. The calcic soil of the dunes is especially well suited for the growing of flowers, whose famous fields here yield a carpet of color in springtime. Peat is found in abundance, and, because the terrain in the western Netherlands serves as an ideal subsoil for pastureland, the meadows are mottled with grazing sheep, goats, and dairy cows.

The flat delta region, including the southwestern islands, contains soils of fertile river and sea clay. Farther inland, the great rivers—the Rhine, the Waal, and the Meuse—and their tributaries cross and crisscross the center of the country. They define the landscape here, although water is omnipresent throughout the country. Navigable rivers and canals totaling 4,830 kilometers (3,020 miles) traverse the Netherlands. The central waterways are contained by hundreds of miles of dikes separated by fertile strips of field and pasture (*uiterwaarden*) between them, which can easily flood in the spring should the rivers carry inordinate amounts of melted glacial water from central Europe. In December 1993 nearly 20 percent of the province of Limburg was flooded by the Meuse River, which overflowed its banks again in 1995. Every century since the Middle Ages has seen at least two major floods.

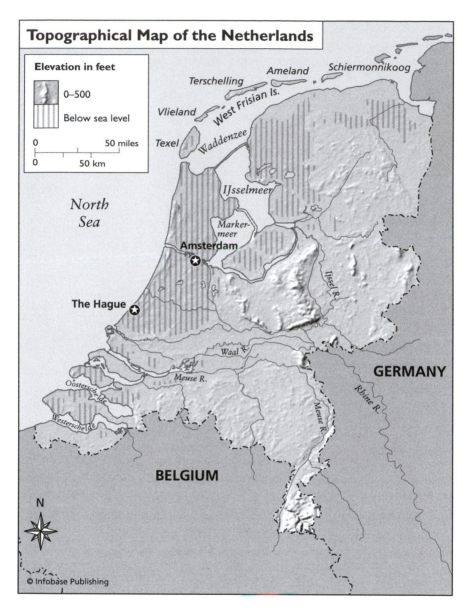

Across the countryside, water is pumped off the land and into drainage ditches and canals by means of windmills, which first appeared in the 13th century, and today by electric pumps. Only about 1,000 of the famous windmills that once dotted the checkerboard landscape survive as private homes and museums, and only a few are still in working order. In their stead, tall, slender-stalked modern turbines now march

Dutch poet Hendrik Marsman (1899–1940) penned the following lines in reminiscing about the country.

Memories of Holland

Thinking about Holland,
I see broad rivers
moving slowly through
endless lowlands,
rows of unthinkably
thin poplars
standing as high plumes
on the horizon;
and sunken within
wonderful space,
farm houses
scattered throughout the land,
clusters of trees, villages,
cropped towers,
churches and elms
in one great association.
the air hangs low
and the sun is slowly
muffled in a gray
mottled fog,
and in all the many provinces
the voice of the water
with its eternal calamities
is feared and heard.

Marsman, Hendrik. "Herinnering aan Holland." In *Verzamelde Gedichten*, 1941. "Memories of Holland." Translated by Cliff Cargo, 2000–02. Available online. URL: http://www.cs-music.com/features/r2c-index. html. Accessed March 19, 2007.

sentinel-like across the land in harnessing the never-ceasing North Sea winds to produce the energy to drive electric power plants. Despite the use of state-of-the-art pumping and drainage technology, the process of reclaiming land remains essentially the same as it was in the 1300s. Once water is pumped off and dikes and drainage canals are built, the land that emerges is largely swamp. Shallow runoff ditches are dug and, to further dry the land as well as to draw the salt out of the soil, the ground is seeded with grass. The entire process takes about five years.

Flood control and land reclamation have been ongoing through history, making the Dutch among the world's leading experts in hydraulic engineering. Dunes and dikes have risen higher and higher. Barrier mounds and walls of sand have given way to stone and then concrete. Early reclamation of small plots of former seabed has progressed over the centuries, culminating in the creation after 1945 of four large polders comprising the entirely new province of Flevoland, the largest manmade island in the world. Altogether more than 3,000 polders exist in the Netherlands.

The land in the east and south is older and rises slightly the farther inland one moves. The Veluwe in the province of Gelderland consist of groups of hills formed in the last Ice Age. Sandy plains, moors, and woods are found here. Woods cover only about 8 percent of the total land of the Netherlands, one of Europe's least forested countries. Flat lands with clay soils that have accumulated over many centuries predominate in the provinces of Drenthe, Groningen, and Friesland. Tidal mud flats (*wadden*) along the Wadden Sea constitute a unique wetlands environment.

The oldest and highest parts of the country are found in the extreme southeast in the province of Limburg, a region made up of marl and limestone. Low ridges and rolling hills rise gradually to form the "Dutch Alps," which attain their maximum "peak" at the Vaalserberg (1,053 feet [321 m] above sea level).

The People

The Netherlands's population of 16,357,000 (est. 2007) reflects rapid growth over the preceding century, the numbers having stood at only 5,104,000 in 1900. At 1,023 inhabitants per square mile (482 per sq. km), the country has one of the highest population densities in the world (the United States has approximately 84 persons per square mile [2006]). The Dutch are ethnically homogeneous. The descendants of Germanic tribes that infiltrated the area beginning centuries before the Christian era, they speak Dutch, a Germanic tongue. Frisian is spoken in the northern province of Friesland and is a co-official language in that province. Several dialects of Low German are spoken in northern areas and Limburgisch, recognized as a minority language in 1997, is spoken in Limburg.

Although the vast majority of the population remains ethnically Dutch (approximately 80.8 percent), the country has seen an influx of newcomers since 1950, including 300,000 who repatriated or emigrated from the Dutch East Indies following the independence of Indonesia in 1949 and 130,000 who arrived from Suriname after the former Dutch Guiana gained sovereign status in 1975. Economic growth and the need for unskilled labor in the 1960s and 1970s saw Italians, Spaniards, Turks, Moroccans, and others arrive, and many have stayed. Recent immigrants have been drawn by the liberal social benefits the country offers residents. Given the Netherlands's compact size and growing ethnic diversity, Dutch demographers have taken to calling their country the "European Manhattan." The newcomers have made exotic contributions to the Dutch culinary scene. The traditional cuisine—herring, cabbage, bread, cheese, endive, vegetables, and the omnipresent potato—has been supplemented especially by fare from the former colonies. Indonesian rijsttafel (rice table) has become a national staple.

The nation's two major religions—Roman Catholic and Protestant (largely Dutch Reformed)—are professed by 30 percent and 20 percent of inhabitants, respectively, although church attendance figures are much lower. Reflecting the outcome of the struggle for independence in the 16th and 17th centuries, the great rivers have served historically as a religious and cultural dividing line, with Protestants predominant to the north and Catholics to the south. Growth in the number of people who acknowledge no religious affiliation has been ongoing throughout the last century, and it is expected that 73 percent of the population will be nonreligious by 2020. The influx of refugees and new residents is altering the religious makeup of the country, which now counts 200,000 Hindus and 920,000 Muslims. Seven percent of the populace is expected to be Muslim by 2020.

In this heavily urbanized country, 60 percent of the Dutch live in the urban agglomeration in the western provinces designated the Randstad (*rand* = edge; *stad* = city), a horseshoe-shaped area that takes in the cities of Rotterdam, Dordrecht, Delft, The Hague, Leiden, Haarlem, Amsterdam, and Utrecht. A term coined by Dutch aviation pioneer Albert Plesman (1889–1953) in the 1930s, the Randstad is the country's core area of political and economic activity. The center of the horseshoe, which is shrinking steadily, is less urbanized and is known as the "green heart" (*groen hart*). The northeastern provinces of Drenthe and Groningen are the least populous.

The Netherlands is a small place packed with a lot of people. Space is at a premium and the Dutch use it thriftily. The land is intensely cultivated. Modern high-rise apartment dwellings abound. Older, gabled houses in city centers sit smack one against another and, because they are tall and narrow, the stairs inside can rise in alpinelike gradients.

Society is egalitarian and the Dutch are characterized as independent, industrious, and stolid, given to small gestures and simple, unostentatious display. They became Europe's preeminent traders in the 17th century, a status that earned for them a reputation for being shrewd in business. They have traditionally maintained close family ties, and, in their personal lives, the Dutch cherish *gezelligheid,* an enigmatic term often heard that connotes coziness, comfortableness, friendliness, and a welcoming openness.

Tightly knit social networks based on religion or class long characterized the Dutch, although the confessional character of society has now largely disappeared. They emerged in the late 20th century as world trendsetters in movements for social liberalization.

The Government

The Netherlands is a parliamentary democracy with a constitutional monarch (at present, Queen Beatrix) as head of state. Parliament is known collectively as the States General (Staten Generaal) and consists of a lower house, or Second Chamber, of 150 members directly elected

Queen Beatrix of the Netherlands (AP Images)

every four years, and an upper House, or First Chamber, of 75 members, one-third of whom are indirectly elected by the provincial councils every two years. The First Chamber can only ratify or reject laws passed by the Second Chamber; it cannot propose or amend bills.

Under the proportional electoral system, each political party is assigned seats based on the number of votes that the party's candidates receive in elections. Candidates are drawn from party lists so that voters focus their choices on parties rather than on individual members. Citizens over 18 are eligible to vote and voting is voluntary. Participation rates have averaged more than 80 percent.

Political parties proliferate in the Netherlands and coalition governments have been the norm since the 19th century. Following elections to the Second Chamber or if the government should fall, the monarch appoints a *formateur*, who is directed to assemble from among the elected parties a governing cabinet. The government (cabinet of ministers) is headed by a minister-president, or prime minister. Governments are not long-lived; only five cabinets having served the full four years since World War II. The sovereign, the government, and the Second Chamber each have the right to introduce legislation, and all bills approved by the States General must be signed by the monarch.

The two chambers of parliament together with three other advisory bodies constitute the high colleges of state (Hoge Colleges van Staat), all of which are explicitly recognized by the constitution as independent institutions. The Council of State (Raad van Staat) is composed of legal specialists, former government ministers, members of parliament, judges, and other experts chosen by the monarch and chaired *ex officio* by the queen. The council advises on constitutional and judicial aspects of proposed legislation. All cabinet bills must be sent to the council, whose opinion, while not binding, often engenders significant parliamentary debate. The council also acts as the country's high court of administrative law. The General Chamber of Auditors (Algemene Rekenkamer), whose members are appointed by the cabinet, audits the national government's accounts, and the National Ombudsman (Nationale Ombudsman), also appointed by the cabinet, hears citizens' complaints of improper government conduct.

The country is divided into 12 provinces (*provincies*), each with its own government: provincial legislatures (Provinciale Staten), directly elected every four years; an executive council (Gedeputeerde Staten), whose members are elected by the legislature; and a queen's (or king's) commissioner (Commissaris), who is appointed by the monarch and the government and who serves as president of both the provincial

The Twelve Provinces of the Netherlands				
Name	Population (2004)	Area (sq. km)	Area (sq. mi)	Capital
Drenthe	482,300	2,655	1,025	Assen
Flevoland	356,400	1,412	545	Lelystad
Friesland	642,500	3,359	1,297	Leeuwarden
Gelderland	1,967,600	5,015	1,936	Arnhem
Groningen	575,900	2,346	906	Groningen
Limburg	1,143,000	2,169	838	Maastricht
North Brabant	2,406,900	4,943	1,908	s'Hertogenbosch
North Holland	2,583,900	2,663	1,028	Haarlem
Overijssel	1,105,800	3,340	1,289	Zwolle
South Holland	3,453,000	2,877	1,111	The Hague
Utrecht	1,159,200	1,363	526	Utrecht
Zeeland	378,300	1,793	692	Middelburg

legislature and the executive council. Provincial government presides over regional matters.

The 12 provinces are further divided into 647 municipalities (*gemeenten*), administered by local councils elected by popular vote every four years. Unlike in other levels of government, non-Dutch citizens who are resident in the country for at least five years are eligible to vote in municipal elections. Local government matters are overseen by an executive board appointed by the local council. Both the council and the board are headed by a mayor (*burgemeester*), who is appointed by the crown. The central government has devolved greater powers to provincial and local authorities in recent years. In addition to elections at the national, provincial, and local levels, voters choose representatives for the European Parliament, for neighborhood councils in larger cities such as Amsterdam, and for the country's 27 water boards. Referenda are also held occasionally.

The judicial system consists of a blend of Roman and Napoléonic law. All cases are heard by independent judges, who are irremovable except for malfeasance or incapacity. There is no trial by jury, and the state rather than the individual acts as the initiator of legal proceedings. Courts include 62 cantonal courts, which hear petty criminal and civil claims; 19 district courts, which handle criminal and civil cases not adjudicated by the cantonal courts; and five courts of appeal. The Supreme Court (Hoge Raad) reviews judgments of lower courts and ensures consistent application of the laws, but it cannot declare them unconstitutional. The death penalty was abolished for most crimes in 1870 and for all crimes in 1982.

The Economy

The geography of the Netherlands has been the means to its fortune. The country's location where western Europe's great rivers meet the sea gave rise to trade in goods that grew from local to international significance, which made the Netherlands a major world power by the 17th century, and the economy today remains to a large degree based on the import-export trade and services that derive from its status as a transportation hub. In the open, prosperous economy that depends heavily on foreign trade, exports account for some 51 percent of gross national product (GNP).

The economy is marked by stable industrial relations and moderate growth and unemployment. Industrial activity centers on electrical machinery, food processing and distribution, and petroleum refining—Royal Dutch Shell/Shell Group is the world's biggest publicly held company and its refinery in the Rotterdam suburb of Pernis is the largest in Europe. Banks, warehousing firms, trading companies, and ship brokerages play prominent roles. The port of Rotterdam is the world's largest in total cargo handled and, together with Amsterdam, processes more than a third of European Union (EU) seaborne imports. Schiphol airport is a major European hub, the fourth in Europe in passenger traffic (44.2 million passengers in 2005).

Dutch investment holdings span the globe—the Netherlands is the third-largest foreign investor in both the United States and Canada. The world buys Dutch food, home, and personal-care products (Unilever), drinks Dutch beer (Heineken, Amstel), uses Dutch-produced electronic goods ranging from compact disc players to light bulbs (Philips), and shops at Dutch-owned supermarkets (Albert Heijn).

Agricultural products account for 20 percent of exports. The bright, green pasturelands dotted with fat black-and-white Holstein cows paint the picturesque portrait of a farming sector that operates in a fully mechanized, highly efficient manner, employing no more than 4 percent of the labor force. Original to the Netherlands, the Holstein breed of cattle produces among the highest yields in milk of any in the world. The world's largest seller of powdered milk, butter, and cheese (half the country's production of milk is turned into cheese), the Dutch rank third worldwide in the value of agricultural exports. The towns of Edam and Gouda along with the province of Limburg have won world fame in giving their names to the cheeses produced there. The country exports more beer than any other. Heineken is the nation's largest brewery and the second largest in the world. The Dutch grow about 65 percent of the world's flower bulbs and lead the world in exporting tulips, daffodils, irises, and hyacinths. The Netherlands is a major EU supplier of vegetables, including exporting a quarter of the world's tomatoes and a third of its cucumbers. Flowers, fruits, and vegetables grow year round in thousands of greenhouses whose glass walls glitter across the province of South Holland from Rotterdam to the Hook of Holland.

Apart from natural gas, which is found in Groningen and off the northeast coast in some of the world's largest fields, the Netherlands has few natural resources, most notably clay and salt. The coalfields of Limburg, once of some importance in supplying domestic needs, are now depleted.

1

FROM EARLY SETTLEMENTS TO FRANKISH RULE (PREHISTORY-C. 1000)

If places are defined in terms of their geography, then no place on earth is more readily identifiable than the Netherlands. The very name denotes its physical character. Since earliest times seas and rivers have set the parameters of life here. The existence of the land itself has been determined by the whims of the water and not until those who dwelled here acquired sufficient technical skill to match and, in time, master its power could a foundation be made on which to build, first, subsistence settlements and, later, organized communities. "If God made the world, the Dutch made Holland," is the oft-heard phrase popularly attributed to French mathematician and philosopher René Descartes (1596–1650), who lived for a time in the Netherlands. Whether or not he actually coined the comment, it contains more than a grain of truth.

The Land Forms

The formation of the Netherlands took place over a relatively short period of time, spanning the youngest geological period, the Quaternary, which began about 2.5 million years ago. From then until the end of the last Ice Age about 10,000 years ago, the place that is the Netherlands today existed as part of a vast, dry tundra pasture reaching far into the present-day North Sea. It formed a boundary region between the sea and higher land. In the northeast Netherlands an inland glacier projected down from Scandinavia and the gravel was partly overlaid with a clay and sand accumulation. The land here and in the south—called the *geest*—is older and higher than in the extreme west.

Over time (after 10,000 B.C.E.) the weather grew gradually warmer. Sometime between 5500 and 3000 B.C.E. the seas pierced the land bridge between Britain and the continent of Europe, creating a spillway—the Straits of Dover—and the resulting constriction led to a buildup, where the Netherlands exists today, of dry areas of marine deposits and sand. Sandbars slowly emerged, which created shallow lagoons. Within the lagoons, clay settled and formed solid ground. When the clays dried out, the sand, aided by the action of wind and tides, began to form into dunes. Stretches of dunes held together by tough grasses and salt-tolerant plants appeared in a long line running roughly parallel to today's coastline from Alkmaar to The Hague. The sand dried out behind those Old Dunes, and deposits of peat built up, facilitating the growth of trees and reed beds in a swampy terrain interspersed by lakes. Coves, bays, and fens were formed.

The warming of the climate following the melting of the great ice sheets permitted the major rivers to meander where they would, and the river flows cut deep channels in their drainage basins. The channels gradually silted up, cleared, and silted again. Drift sand deposits along the river channels in time became covered with clay and peat, allowing vegetation to grow. The fast-flowing rivers, together with the action of the tides, tore large gaps in the coastal, protective dune belt, exposing the low-lying marshland to flooding from both rivers and sea. The funnel-shaped estuaries fanned out and islands emerged between the Rhine and Scheldt rivers.

The area of Holland emerged as Europe's lowest. Between the islands of sand along the seacoast and the firm ground inland at least two-thirds of Holland's land lay below sea level, made up mostly of mud flats and shallows, salt marshes, brackish lakes, and flood banks, but also with patches of woodland (Holland or *Holt-land* means "Woodland").

The geology of the Netherlands has been one of continuous topographical change. Coastal dunes alter their formations constantly. The Rhine Delta was the most recent and the most changeable of Europe's landmasses. Formed since the last Ice Age ended, it has been shaped by the competing forces of three north-flowing rivers—the Rhine, the Meuse, and the Scheldt—and of the westerly winds and tides of the sea. The Rhine carries, at an average level, about 84,744 cubic feet (2,400 cu. m) of water per second and five times these amounts at high water, which has made it a formidable terrain-altering force. The interlacing web of streams and rivulets in the central riverine areas have formed and re-formed. The estuaries of the Rhine and Meuse have shifted southward over time, reflecting northeastern tidal flows. And so the estuary of the Rhine that lay near Leiden in Roman times has long silted up.

The Earliest Inhabitants

No one knows exactly when the first inhabitants trudged into the territory of what is today the Netherlands, but flint artifacts found in quarries show that the country was already occupied before the advance of glacial ice in the middle Pleistocene epoch, about 150,000 years ago. Groups of hunter-gatherers remained the sole occupants until the last Ice Age froze the flatland and forced humans to flee.

They began to drift back as the climate grew warmer and sea levels fell. Herders arrived seeking places to graze their reindeer and nomadic hunters and fishermen penetrated the region. Wooden canoes have been unearthed that date to around 6500 B.C.E. They were followed by the first farmers, who arrived in southern areas of the present-day Netherlands and on the gentle hills in the vicinity of present-day Utrecht in the early Neolithic period (c. 5300 B.C.E.) to establish small sites on the sandy ground on which to construct farmsteads to grow wheat and domesticate cattle. The Funnel Beaker Folk settled the sandy plateau of the province of Drenthe around 3400 B.C.E. They left behind dolmens (*hunebedden*), megalithic tombs of standing stones capped by giant lids, of which some 54 survive. The sparse, bleached soil in the east offered limited prospects for farming but the higher elevation made it safer to live here than in areas farther west. Barley, millet, and linseed were grown, and sheep and cattle, much smaller than today's animals, grazed on heath and moor.

The forests that covered the riverine areas began to be cleared. The first fellings were made possible by simple stone-bladed axes hafted in a wooden handle, which were used to build houses, wagons, dugout canoes, and pathways through the bogs. Flint was mined in Limburg in the Neolithic period (c. 4400 B.C.E.) and used to fashion axes, knives, arrow points, and scraping implements. Over time, hunter-gatherers would borrow equipment from the farmers, including axes, pottery, and primitive hand-operated grain mills, to supplement their subsistence living with crop cultivation and stockkeeping. In the Middle Bronze Age (c. 3500 B.C.E.) farmers began to enrich the soil with manure. Settlements began to appear made up of two or three farmyards with a longhouse dwelling at the center surrounded by several granaries and perhaps a water well and a shed or barn, where cattle would be stalled. The wooden shoes (*klompen*) so identified with the Netherlands date from the first farmers who clomped through the sodden soil.

Colonization of western sections of the province of North Holland (West Frisia) commenced in the Middle Bronze Age and the northern marshes and tidal flats in North and South Holland in the Iron Age

(c. 8th–6th centuries B.C.E.). Travel here was usually by boat, except in the winter when the shallow waters froze to create roads on the ice. Starting in the sixth and fifth centuries B.C.E. in areas of Friesland and Groningen exposed to periodic flooding, the inhabitants constructed artificial mounds called *terpen* out of sod and turf dug from the surrounding ground, which they combined with refuse produced by humans and animals, especially manure. The arable land lay on or around the mounds. These raised dwelling sites continued to be built until the end of the Middle Ages, at around the 11th century, when construction of dikes began in earnest. The *terpen* provide the first visible proofs of the inhabitants' determination to confront the elements and shape the circumstances and conditions of their existence.

The first Teutons and Celts appeared about 800 B.C.E. Celts were living in the vicinity of Maastricht around 500 B.C.E. A branch of the Teutons, the Frisians, moved into the Netherlands about 300 B.C.E., probably from the area of present-day Schleswig-Holstein in Germany. They were cattle breeders who established settlements on the rich clays of the northern seacoast.

Agricultural homesteads remained open and exposed in the Late Bronze Age and Early Iron Age but after about 500 B.C.E. fortified sites began to appear in the hillier regions around the lower Rhine basin. Some of these were probably only temporary refuges, but others devel-

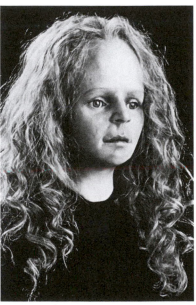

Found in a bog near the village of Yde in 1897, the "Yde girl" died between 54 B.C.E. and 128 C.E. at about 16 years of age. The reconstruction is based on anatomical features of the girl's skull and on remains of her hair. (Drents Museum, Assen)

oped into politically and economically important centers. Consisting of clusters of huts surrounded by stone defenses or timber-framed stone and earthenworks, they served as focal points of the tribal groupings that gradually evolved. Warriors defending these places would be the first of the area's inhabitants to meet the first recorded invaders when the Romans arrived.

A Roman Frontier Outpost

Julius Caesar's account of his conquest of the Gauls provides the earliest historical record of the Netherlands. "The Belgae are the bravest of them all," he writes at the beginning of his *Commentaries on the Gallic Wars* in referring to the Belgic Gauls, Celtic peoples whose territory extended from northeastern France into Belgium and parts of the southern Netherlands. They were gradually pushed south into southern Belgium by Roman armies that laid waste their territories and by Germanic tribes allied to Rome, who were encouraged to settle Roman borderlands.

Caesar moved progressively northward until, by 60 B.C.E., Roman legions stood on the banks of the "Old Rhine," which then flowed north of its present course. In the late first century B.C.E. the Roman commander Drusus (38–9 B.C.E.) built a dam and a ditch (*Fossa Drusiana*) near present-day Herwen to connect the Rhine with the IJssel River. The ditch is today a big stream. The Romans fixed the Rhine as the boundary of Gaul, and they permitted several Germanic tribes from north and east of the river to settle the delta area. They included the Batavi, a Frankish tribe that arrived from central Germany in the first century C.E. to settle the dry lands between the Rhine and Waal rivers. The Batavi were not incorporated into the empire as were Celtic tribes to the south. Considered *socii* (allies), they paid no taxes but were compelled to contribute troops to the Roman legions. Roman historian Tacitus called them the bravest of the Germans, and the Batavian cavalry became famous throughout the empire.

Flush with wealth and power, the newly proclaimed Roman Empire sought to extend its might in launching invasions of Germanic lands through the course of the first century C.E. First in the line of march were the Frisians. Capitulating almost at once, in 12 B.C.E., they allied themselves to Rome; over the succeeding years, Frisia became a conduit through which Roman armies trudged back and forth to and from Germany in a cycle of invasions and withdrawals, the Romans always falling back to the series of riverside forts they built that defined the Rhine defenses.

PLINY THE ELDER VISITS THE NETHERLANDS

The Roman author and natural philosopher Pliny the Elder (23–79 C.E.) participated in a campaign against the Frisians in 47 C.E. He visited the northern coast of the Netherlands and recorded his impressions:

> There the ocean pours in its flood twice every day, and produces a perpetual uncertainty whether the country may be considered as a part of the continent or of the sea. The wretched inhabitants take refuge on the sand-hills, or in little huts, which they construct on the summits of lofty stakes, whose elevation is conformable to that of the highest tides. When the sea rises, they appear like navigators; when it retires, they seem as though they had been shipwrecked. They subsist on the fish left by the refluent waters, and which they catch in nets formed of reeds or seaweed. Neither tree nor shrub is visible on these shores.

Source: Thomas Colley Grattan, *Holland: The History of the Netherlands* (New York: Peter Fenelon Collier, 1898), p. 18.

Behind the military frontiers, adoption of Roman styles of life proceeded gradually. Towns developed to serve the great fortified camps, such as Nijmegen, and some emerged at crossroads where trade routes intersected, such as Heerlen in present-day Limburg. During the reign of Augustus Caesar (r. 27 B.C.E.–14 C.E.), the Romans built a bridge at a shallow spot on the Meuse River where Celts had already established a settlement. They named it Mosae Trajectum (Meuse crossing), the origin of the city of Maastricht. The distinctive Roman villas with their red-tiled roofs appeared, and the Romans introduced poultry culture. Dates, fish sauce, olive oil, and wine from Mediterranean climes arrived over Roman-built roads. The old druid-based religions of the Celtic inhabitants did not so much disappear as continue to exist side by side with the official and unofficial cults of Rome.

Roman influence beyond the lower Rhine spread in degrees that steadily diminished the greater the distance from the frontier. The Frisians, though not ruled or taxed by Rome, were required to pay tribute, set at a certain number of cowhides. If payments faltered, the Romans would launch raids, seizing cattle, land, and women and

Otto van Veen, Batavians Defeating the Romans on the Rhine *(1613). Oil on panel, 38 × 52 cm.* (Collection Rijksmuseum Amsterdam)

children, and the Frisians would strike back. Only 40 years after first coming under Roman domination, the Frisians revolted, in 28 C.E., not meeting defeat until 47 C.E.

Within the first century of Roman rule, troubles with the native peoples remained endemic. The unstable conditions engendered by the struggles over the imperial throne following the murder of the emperor Nero (68 C.E.) led to a testing of Roman power in the region. In 68 the Batavi rallied under the leadership of their prince Gaius Julius Civilis to resist Roman spoliation of their lands. Joined by Batavian deserters from Roman armies and allied with tribes both Germanic and Celtic, the one-eyed Civilis, who wore his hair long and dyed it red, waged a successful guerrilla war. Part of the Rhine was diverted to flood the country—a military tactic to be repeated over the centuries—and Roman forts, including Traiectum (modern Utrecht), were attacked. Sometime after 70 (the Roman chronicler is uncertain of the date), the Batavi made peace—the fate of Civilis is unknown—and they returned to their status as a client state subject to military levies but not taxation.

THE BATAVI

The Batavi remained allies of Rome until the Silian Franks over-ran their lands at the end of the third century. They disappeared from history's annals at that time, but they remained very much alive in popular imagination. They are viewed by the Dutch as their founding forefathers and the name survived as *Batavia* (Latin for Holland). In the 17th century, the capital of the Dutch East Indies was named Batavia, and the Dutch East India Company gave the name Batavia to a famous ship that was wrecked after a mutiny on its maiden voyage in 1628–29. Batavia was used as a poetic name for Holland in the 18th century and the "Batavian Republic" designated the French-backed regime at that century's end. Dutch settlers in the United States named cities and towns Batavia in New York, Illinois, Iowa, Ohio, and Wisconsin. The Dutch today cycle on Batavus brand bicycles. Cafés, apartment complexes, sports competitions, and retail outlets bear the name.

In 69, the Frisians broke free from Rome's grip, and they remained independent for the duration of the empire. From their location just north of the border, they remained an important contact people between Romans and Germans, and they became major traders, carrying on commerce throughout northern Gaul, selling their own produce as well as goods ranging from Scandinavian amber, English wool, lead, and tin, and Rhineland wine. Both the Frisians and the Batavians practiced animal husbandry, breeding their existing stocks of dairy cattle. Black cows and white cows were carefully culled to obtain animals that made the most efficient use possible of relatively small areas of rich grasslands, and the breed that, in time, evolved—the black-and-white Holsteins—became, and remain, ubiquitous in the country.

Around 80 C.E. the military zone on the Rhine was converted into the province of Lower Germany (Germania Inferior). Relations between Roman and Celt became more settled. *Civitates*—Roman towns whose inhabitants remained citizens of their tribes—flourished, notably Noviomagus (Nijmegen), the new chief town of the Batavi that replaced the old settlement destroyed by order of the Romans following the revolt under Civilis. Area tribesmen served in imperial armies across the empire. A Batavi even gained the title *caesar* in 258 when the general M. Cassianus Latinius Postumus, legate of Lower Germany, proclaimed himself ruler of a "Gallic Empire," which comprised one-half of the western Roman Empire that he shared with the emperor Gallienus. Postumus owed his success to beating back pillagers from tribes who emerged from the dense forests east of the Rhine in present-day Germany to periodically plague the province. By the fourth century, these peripatetic marauders had become a constant menace.

Germanic Tribes and Christianity Arrive

The influx of Germanic tribes from over the Rhine at first proved manageable. Treaties granted them lands between the Meuse and the Scheldt in return for military service, and soldiers and settlers gradually integrated into society. By the fourth century, they existed in great numbers in Germania Secunda, the lower Rhine province remodeled under the reforms of Emperor Diocletian (c. 245–312), and soon what had been a slow, steady trickle turned into a flood. In the winter of 406 Vandals, Swabians, Burgundians, and Alamans crossed over the frozen Rhine at Mainz. The military frontier collapsed and with it the provincial government, many of whose elites, including Romano-Gaullish landowners, lived as absentee lords in Italy, far from the troublesome borders.

By the middle of the fifth century, the Franks, a confederation of west Germanic tribes, held predominant power in the Roman lowlands, their leader Childeric I (c. 436–81) securing imperial recognition as head of the provincial government. The Frisians remained firmly ensconced in the swamps and on the *terpen* along the northern coast and even moved into parts of the Rhine delta region yielded to them in wars with the Franks. Saxons dominated the northern inland areas. Settlement patterns recognizable today began to take shape. In inland areas, farms were often concentrated around a central clearing (*brink*) in swamps and woodland, and clusters of dwellings would emerge gradually. In places the number of inhabitants would steadily increase, and villages, strung out in long, straggling lines along sandy ridges, would grow, in time, into towns.

Christianity first arrived during the fourth century, brought to the area around Maastricht by Saint Servatius (died c. 384), a bishop at Tongeren in present-day Belgium who proselytized in areas to the east. He built a church on the site of a Roman temple (present-day Church of Our Lady) in Maastricht, and a wooden chapel built on the site of his tomb in that city became the foundation edifice for the current Basilica of Saint Servatius. Christianity, however, did not begin to take hold until sometime after 496, when Childeric's son Clovis (c. 466–511), who unified the Franks and founded the Merovingian

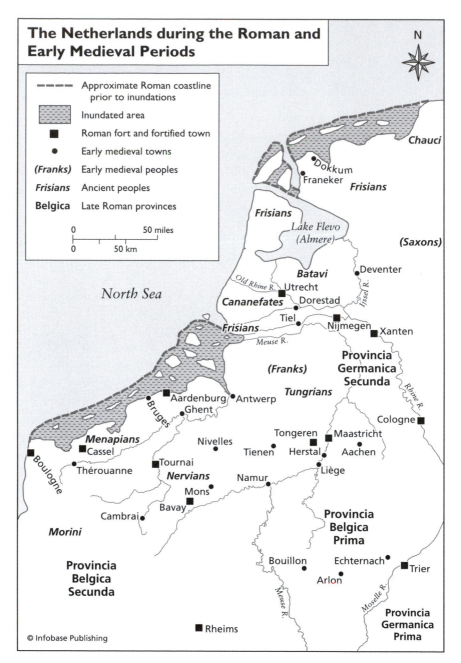

The Netherlands during the Roman and Early Medieval Periods

N

Legend:
- – – – – Approximate Roman coastline prior to inundations
- Inundated area
- ■ Roman fort and fortified town
- • Early medieval towns
- *(Franks)* Early medieval peoples
- *Frisians* Ancient peoples
- **Belgica** Late Roman provinces

0   50 miles
0   50 km

Chauci

Dokkum
Franeker
Frisians

Frisians

Lake Flevo (Almere)

(Saxons)

Deventer

Batavi

Old Rhine R. Utrecht
Cananefates Dorestad

Ijssel R.

North Sea

Tiel
Nijmegen
Xanten
Frisians
Meuse R.

Provincia Germanica Secunda

Rhine R.

(Franks)

Tungrians

Aardenburg • Antwerp
Ghent
Bruges

Cologne ■

Tongeren ■ Maastricht
Nivelles
Menapians   Tienen   Herstal   Aachen
■ Cassel
Boulogne
Thérouanne   Tournai
Nervians   Namur   Liège
Mons
Bavay
Cambrai
Morini

Provincia Belgica Prima

Bouillon   Echternach
Arlon
■ Trier

Provincia Belgica Secunda

Meuse R.
Moselle R.

© Infobase Publishing

■ Rheims

Provincia Germanica Prima

dynasty (481–751), was baptized by Remigius, the bishop of Reims. Royal house retainers and the nobility followed suit and, in so doing, promoted the fusion of the remaining Romano-Gaullish aristocracy

10

with their Frankish counterparts. However, most of the population clung to the old faiths.

Systematic efforts at conversion began around 500 under the sponsorship of the Frankish kings, who by then ruled the Netherlands as the subkingdom of Austrasia following a complex series of divisions of Frankish lands after the death of Clovis's grandson Chlotar in 561. Irish monasteries, founded among the Franks most famously by Saint Columbanus (c. 543–615), who left Ireland in c. 590, soon became mission stations and training centers for preachers. The latter, in turn, established their own monasteries. Endowed by wealthy nobles, many of these communities came to own substantial lands, and they would assume an important role in the economic, social, and intellectual life of the surrounding territories.

Itinerant preachers met stubborn resistance from the Frisians, who rejected Christianity as the religion of Frankish royalty. By the late seventh and early eighth centuries, the "kingdom" of Frisia—records refer to Frisian leaders as "kings," "counts," or "dukes"—was centered at Utrecht, where the rulers resided, having moved here from farther north, perhaps in the wake of extensive flooding or to be nearer to profitable river trade. Relatively coherent and prosperous among the welter of Germanic peoples scattered across northwestern Europe, the Frisians in the seventh century controlled an area stretching from northern Jutland in Denmark to Flanders. They dominated seagoing commerce in the region, trading in Frisian cloth, fish, and Baltic timber using a silver currency ("sceats") at a time when bartering constituted the dominant method of exchange.

Missionaries came to Frisia not from the Christianized south but from Northumbria in Britain, where the Anglo-Saxons had been converted two generations before. Saint Wilfrid of Hexham landed in 678 and began evangelization work that was largely completed in the regions around the Rhine under Saint Willibrord, who arrived in 690. Willibrord's successor Winfrid (c. 672–754), who was given the name Saint Bonifacius (Boniface) by the pope and ordained by him as a bishop, continued the work from Willibrord's base of operations at Utrecht, which would become Christianity's power center in the Netherlands. He met his death at Dokkum on June 5, 754, martyred while bringing the new faith to northern Frisia.

Conversion was largely complete by the late eighth century. Having been won over, the Frisians now proved to be as fervent proponents as they once were opponents of Christianity. Saint Ludger (Liudger, c. 744–809), who was born at Zuilen near Utrecht and trained at

11

SAINT WILLIBRORD

Styled the "Apostle of the Frisians," Willibrord (c. 658–739) was born in Northumbria in Britain. He studied at Ripon as a pupil of Wilfred of York (c. 633–709) and entered the Benedictine order. Commissioned to carry out a mission to the Frisians, he twice received papal authorization for his labors, finally being consecrated bishop of the Frisians by Pope Sergius III on November 21, 695. Working under the protection of the Austrasian "mayors of the palace," powerful court officials of the Merovingian kings, Willibrord founded a monastery at Utrecht, raised many recruits, and preached throughout the lands bordering the Waal and Meuse rivers and into North Brabant. He was forced to leave the area when the Frisian king Radbod, at war against the Franks (714–719), restored pagan shrines and temples and killed many missionaries. He returned after Radbod's death (719), assisted now by Boniface. Willibrord is interred at Echternach, in Luxembourg, where he founded an abbey, and his burial site became a place of pilgrimage. His feast day is celebrated on the day of his death, November 7.

the school of learning in the latter city, preached beyond the IJssel River into Saxon lands and brought monastic learning to the court of Emperor Charlemagne.

Christianity revolutionized cultural and social life in the Netherlands. Architecture and the arts now centered on building churches, painting and carving church furnishings, and copying and embellishing books. New beliefs brought new rituals that formed the foundation of subsequent social developments. Gone were the ancient, pagan practices of animal and human sacrifice, replaced by the Mass and the sacraments, the cult of the saints, and, most especially, moral standards embodied in acts such as alms giving and care for the sick and elderly, works of charity that are displayed in the famous Utrecht psalter produced about the year 800.

The Holy Roman Empire

The Frankish empire under the Merovingians grew to include the territory of the Batavi, and, by 690, Pepin II of Heristal (d. 714) had conquered large swaths of the central Netherlands. Charles Martel (688–741), founder of the Carolingian dynasty, expanded the empire further. In 718 he drove off the Saxons, captured the pagan Frisian court of Radbod at Utrecht, and took lands farther north. Under Charlemagne (742 or 747–814) the empire reached its zenith and the Netherlands formed part of a vast domain that extended to Italy and Spain. The emperor's wooden palace at Nijmegen became a subsidiary residence. The Frisian settlement of Dorestad (present-day Wijk bij Duurstede) on the Rhine southeast of Utrecht flourished as the largest mercantile town in northern Europe. An imperial mint here produced coins (the Dorestad coin) much imitated across Europe.

Territorial divisions soon appeared that narrowed borders. The Low Countries—defined at this time as the low-lying regions around the deltas of the great rivers including not only the present-day countries of the Netherlands, Belgium, and Luxembourg but also Westphalia and the Rhineland in Germany—formed part of the lands of the Middle Kingdom assigned to Charlemagne's eldest grandson Lothair I (795–855) by the Treaty of Verdun (843). Before his death, he subdivided his kingdom, establishing a Kingdom of Lotharingia ruled by his son Lothair II (r. 855–69). On Lothair II's death in 869, his uncles Charles the Bald (r. 843–77) and Louis the German (r. 817–76)) signed a treaty at Meersen in present-day Limburg dividing the kingdom between them. Charles took the territories comprising today's Netherlands and Belgium to join them to his West Frankish kingdom while Louis, king of the East Franks, took Alsace and the left bank of the lower Rhine. After a period of confusion and warfare during which all these lands were once again reunited under the rule of Bruno, archbishop of Cologne (Saint Bruno, 925–65), in 959 Bruno divided the region into the duchies of Upper Lotharingia (Lorraine in present-day France) and Lower Lotharingia, of which the Netherlands formed part.

Titles to the dukedom were subsequently awarded to various noble houses, but effective power gradually passed to holders of smaller units of territory. The significance of the title eventually lapsed entirely in the wake of the rising power of feudal lords—dukes and counts—who held smaller units of territory as fiefs of the Holy Roman Empire. The growth of local autonomy proved inexorable, a growth necessitated to some degree because only leaders located onsite could exercise effective control in managing the resources needed to administer and, most essentially, defend their territories. Threats, when they came, arrived by sea.

The Vikings, Scandinavian seafarers, had been raiding isolated monasteries in the northern British Isles since the 790s, when they began to move south. They launched their first major attack in the Netherlands in 810 when a fleet of 200 long ships arrived off Frisia. In time, raids grew bolder. Dorestad was plundered three times from 834 to 836 and never recovered its commercial strength. Hit-and-run raids on coastal and riverine communities were followed by wars of conquest. In 881 the Vikings moved out of their winter quarters near Nijmegen and Roermond to sack towns in the valleys of the Rhine and Meuse. Besieged at their main camp at Asselt by forces of the east Frankish king Charles the Fat (839–88), they reached a settlement whereby the Rhine delta and the coast to the north were granted to their leader, Godfrey. Titled the "sea-king," Godfrey accepted baptism and married Gisela, an illegitimate daughter of Lothair II. Godfrey faced opposition to his claims to the title from Gerulf, the count of Frisia, who killed him at a meeting to discuss the dispute in 855. Godfrey's lands were ceded to Gerulf and, about 916, they passed to his younger son Dirk (Dideric, r. c. 916–39)), who became the first count of territories that were known, before 1100, as the county of West Frisia. By about that date the region came to be called Holland. Effective military organization by the rulers ended the Viking menace, with sporadic raids sputtering out by the 10th century. The beginnings of a new locus of power had been made.

Feudalism Takes—Partial—Hold

By the 10th and 11th centuries the historically unique social organization that was feudalism had fully developed. The practice of a free man (lord) receiving the personal service of another free man (vassal) dated to late Roman times and, under the Frankish kings, had evolved to such a degree that the obligations of vassal and lord had become virtually hereditary, a lord charging a fee ("relief") in renewing an agreement with a vassal's son. Under the improved agricultural conditions of the 11th century, which included the introduction of new technologies (the heavy plough, the horse collar) and new techniques (the adoption of three-year crop rotation) the system solidified, and both serf laborers and free peasantry, who also entered into contractual relationships, were drawn in.

Counts, who represented royal authority at local levels under the Frankish kings, and dukes, who organized and commanded regional defenses, wielded increasing power. They built castles, levied taxes, minted coins, raised armies, and granted land, in return for homage from lesser lords and knights. Castles and fortified manor houses appeared where groups of scattered farmsteads would tend to cluster around the parish church, forming the nucleus of future villages. A welter of lordships and counties competed for the additional titles that brought with them the land on which wealth resided.

In no case, however, did rulers acquire the power to appoint high clerics. Bishops, who as clergymen acquired title to nonheritable lands, were appointed by the Holy Roman Emperors in a bid to stem the erosion of imperial authority by dukes and counts. In the region that is today the Netherlands, the bishops sitting at Utrecht held ecclesiastical authority over wide swaths of territory. To the chagrin of their imperial overlords, they too, like their nonclerical counterparts, began to acquire secular power over surrounding areas.

Feudalism emerged most prominently in regions south of the Rhine River. Frisia (Friesland), however, remained a land apart. The Frisians were traders, stockbreeders, and fishermen, and feudalism took little hold in the swampy soil here. In Frisia, chivalric battles were replaced by private warfare involving family blood feuds waged by headmen and their armed retainers.

Even in areas where feudalism held sway, its grip was lessened by the continuing existence of towns. Urban life never entirely vanished following the collapse of Roman rule and the centuries of migrations and invasions that ensued. Urban centers that dated from Roman times lay along the three main river systems—Maastricht on the Meuse, Nijmegen and Utrecht on the Rhine delta, and Middelburg on the Scheldt estuary—and at these places major castles and churches were located. Over time, merchants and craftsmen arrived to set up shop, drawn by the money to be made in trade with local, wealthy residents. Freed from the binding feudal obligations that confined nobles, knights, and serfs to a rigid social hierarchy, townsmen—coopers, tanners, fishmongers, weavers, and a host of other tradesmen—reaped material gain. These riverine towns began to flourish again as early as Merovingian times. The end of the Viking menace meant that trade could revive. They were few in number, but, by the end of the first millennium, these small urban clusters were being joined by others.

2

POLITICAL STRIFE AND THE RISE OF URBAN LIFE (C. 1000–1515)

At the end of the first millennium, the area of the present-day Netherlands retained a frontierlike character. One of the more remote districts of the Holy Roman Empire, the country lay entirely at the mercy of its geography. Sparsely populated settlements lay scattered over the low-lying landscape, pockmarked by swamps and marshland. By the 11th and 12th centuries, however, improved technologies to control the water-threatened environment led to a growth in the number of inhabitants, for whom greater security brought opportunities for expanded economic activities. In time, the rise of commercial trading and protoindustrial trades created wealthy urban communities, which transformed the character of life and attracted the attention of covetous rulers from near and, then, far.

Reclaiming Land from the Sea

The threat of flooding remained endemic. In 839 a great flood diverted much of the Rhine River flow into the Meuse, creating the interconnected channels of Waal, Lek, and "New Meuse." The sea broke through the narrow belt of barrier dunes near Texel in 1282 and, in time, transformed the Almere, the lake on the central coast known to the Romans as Flevo Lacus (Lake Flevo), into the Zuider Zee, an arm of the sea. A landscape of bogs and lakes became one of creeks, peninsulas, and small islands. West Frisia, which today refers to the extreme northern sections of the province of North Holland, was almost completely severed from the rest of Frisia. On the northern coast, the great inundation of December 14, 1287, ravaged the land.

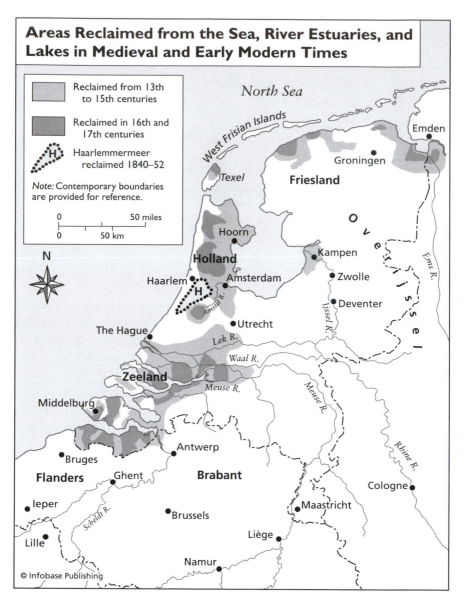

Areas Reclaimed from the Sea, River Estuaries, and Lakes in Medieval and Early Modern Times

Reclaimed from 13th to 15th centuries

Reclaimed in 16th and 17th centuries

Haarlemmermeer reclaimed 1840–52

Note: Contemporary boundaries are provided for reference.

0   50 miles
0   50 km

N

North Sea

West Frisian Islands

Emden

Groningen

Texel

Friesland

Overijssel

Ems R.

Hoorn

Kampen

Holland

Zwolle

Haarlem

Amsterdam

Deventer

Amstel R.

IJssel R.

The Hague

Utrecht

Lek R.

Waal R.

Zeeland

Meuse R.

Meuse R.

Middelburg

Rhine R.

Antwerp

Cologne

Bruges

Flanders

Ghent

Brabant

Maastricht

Ieper

Brussels

Scheldt R.

Liège

Lille

Namur

© Infobase Publishing

The first dikes of significance started to appear in the seventh and eighth centuries, and systematic building began about 1000. Coastal dwellers would surround lowlands, where tides could enter and retreat freely, with walls made of sand, carried into place with carts and shovels and planted with grass to keep the sand in place. Preventing the inflow of salty seawater made the soil more fertile, promoting pasture and farmland. In areas farther inland, polders were formed, patches of reclaimed land enclosed by dikes in which the water level could be artificially contained. Unlike in coastal areas, drainage of polders could not rely solely on the release of water during low tide. Here pumps were required to lift the polder water to the higher level of the surrounding drainage channels, a technique that became possible only in the 15th century when the Dutch learned to build windmills whose blades could be rotated to face into the wind from any direction (*wipmolen*).

To direct and manage flood prevention and land reclamation, farmers, landowners, and townspeople formed governing councils, and these water boards (*waterschappen*), which first appeared in 1196, laid the foundations of civil society. Among the world's oldest democratic bodies, the water boards continue to exist today, one for each of the country's 27 water districts.

Only through technological and organizational innovations were the inhabitants able to battle the water. The work of land reclamation never ceased. It also never went unchallenged, because throughout the Middle Ages, what the sea surrendered it could also as easily take

Windmills account for much of the topography in the country's low-lying areas. (Library of Congress, Prints and Photographs Division)

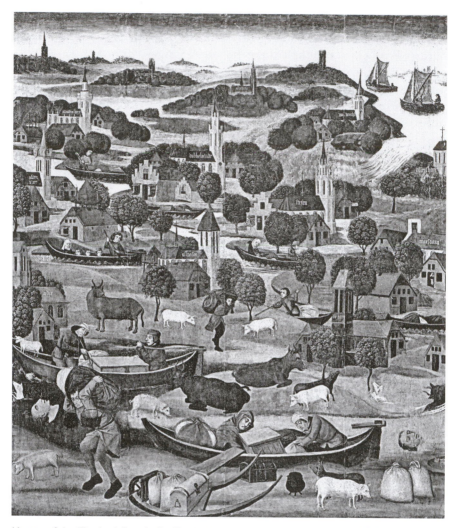

Master of the Elizabeth Panels, St. Elizabeth Flood in the Night of 18 to 19 November 1421 *(c. 1470). Oil (?) on panel, 127 × 110 cm* (Collection Rijksmuseum Amsterdam)

back. The 14th century witnessed nine major floods—three between 1373 and 1376 alone—and nature's elements seemed more threatening than ever in the 15th century. Frequent storms pounded the coastal dunes, eroding the coastline, shifting its contours hundreds of meters inland, and covering once fertile lands behind the dunes with sand. Floods expanded the size of sea inlets, creating a vast inland lake (the Haarlemmermeer) and submerging large portions of the Zeeland islands, while the infamous St. Elizabeth's Day flood of November 18–19, 1421,

THE SAINT ELIZABETH'S DAY FLOOD

With the exception of the flood of 1953, no natural disaster is so embedded in the historical memory of the Dutch as is the St. Elizabeth's Day flood. During the night of November 18 to November 19, 1421 (the medieval feast day of St. Elizabeth of Hungary), a heavy storm on the North Sea generated a high tide that surged up the rivers of the delta region, tearing wide gaps in dikes that were weakened because of age—many were more than a century old—and that were badly maintained due to poor economic conditions and the unstable political environment caused by Cod-Hook factional infighting then prevalent in the area. The floodwaters poured into a large sea arm between southern Holland and northern Zeeland, devastating the islands of South and North Beveland and destroying an area called the Groot Zuidhollandse Waard (the extreme southwestern sections of the present-day province of South Holland). The waters swallowed an estimated 72 villages and caused between 2,000 and 10,000 casualties (no exact records were kept). Most of the region remained flooded for decades. The island of Dordrecht and northwestern areas of the present-day province of North Brabant were reclaimed, but approximately 193 square miles (500 sq. km) of polderlands in the Groot Waard were never drained, and they remain submerged today. Over decades, a network of interlacing small rivers and creeks emerged, mottled with mudflats and islands on which willow forests, grasslands, and reedbeds appeared. At first called the Bergse Veld and now known as the Biesbosch ("forest of sedges"), the area is one of the largest national parks in the Netherlands and one of the last freshwater tidal locales in Europe.

devastated the Rhine river region around Dordrecht, wiping out two centuries of progress in land reclamation.

The physical environment, while it posed a never-ending threat, also offered unique opportunities in patterns of settlement and means of livelihood, opportunities that were realized in the rise of commercial life.

Town and Country in the Middle Ages

At river crossings, on seacoast deltas, and astride sheltering bays, settlements appeared by the start of the second millennium. Many were founded literally where dams were built on rivers and streams, and these "dam cities" (*damsteden*) include Rotterdam, Volendam, and Edam. Of particular note, where dikes appeared at the mouth of and on the west bank of the Amstel River, a small stream running south out of the Zuider Zee, a few fishermen's shelters could be found around 1000 on firm ground along the river's east bank. In the 12th century, traders built the first rough huts and houses made of wood, which they brought with them to this treeless place when they arrived to help the fishermen market the stocks they caught in the IJ estuary and on the Zuider Zee. Stocks were sold to neighboring villages such as Haarlem, which was already in existence. In the 13th century (c. 1240), a dam erected across the river gave the settlement, now called Amestelledamme, both a river and a sea harbor. In 1275 Count Floris V of Holland (1254–96) granted the residents toll-free passage on the waterways. Growth proved rapid. By the turn of the 15th century, Amsterdam had emerged as Holland's largest town, with a population of about 12,000.

Seas and rivers were the instruments that propelled the birth of towns everywhere in the Netherlands, and it was trade in fish that spawned the earliest commercial activity. The creation of the Zuider Zee produced a vast inland sea rich in fish, and fishing villages soon dotted its coastline. Thanks to preservation in salt, a Swedish technique perfected in the Netherlands in the mid-13th century, herring—a centuries-old staple of northern European diets—could now be caught in large quantities, and the Dutch came to dominate the trade.

The Zuider Zee offered sheltered sailing conditions that made it an ideal route for vessels to ply, and the connection south afforded by the IJssel River, which linked the Zuider Zee with the Rhine, created a waterborne highway ready-made for trade. Along the IJssel emerged towns—Deventer, Kampen, Oldenzaal, Zwolle, and Zutphen—built on the exchange of commodities that grew to include salt, timber, wax, amber, resins, and grain, as well as fish. These towns joined the Hanseatic League, the alliance of trading towns that, from the 13th to the 16th centuries, maintained a trade monopoly covering the Baltic Sea and parts of northern Germany. Membership reflected the strategic significance of these communities as trading places along the route that linked the forests and farming lands in Scandinavia and northern Germany with bustling towns in Flanders and Brabant such as Bruges, Ghent, and Antwerp, busy producing cloth, in the southern Low Countries.

Nowhere else in northwestern Europe did urban centers appear so early, become so numerous, and play so central an economic role as in the lands that today comprise the Netherlands and Belgium, specifically in Holland, Flanders, and Brabant. Maritime trade created the conditions for craftsmen to emerge, most especially, those engaged in the production of cloth from wool—some if it imported from England and some, together with flax for weaving linen, brought to the towns by farmers from the surrounding countryside. Gouda, in particular, became a center of the medieval cloth trade. Crafts began to be traded for cash, meaning that a money economy was fast overtaking bartering as a means of exchange.

And crops too began to be sold for ready money. The emerging urban landscape profoundly changed agricultural practices. Dairy farming and the growing of food crops, including cabbage, turnips, and beets, to supply nearby towns became so predominant that by the 13th century grain was imported in increasing quantities from the Baltic coast, East Anglia in England, and the Rhineland. In the early 14th century, an important consumer innovation appeared when cultivation of hops led to the brewing of beer. A replacement for spiced ale, beer soon became widely popular and was sold abroad. In Holland and Frisia farmers found additional income sources in fishing, fowling, and reed gathering.

Towns served not only as outlets for products of the land but also as sources of raw materials for the farms. Urban dwellers supplied rural residents with fertilizers in the form of leather shavings, rags, rubbish, and even human excrement to supplement animal manure. Intensive manuring facilitated abandonment of three-year crop rotation cycles, and cereals and other crops began to be grown year round, a practice not adopted in other parts of Europe until the 18th century. Feudal relationships broke down as labor services were converted to cash rents and peasants secured land of their own or moved to the burgeoning towns. By the end of the 13th century, serfdom had largely disappeared except in areas of Gelderland and Overijssel, although it was not legally abolished until the 1790s.

Merchants or landowners—in some cases both—began to acquire great wealth, and economic might led, in time, to demands for political rights. Regional rulers, loath to incur the ire of subjects who possessed the means to finance their power schemes, acquiesced in issuing charters of municipal self-governance. The earliest town charters granted by dukes and counts date from the late 12th and 13th centuries, including Zutphen (1191), Maastricht (1201), Middelburg (1217), Haarlem (1245), Delft (1246), Alkmaar (1254), and Gouda (1272). Amsterdam secured rights in 1306 and Rotterdam in 1328.

The wealthiest town residents—the patricians—would come to control municipal government, which was run by town councils (*vroedschappen*) composed of from about 20 to more than 80 members chosen from among their peers. Councilmen served for life, or until they moved elsewhere. These closed colleges drew up shortlists for appointment by regional rulers of burgomasters and aldermen (*schepenen*), who, as the "magistracy," levied local taxes and administered justice, often in conjunction with a sheriff (*schout*), representing the count or duke, or, in Utrecht, a prefect, representing the lord-bishop. To keep order, militia companies (*schutterijen*) were formed made up largely of master craftsmen, shopkeepers, and trades dealers, officered in the higher ranks by leading, wealthy citizens. The poor were excluded because members had to buy their own outfits and contribute funds to help defray the militias' costs, which included food and drink. Members of the militias patrolled town streets, walls, and gates, and the groups also served as fraternal social organizations. Well-armed and highly disciplined, these civic guards supplied the military muscle to match municipal economic power, and so their support was sought by rulers and would-be rulers at regional and, later, national levels. They played an important role in Dutch political history until the end of the 18th century.

Service in the militias reflected the swelling social and economic status of craftsmen and tradesmen. Artisans grew in numbers and wealth as demand for the products they produced expanded. To regulate wages and working conditions and provide material aid, they formed craft guilds, which first appeared in the 12th century. In the 13th century, they began to press for a voice in public affairs.

Patricians, however, did not willingly surrender their monopoly on power. They fought pitched battles in places with guildsmen, who themselves raised militias of their own. At times, guilds even fought guilds. In time, the success won by guildsmen in the cities of Flanders in forcing patricians to share and, in places, even surrender civic power spread north. By the 14th century, craft guilds were demanding the right to participate in government in every town in the Netherlands, and, by century's end, they had won that right in varying degrees everywhere. They even seized power for a time in Utrecht as early as 1304.

Town magistracies would be elected in rotation by patricians and guildsmen, an arrangement that, because the cast of characters changed constantly, led to the establishment of a new element in urban government—the professional administrator. Clerks employed as permanent civil servants gave continuity to town affairs. They began to be hired in the 14th century and by the end of the Middle Ages (late 15th century) administrative staff had grown to include secretaries, who drafted edicts and kept records, and "pensionaries" (or "syndics"), lawyers who served as advisers to magistrates and represented the town to outside authorities.

Settlement of struggles between patricians and guildsmen for control of urban rule give rise, in turn, to new divisions. Those now in power found themselves challenged by rival have-nots who sought to break their grip on government, and the two sides formed factions whose partisans battled each other to compete for municipal authority in towns across an entire county or duchy. In the 14th century, fighting between factions became rife, with supporters of one side warring with partisans of the other in contests that kept the country in a condition of continual disorder amounting to near civil war. Lichtenbergers fought Fresings in Utrecht; Schieringers struggled against Vetkopers in Friesland; Bronkhorsts battled Hekerens in Gelderland and Overijssel; and, most famously remembered in the municipal mayhem, Cods (Cabeljauwen) clashed with Hooks (Hoeks) in Holland. The Cods, who were strongest in the largest towns, backed the ruling elites as partisans of the powerful status quo. The Hooks fought on behalf of those among the populace, namely, the lesser nobles and the poorer townsfolk excluded from any share in government, who sought a voice at the governing table. While the factional infighting revolved around struggles for local power, at the same time, opposing parties sought support from, and in turn sided with, ruling overlords, who were themselves engaged in their own dynastic scheming.

Counts, Dukes, and Bishops Compete

By the 12th century, the dozens of counties and many minor lordships that had emerged following the disintegration of the Frankish kingdoms had been consolidated into a handful of territorial principalities governed by quarreling rulers still under imperial authority. That authority, however, had dwindled largely to the prestige that came to the holder of the title "Holy Roman Emperor"; emperors were no longer able even to invest bishops. The imperial crown itself, an elective office, was open to dispute among the local princes, who now wielded the effective power. In the northern Low Countries, the main rulers were the count of Holland-Zeeland, the lord-bishop of Utrecht, the dukes of Brabant and Limburg, and the count (duke from 1339) of Gelderland.

Holland emerged as a relatively compact territorial state. From their central holdings at the mouth of the Rhine and along the coast to the north, the counts, beginning with Dirk I (r. c. 916–39), the descendant of Vikings who had established a base in the river's delta in the ninth century, eventually acquired the whole of the delta. The first to use the name of Holland in his title, Count Dirk III (r. 993–1039) set up unauthorized tolls on the lower Rhine in defiance of Holy Roman Emperor Henry II (r. 1014–24). The emperor sent imperial forces against him but Dirk III solidified his position by winning a battle on the dikes in 1018. Dirk IV (r. 1039–49) fought Bernold (r. 1027–54), the lordbishop of Utrecht, who allied with Holy Roman Emperor Henry III (r. 1039–56) in seizing Flushing (Vlissingen). The emperor's forces sacked Leiden in 1047 and Dirk met defeat. His successors, however, proved more fortunate. From their castle at Haarlem, the counts waged nonstop feudal strife in winning the Scheldt estuaries in battles with the counts of Flanders and in wrestling for control of the west coast of the Zuider Zee with the rulers of Utrecht and Gelderland. In both cases, the counts of Holland proved victorious. Together with Zeeland, originally a separate county that became aligned with it, Holland grew by the mid-15th century to become the wealthiest and most politically powerful of the states in the area of the present-day Netherlands.

Before then the bishops of Utrecht were the most prominent of the rulers north of the Rhine. Their power encompassed both ecclesiastical jurisdiction over almost all of the Netherlands north of the great rivers and temporal rule over a much more restricted area, namely, the territory around the city of Utrecht (the Sticht or Nedersticht) and holdings over the IJssel north and east of Deventer (the Oversticht, including present-day Overijssel and parts of Drenthe). Rural and sparsely populated, the Oversticht was for much of the time ruled by the bishops in name only. No longer imperial appointees after 1122, the bishops were elected by the canons of the five collegiate churches of Utrecht. They proved as covetous to acquire additional lands as their lay neighbors.

Between the Oversticht and the Nedersticht a territorial vacuum existed. The lands here—Gelderland (Guelders), Zutphen, the Veluwe, and the Bommelerswaard—were united under Otto I (r. 1184–1207), the first count of Gelderland. In the east, a fragmented political landscape existed. The rulers of Brabant, Limburg, and Gelderland competed here for overlordship of fragmented bits of territory with varying legal powers; however, the bits were wealthy ones. They included towns that controlled river trade, such as Arnhem on the Waal, Kampen on the IJssel, and Roermond on the Meuse. Maastricht came under the joint rule of the dukes of Brabant and the prince-bishop of Liège (in present-day Belgium) in 1284. Limburg's scattered lands were joined with Brabant in 1289.

Only Frisia had no settled princely ruler. West Frisia was an integral part of Holland by 1297, but wealthy families, battling the sea, invaders, and each other, predominated along the North Sea coast from Holland to Denmark. The men of the wealthier families would gather regularly in public meetings in area districts to make policy and, beginning in the 12th century, representatives of the districts would meet in annual assemblies to settle major quarrels and harmonize large-scale actions. Factional fighting intensified in the 14th century to such a degree that, by the early 1400s, all of Frisia acceded to dominance by Holland as the only way to overcome the incessant warring. In the far north, the city of Groningen and the surrounding lands (the Ommelanden) fell under the authority of the lord-bishop of Utrecht in the 11th century, and the city itself became virtually independent in 1251. These areas formed a wedge separating the lands of the Frisians. Those areas to the west of the Ems River would evolve into the Dutch province of Friesland while those to the east would become German Friesland.

The demise of rulers would ignite dynastic duels. The death of Count Dirk VII of Holland in 1203 led both the late count's son-in-law and brother to vie for the title, each backed by neighboring sovereigns. Powerless to assert their authority, emperors bowed to the inevitable. In 1231, Holy Roman Emperor Frederick II (r. 1220–50) effectively recognized the independence of regional rulers. Count William II of Holland (r. 1235–56), a ruler who marked his rising status by having a hunting lodge constructed for him on the sand dunes at s'Gravenhage, or "Count's Hedge," in 1242 (the beginnings of The Hague), succeeded to the imperial throne itself when, in 1247, he was elected anti-king by the German princes who were rebelling against Frederick II. The counts would be based at The Hague after 1351 following a fire at Haarlem that destroyed their castle there.

Rulers would seek confirmation of their titles—and additional lands besides—through judiciously arranged marriages. William II's son Floris V (r. 1256–96), a ruler much beloved for liberties granted to peasants after revolts in 1275 and much remembered for his battles to gain West Frisia, affianced his infant son John to Elizabeth, the daughter of Edward I of England (r. 1272–1307). The marriage took place in 1297, the year after Floris's brutal murder; he was the victim of an international conspiracy against him led by Guy of Dampierre, count of Flanders, Floris's rival for control of Zeeland, and by Edward, now an ally of Flanders who had moved the lucrative trade in English wool from

Dordrecht in Holland to Mechelen in Brabant. Ironies could abound in the complicated diplomatic maneuverings of medieval Europe.

Floris V was followed by his son John I, who, at 15 in 1299, died childless, and with him the dynasty that had ruled Holland in the male line for almost 400 years. The son of a sister of William II, John II of Avesnes (r. 1299–1304), the count of Hainault (in present-day Belgium), succeeded, with the backing of Holland's merchants, grateful to John for making Dordrecht a staple market by requiring that all imported goods coming into the county had to be offered for sale in the city. The House of Avesnes ruled Holland and Zeeland under his son William III (r. 1304–37) and grandson William IV (r. 1337–45).

The notion of a contract between ruler and subject, evident in the grant of rights of self-government to townsmen, emerged equally in the gradual recognition by the region's rulers of power-sharing arrangements at the territorial level. The 14th century witnessed the first participation by representative assemblies in governing the duchies and counties. By the 15th century, full-fledged parliamentary bodies, called Estates, began to meet to offer advice to and be asked for support by ruling princes. In Holland the towns and nobility shared power in the provincial assembly. In the bishopric of Utrecht, townsmen and nobles were joined in the Estates by the higher clergy. In Gelderland, where agriculture held sway as the economic mainstay, the landed nobility held preponderant power.

The chronic political instability engendered by contentious counts and dukes continued into the mid-14th century, centering on Holland's drive to secure regional hegemony. By that time, however, conditions proved less than propitious. Scarcity and sickness stalked the area that is today the Netherlands. Famine resulted from loss of agricultural land to repeated flooding, deforestation, and drifting coastal sand. Populations and, with them, incomes fell in the wake of plague, the infamous Black Death, which reached the region in 1350. Holland's dynasty itself died out. The House of Avesnes ended with the death of Count William IV, the last in the male line, in 1345. One of William's sisters, Margaret (r. 1345–54), the wife of Louis of Bavaria, succeeded him. The House of Bavaria presided over a brilliant court life at The Hague, but its territorial ambitions were checked by recurrent family squabbling that led to a series of civil wars when Cods and Hooks backed opposing sides. In 1350 Margaret, supported by the Hooks, battled the Cods allied with her son William, who succeeded her as Count William V (r. 1354–89). The internecine wrangling finally ended at the death of William VI (r. 1404–17), only to start again when a struggle for the title between the acknowledged successor, his daughter Jacqueline, countess of Hainaut (1401–36), backed by the Hooks, and his brother John III, with help from the Cods, ended with John's death (1425). Jacqueline, with the aid of English allies, then battled opposition from the Hooks allied with her estranged husband John, the duke of Brabant, and Philip III the Good, duke of Burgundy (1396–1467), which ended with the duke of Brabant's death (1428). The duke had mortgaged Holland and Zeeland to Philip, and a settlement in June 1428 (Reconciliation of Delft) left Jacqueline in possession of the title of countess of Holland-Zeeland in name only, with Philip in charge of administration. Philip assumed full powers in April 1432, after Jacqueline was forced to abdicate for marrying against his wishes. He acquired title to Frisia in the same year.

Transcending all these changes in ruling regimes and governing machines, the one constant throughout the Middle Ages remained the pervasive influence of the Roman Catholic Church.

New Religious Movements

The call to crusade made by Pope Urban II on November 27, 1095, produced as profound an effect in the area of the Netherlands as it did elsewhere in western Europe. Noblemen and knights traveled east to liberate the holy places from Muslim control. They were led most prominently by Count Floris III of Holland (r. 1157–90), who accompanied Emperor Frederick I Barbarossa (1122–90) in serving as a major leader of the Third Crusade (1189–92). Floris died of pestilence in Antioch.

The region felt the effects of all the religious developments periodically sweeping western Europe from the 12th through the 15th centuries. The new monasticism founded at Cîteaux in Burgundy by St. Benedict in 1098 found a foothold through the influence of Bernard of Clairvaux (1090–1153), who, having established his order of Cistercian monks, twice journeyed to the Low Countries where he founded two abbeys. True to the order's call to build monasteries in remote locales and thus develop the wilderness, houses were planted on polders and in sand dunes, notably the Abbey of Klaarkamp, where the monks, assisted by lay brothers, built dikes and cultivated land on the island of Schiermonnikoog.

Norbert of Xanten (c. 1080–1134), from the Rhineland, founded a house of canons based on the rule of St. Augustine. Norbert, like Bernard, journeyed in the Low Countries, leaving monasteries behind him, and his order, whose members were known as Norbertines or Premonstratensians, could be found throughout the region.

29

Franciscans and Dominicans arrived in the mid-13th century, and the mendicant orders' message of poverty and spirituality resonated as a counterweight to the growing market-oriented materialism. Based in the towns, the friars preached throughout the countryside, and they were joined by an order native to the Netherlands, the Brothers of the Cross (the Crutched Friars), founded by Theodore of Celle, a canon of Liège. The most significant of indigenous movements, which proved popular across northwestern Europe, were the beguines and beghards, groups of secular women and men, respectively, who lived collectively as a means to religious edification but who were not bound by perpetual vows. Clusters of these communities, with an adjoining church, could be found, often several in one town, throughout the Netherlands.

Cultural Stirrings

The earliest cultural expressions were the exclusive preserve of the church, and these consisted largely of church buildings, paintings, and manuscript illuminations. In areas where stone deposits existed—largely the river region along the Rhine and Meuse—churches appeared that followed prevailing architectural styles. Romanesque ecclesiastical architecture is evident in the Church of Our Lady in Maastricht, a stoutly built edifice that reflects, on a smaller scale, the Carolingian and Ottonian influences evident in imperial cathedrals located farther upstream. Gothic became the style for architecture and sculpture at the end of the 12th century though no outstanding examples exist in the Netherlands today. In low-lying coastal areas builders were obliged to use wood for construction and few structures survive. Brick replaced wood in the 13th and 14th centuries. Only a few paintings have been preserved, but illuminated manuscripts, a more widely practiced art, are more numerous. Abbeys and large churches exchanged manuscripts, which accounts for the larger output.

The Dutch language began to form in the late fifth century, developing gradually through an admixture of Old Lower Frankish, Old Frisian, and Old Saxon, early Germanic dialects. Writings in these idioms, such as the ninth-century Wachtendonk Psalms, are considered protoworks of both Dutch and German.

The emergence of Dutch as a vehicle of literary expression began in the 10th century. The earliest examples of Dutch literature in the Netherlands appeared, as in the rest of western Europe, in the form of courtly romance poems, chivalric epics, and fables, penned largely for aristocratic and religious readers. They include, notably, the poems and epics of the 12th-century poet Henric van Veldeke, the first writer in the Dutch language whose name is known. Most early literature consists of translations and adaptations of French works (*Of Reynard the Fox [Vanden vos Reynaerde]*, for example), but originals were also occasionally produced, such as the anonymous *Karel ende Elegant,* written in Flemish, a southern dialect.

New chronicles, histories, and hagiographies replaced chivalric tales as central literary types, and the miracle story, exemplified in the 13th-century Flemish narrative poem *Beatrijs,* gave expression to the new emphasis on inner spirituality. Jan van Ruysbroec (John of Ruysbroeck, 1293/94–1381) penned mystical sermons and is considered the father of Dutch prose. An Augustinian friar, he wrote at his monastery at Groenendaal, near Brussels in Brabant, where, together with Flanders, the preponderance of works written in the Middle Dutch of the Middle Ages (c. 1150–c. 1500) appeared, reflecting the greater population and economic wealth found here.

Jacob van Maerlant (c. 1235–c. 1300) links the northern and southern literary strains. A Flemish scholar who served as a churchwarden at Maerland on the island of Voorne in Zeeland, he wrote thousands of lines of verse, his masterpiece the 90,000-line *The Mirror of History* (*De spieghel historiael,* c. 1284), a world history from the Creation to the First Crusade, which he dedicated to Floris V. Although Maerlant wrote for the nobility, the bourgeoisie emerging in the towns commissioned many of his works, which included some of the earliest printed in Dutch.

The new audience reflected the growth of a literate, urban middle class that accompanied the rise of civic life. Subject matter catering to secular tastes began to be written. In addition to histories and collections of satirical and moral tales aimed at all classes of society, secular dramas staged by chambers of rhetoric—amateur dramatic groups—began to be performed in the 15th century, a departure from the religious plays that had been performed in monasteries since the 10th century. New themes emerged in works that included the 14th-century *Gloriant* (a love story), *Vanden winter ende vandem somer* (an allegorical debate between winter and summer), and the 15th-century morality play *Den spyeghel der salicheyt* (or *Elcerlyc*). Art and literature would flourish with the arrival of a regime in the 15th century with the power to give them brilliant effect and official respect.

The Burgundian Era, 1432–1477

The acquisition of Holland and Zeeland by Duke Philip the Good of Burgundy in 1432 marked only the latest in a steady series of moves he made in seeking to win control of all the Low Countries. A fief of France since French king John II bestowed the territory on his son Duke Philip the Bold in 1364, Burgundy became the base territory from which the rulers expanded their power to the east and to the north. Eyeing the rich trading cities of the Low Countries, the duke's son Philip the Good (r. 1419–67) set out to secure that wealth using a tried-and-true medieval diplomatic tool, namely, marriage. Philip's betrothal in 1384 to the count of Flanders's daughter Margaret of Male left him in possession of Flanders, then the jewel of the region as the richest and most populous province. Most of the rest of the Low Countries—both in the South (present-day Belgium, Luxembourg, and parts of northwestern France) and in the North (present-day Netherlands)—gradually fell to the duke through purchase and inheritance. He secured Utrecht through invasion (1455), putting his bastard son David (r. 1455–96) in place as lord-bishop.

Considered the founder of the countries that would emerge as the Netherlands and Belgium, Philip united the two areas, tying them together with a jumble of French and German lands and bringing them, for the first time since the Carolingian era, into the territory of a large and powerful European state.

To give cohesion to the region Philip created new central institutions. The Council of State was established, composed of leading noblemen to advise the duke on matters of state, and the Order of the Golden Fleece, first called to order on January 10, 1429, was created as a fraternal knighthood whose members, chosen by the duke, swore fealty to him. A common currency (*vierlander*) began to circulate, and a uniform system of weights and measures was implemented. Most significantly, to unify and better regulate the collection of revenues—the regime's chief need—a States General, an assembly composed of representatives from the various provincial Estates, was set up whose consent was required to approve taxes. The first session was held January 9, 1464, at Bruges, in Flanders. In each of the provinces, governors (stadholders) were appointed. The stadholder (*stadhouder*, literally "stead holder") traced its antecedents to those officials appointed by feudal lords during the Middle Ages to represent them in their absence. In Holland and Zeeland the first stadholder was Hugo van Lannoy, who held the post from 1433 to 1440. Responsible for overseeing the prince's prerogative in the province, the stadholders would call the Estates into session and would appoint burgomasters and aldermen from shortlists submitted by town councils. Trusty lord lieutenants, they came largely from Flanders and Brabant, the locus of power of the regime. Duke Philip rarely, and then only briefly, visited his lands north of the great rivers.

By now towns dominated in Holland and Zeeland to a greater extent than elsewhere in the Netherlands, but town councils remained riddled with disaffected nobles and artisans. To lessen the influence of the guilds and factions, Philip purged Hooks from town councils, banned the use of the labels "Hooks" and "Cods," and sharply reduced the number of council members, cutting them from 80 to 40 in Haarlem, for example. Burgomasters, the chief municipal officeholders, had been chosen by broadly based colleges of electors composed of representatives of the guilds and town councils; under Philip, they came to be appointed by the councils exclusively. Thus he sought to strengthen the power of the wealthier citizens, who were the primary force for stability. The duke's policies gave birth to the urban patriarchate of economically and politically privileged regents who would dominate civic affairs until the end of the 18th century.

At the same time, urban patriciates increasingly dominated the provincial assembly, the Estates of Holland. The Estates provided a ready instrument to enable the towns to come together to consult and coordinate actions. Unlike provinces in the southern Low Countries where towns won and kept power by acting on their own, towns in Holland found they could garner more clout by working together. Just as necessity demanded that town and countryside act jointly to maintain dikes and sluices, so too the aim to thrive economically called for coordinated action. The six large towns of Amsterdam, Leiden, Haarlem, Gouda, Delft, and Dordrecht cooperated in the Estates to create joint policies to gain for themselves a greater share of the trade—essentially carrying bulk goods and catching herring—that, in the 15th century, were concentrated in and around Rotterdam and in small ports such as Edam and Enkhuizen.

In the mid-1400s Amsterdam launched the drive that would see it later thrive with an aggressive challenge by its merchants to the Hanseatic cities that controlled so much Baltic and northern European trading wealth. The city secured support from Hansa cities in Prussia and Poland and, backed by a Burgundian fleet, the allies defeated the main north German Hansa towns between 1438 and 1441, which decisively broke the latter's monopoly hold. Grain, timber, and naval stores began to appear in growing amounts on Amsterdam's wharves.

Thoroughly French in language and culture, the Burgundian dukes, anxious to match the splendor on display at the French court, assiduously promoted artistic activity and oversaw a striking surge in the production of tapestries, sculptures, paintings, jewelry, and courtly music, although output was largely confined to cities in Brabant and

Flanders where the Burgundian court presided. Flemish masters served to inspire those working in the North—Jan van Eyck (c. 1385–1441) worked for the counts of Holland before returning to Flanders. The few Dutch painters to do important work include Dierik Bouts (1415–75) and Geertgen tot Sint Jans (c. 1460/65–after 1495), both of Haarlem, and Albert Ouwater (active 1440–65). Bouts moved south and little is known of Ouwater, but Geertgen seems to have spent his entire life in Haarlem, where he produced landscapes striking for their ease and natural look. The first printing presses arrived in the country in the 1460s, less than a decade after Johannes Gutenberg (c. 1390–1468) had perfected movable type. Printing works were first set up in eastern towns—Utrecht, Deventer, and Zwolle—that maintained close connections with Germany, and from there they spread west. Basic devotional tracts constituted their earliest stock in trade.

Chambers of rhetoric grew in numbers. Their members became known as *rederijkers*—rhetoricians, or those who were "rich in words." They met regularly, wrote and recited verse, and rehearsed. The groups put on plays at fairs and during special occasions and, in time, they became virtual theatrical guilds adopted by towns and given semiofficial status in being responsible for dramatic presentations. Competitions held between communities could be fierce.

The Burgundian era marked the start of one of the great ages of church building in the Netherlands. Edifices with lofty spires and richly furnished interiors appeared all over the country by the mid-1500s. The church at Haarlem, built in the late Gothic style, was completed between 1456 and 1470 and the tower between 1518 and 1520. In Gouda, the Grote or Sint Jans Kerk, begun in the 13th century, was finished in the early 1500s, its completion crowned by 40 stained glass windows installed between the 1530s and 1603, the largest collection in the country. Most building was driven by the need for numerous side chapels to accommodate growth in demand for services during this last medieval century, which was characterized by a surge in piety evidenced also in a host of monastic and semi-monastic communities that blossomed in towns beginning in the early 1400s.

The regime attained its apogee in fame and fortune under Duke Charles the Bold (r. 1467–77). Strong-willed and autocratic, Charles strove to centralize administration, touring Holland and Zeeland in 1468 and appointing loyal retainers, again mostly from the southern provinces, to provincial and municipal offices. Gelderland was seized by force in 1473. Ambitious to forge a strong state free from feudal dependence on and challenging the very power of France, Charles relentlessly waged war, paid for by ever-higher taxes, which proved highly unpopular. Poised to win success against his great enemy King Louis XI of France (r. 1461–83), the proud duke fell in battle against the Swiss, allies of the French king, outside Nancy in January 1477, his body lying naked and frozen in a ditch for days and his face gnawed away by wolves. Given an opportunity to act by this single, sudden blow, his subjects, grown weary of exactions of money and men to fund and man the duke's armies, promptly took advantage of the resulting royal limbo.

The Habsburgs Take Hold, 1477–1515

The pent-up grievances against Charles's methods and policies burst into open revolt under his daughter Mary of Burgundy (r. 1477–82), who succeeded him. With neither money nor troops and faced with a French army invading the southern Netherlands, Mary had no choice but to grant the Grand, or Great, Privilege (Joyous Entry) in February 1477, a charter that gave the States General the right to meet at a time of their choosing and checked the power of the ruler to levy taxes or obtain troops without the consent of the towns and provinces. Holland and Zeeland sought and secured a second Grand Privilege (Groot Privilege) in March 1477 that excluded outsiders from holding administrative and judicial posts in the two provinces and acknowledged Dutch rather than French as the language of administration.

Mary sought to thwart French designs by marrying Maximilian (1459–1519, Holy Roman Emperor 1493–1519) of the powerful House of Habsburg, whose resources would allow her not only to battle foreign foes but also to win back concessions granted her subjects. However, her reign was cut short when she fell from a horse, and Maximilian served as regent for their four-year-old son Philip. Brave, idealistic, but as perennially short of funds as his wife had been, Maximilian found little allegiance awaiting him in the northern Netherlands. Utrecht and Gelderland broke away. He faced open revolt in Holland, where Hook insurgents, traditional opponents of the ruling house, captured Sluis, Rotterdam, and surrounding towns. Led by their leader Frans van Brederode (1465–90), they allied with the anti-imperial party in Utrecht and waged a bloody guerrilla war against forces led by Duke Albert of Saxe-Meissen (1443–1500), a German general brought in by Maximilian. The insurgents were finally subdued in fighting at Brouwershaven in 1490 during which Brederode was killed. Because he had no money, Maximilian settled his debt to Duke Albert by awarding him the hereditary governorship of Friesland in 1498. Holland and Zeeland settled down to relative stability, lending vital support in Habsburg moves to nail down power to the north and east. Utrecht was won back, but rebellion raged on in Gelderland, where a concerted effort was not made until the accession of Maximilian's son. Philip I, who assumed power in 1494, launched a full-scale invasion in 1504, but failed to subdue the rebels. Nor did he succeed in Friesland, which, although subjected to Habsburg rule in 1498, remained loosely held in the regime's reins. Opponents here, allied with Gelderland and Groningen, beat back Philip's forces.

Philip relinquished his claims to these areas and, in so doing, abandoned the expansionism that had characterized the actions of his Burgundian grandfather and great-grandfather. He maintained the centralizing policies of his predecessors until distracted by dynastic struggles occasioned by his marriage to Joanna, heiress of the Spanish kingdoms of Castile and Aragon. On the death of Joanna's mother, Queen Isabella of Castile, in 1504, Philip claimed the title of that kingdom in his wife's right, but, after a brief fight with his father-in-law, Ferdinand of Aragon, in which he won his claim, died in 1506. Joanna went mad with grief. Their son Charles, only six years old, assumed title to the Netherlands, his grandfather Maximilian serving as regent until his coming of age in 1515.

Early Habsburg rulers, like their Burgundian predecessors, depended on support from the greater and lesser nobility and the patrician elites who held most administrative and judicial posts, including the provincial governorship (stadholderate) and the municipal law-enforcement office of sheriff. At the same time, the late 15th century witnessed the spread of grammar schools, which had been growing steadily since early in the century, a development that reflected a new respect for learning. Wider segments of the population became increasingly better read, fed by an explosion of books that could now be printed en masse. By the early 16th century, an educated class existed in numbers sufficient to staff the state administration, thus displacing the regime's need to rely on nobles and wealthy merchants. These latter groups eyed the growing trend with increasing unease. From a force that, in the 1400s, served to strengthen central authority, patricians and landed aristocrats would lead a drive, in the next century, to deprive the sovereign of his claim to reign.

3

WARS OF RELIGION AND EMANCIPATION (1515–1609)

A native Netherlander born in Ghent, Charles, having come of age, was proclaimed sovereign of the Habsburg Netherlands in a solemn ceremony before the States General at the capital Brussels in January 1515. As Holy Roman Emperor (r. 1519–56), Charles V ruled a vast European realm and New World empire. In the Low Countries, he sought, and was largely successful in achieving, territorial consolidation. The addition of Friesland in 1515, Utrecht in 1538, and Gelderland in 1543 brought all the northern Netherlands under Habsburg rule. The Pragmatic Sanction of 1549 stipulated that a single heir—Charles's son Philip—would inherit a Netherlands united north and south, and a law of 1550 imposed a uniform policy to combat heresy throughout the whole country. The need for unity in matters temporal and spiritual was urgent. Religion-driven passions were dividing society and a coherent, forceful response by government was essential. In trying to enforce the heresy law, Philip II (r. 1555–98), the beneficiary of the inheritance law, would find himself waging a war that was both religious and political in nature and that was at first civil and then international in scope. In the end, he would lose half the lands his father had called home.

The Reign of Charles V

The Netherlands continued to experience rapid urban growth in the first decades of the 16th century. Maritime towns grew the fastest. Amsterdam and West Frisian ports served as depots for Baltic grain and timber as well as centers for the herring fishery trade and for shipbuilding, which began in earnest during these years. Some 1,000 seagoing vessels are estimated to have been based in Holland in the 1560s. In contrast, textile crafts that had dominated in inland towns in the 15th century declined. Places such as Zwolle, Zutphen, Kampen, Oldenzaal, and others that had grown prosperous on the trade monopoly they enjoyed as members of the Hanseatic League now experienced a drop in maritime traffic, due in part to silting of the IJssel River.

The highly urban character of the Habsburg Netherlands made these lands unique in western Europe outside northern Italy. In agriculture as well, unlike elsewhere, the country was distinguished by the high number of independent farmers who owned small plots outright or paid money rents to nobles, the church, or townspeople—the latter owned a third of the land in Holland, Zeeland, and western Utrecht, where profits earned in commerce were used to buy and reclaim plots.

In the countryside peat harvesting, carried out for centuries, intensified in the first half of the 1500s. Peat had been used for fuel since earliest times in the Netherlands, which possessed extensive deposits. At first small-scale and localized, production expanded in the mid-16th century in the face of rising demand coupled with development of new tools, notably a sharper, larger shovel (*baggerbeugel*), that permitted diggers to cut peat below the water level. For the first time, peat digging became a major economic activity while it both eroded the tax base and posed a threat to the environment when exhausted bogs formed lakes, which expanded throughout the century to cover large areas in central Holland and western Utrecht. Water authorities fought back by imposing taxes on the removal of peat, the proceeds used to finance the reclamation of bogs.

Trade guilds remained prominent in the towns, but by now governments here were run exclusively by the regents, namely, the members of the town councils. No one could be a regent without holding a civic office and, although in theory officeholding was never limited by birth or social status, the Burgundian dukes, in fact, had furthered the growth of a closed, patrician oligarchy by promoting appointment of only the richest townsmen. Indeed, by the 16th century, wealth had become a defining, although by no means a universal, characteristic of the urban patriciate, whose elite families not only controlled government but also dispensed patronage. As council members, they would submit lists of candidates for the town magistracies to the provincial stadholders, who would make the selections.

Territorial unity, interrupted under Philip I, proceeded under Charles V. In 1515 Charles bought the lordship of Friesland, although he did not exercise real power until 1524 following a mutual understanding reached with the Frisian Estates. In 1527 Henry of Bavaria, lord-bishop of Utrecht, sold Overijssel to Charles. The following year he transferred title to Utrecht to him, but Charles only won secure possession in 1538 following the death of Charles of Egmond, duke of Gelderland, who disputed the Habsburg claim and held the territory under his governor Maartin van Rossum. Gelderland itself became part of the Habsburg Netherlands in 1543 when Duke William II died and named Charles his heir. Lands in the southern Netherlands were also acquired. By the end of Charles's reign, the Habsburg Netherlands consisted of 17 provinces of varying size and influence.

Under Charles, the term *Netherlands*, came into general use in designating the lands that make up the modern-day nations of Belgium, the Netherlands, and Luxembourg together with portions of extreme northwestern France that were then under Habsburg rule. Charles's central aim was to establish unity of administration to subordinate all authority to royal power. A coherent monetary system was created to coordinate financial activity throughout the provinces. Edicts of 1521 and 1548 supplemented that of 1496 by which the guilder (*gulden*), also called a florin, was established as the unit of account. The authorities introduced bimetallism in issuing gold and silver coins at a fixed rate of exchange. Rapid inflation subsequently forced the gold coins out of circulation, replaced by a variety of foreign coins of differing weights and qualities. The guilder, however, remained the unit of account, divided into *stuivers* and the *stuivers* into *penningen*.

In 1531 the organs of government, which had hitherto resided with the court as it traveled to Bruges, Mechelen, and Brussels, were firmly fixed in Brussels. In the same year, the Great Council was divided into three ancillary councils: a Council of Finance to oversee the financial administration, a Privy Council to provide advice on judicial decisions and other policies, and a Council of State of leading noblemen—largely stadholders—to be consulted on major matters of state. In each province new governmental organs—high courts of justice, chambers of accounts—were intended to lessen the ancient privileges of town and province. Charles capped his measures with the Pragmatic Sanction (1549), an edict intended to consolidate Habsburg rule by ensuring the succession. Under its terms, towns and provincial Estates swore fealty to their future prince, Charles's son Philip.

Charles V brought unity to the northern Netherlands but his efforts to centralize administration under trained professional officials loyal only to the royal regime strained relations with local authorities, namely, the nobility and the wealthy urban patriciate. The growth in the number of educated non-nobles appointed to offices at court, ongoing since the late 15th century, riled the lower nobility, who complained at the loss of the patronage powers that these posts held. Creation of the new councils had the effect of limiting the authority of the States General. While that body retained its power to rule on taxation, Charles, in his annual budget submissions, never failed to impress on the members the imposing powers of the state when explaining the need for them to consent to contribute revenues. The introduction of the new provincial organizations was accepted only reluctantly. In addition, incessant warfare against France, a policy carried forward from Burgundian days, subjected all the provinces to onerous demands for taxes, troops, and provisions, spreading resentment across the social classes.

One institution beyond all others appeared impermeable to wide-scale disrepute. Although it provoked criticism, largely from learned clerics, the Roman Catholic Church, a close ally of the sovereign, reigned powerfully and placidly. When Charles began his rule, there were faint stirrings in calls for reforms that had been percolating for a century, but religious unrest, when it came in the 1520s, would arise very suddenly.

Humanism and the Reformation

Northern European humanism began in the Netherlands in the 1470s and 1480s in the remote provinces of Groningen and Overijssel with the appearance of a simple little book, the *Devotio moderna* (Modern Devotion), written sometime in the late 14th century by Geert Groote (1340–84). Groote, a wealthy and worldly professor at Cologne, experienced an inner conversion after retiring to a Carthusian monastery near Arnhem. Compelled to record what he felt, he stressed in his book the inner development of the individual as the main motivation of the truly holy.

Ordained a deacon but never a priest, Groote preached throughout the Netherlands denouncing the worldly abuses of both clergy and laity. He formed the Brethren of the Common Life, a movement of followers, including both men and women, inspired by his preaching and advice. Members resembled the beguines and beghards in neither taking vows nor begging for alms. Those who were not priests practiced trades and professions, living together as a community so as to better cultivate the interior life. Schools were founded by adherents in the Netherlands and Germany that brought learning for the first time to a largely ignorant populace, including many among the lower clergy.

Humanism hailed a faith based on humility and simplicity. Adherents shunned showy displays of faith in word and deed—Groote denounced the great clock tower at Utrecht as a symbol of worldliness. The message was most famously expressed by a German-born priest and member of the Brethren who, it is believed (some scholars contest the authorship), wrote a follow-up volume to the *Devotio* titled *The Imitation of Christ* (*De imitatione Christi*) by Thomas Hemerken (or Haemerken), known as Thomas à Kempis (c. 1379–1471), first published anonymously in 1418. In this small book of spiritual writings, which still remains widely read, Kempis affirmed that true Christian faith is not to be found in church rituals or dogmatic decrees but rather in the cultivation of a personal communion with Jesus Christ. He wrote: "He who knows from within how to go, and expects little from outward things, neither needs places, nor looks for times for keeping devout exercises" (à Kempis 1950, 55). The book circulated widely, and Dutch humanism spread rapidly after 1490.

Although sentiments such as these drew little reproof from theologians, they would raise greater ire when they emerged full-blown in the writings of northern humanism's quintessential spokesman, Desiderius Erasmus (c. 1466–1536). Erasmus forged a synthesis of new doctrines with new techniques, systematically integrating the new Christian truth rooted in the *Devotio* with the study of Greek and Latin thought, just now being undertaken in northern Europe.

Christian humanism precipitated a revolution in religious philosophy. A faith based on individual initiative looking less to formal styles of worship and more toward self-study of the Scriptures was now in vogue. The movement launched teaching reforms in the grammar schools that, in the second and third decades of the 16th century, produced an educated urban element characterized by a sober piety sustained by Bible reading. While humanism produced no lessening in faith-based feelings, it sparked a marked decline in respect for the piety of the late Middle Ages, expressed in more critical attitudes toward the church's organization and its ordained ministers. The privileges enjoyed by the secular clergy and monastic orders, most especially their exemption from taxation, riled the laity, most acutely during hard economic times. The financial exactions extracted by a remote papacy in Rome, the wealth ostentatiously displayed by the high clergy, and the scandalous conduct much attributed to clerics of all ranks fed the disaffection felt by those in search of spiritual sustenance.

It remained only for Martin Luther (1483–1546), the German Augustinian monk from Wittenberg, to open the floodgates to full-scale reform, a reform that Erasmus, although a caustic critic of the papacy,

DESIDERIUS ERASMUS

Desiderius Erasmus was born Gerrit Gerritszoon, probably on October 27, 1466, in Rotterdam. He was raised by his parents although he was almost certainly illegitimate. Ordained a priest and then taking vows as an Augustinian monk, he never practiced as the former and railed against the latter as a caustic critic of the Roman Catholic Church. Erasmus spent his life as an independent scholar studying and writing in Paris, Leuven, Basel, and in England, befriending leading thinkers of the day. He published new Latin and Greek editions of the New Testament, and his books include *Handbook of the Christian Soldier (Enchiridion militis Christiani,* 1503), a work in which he describes the true Christian life as one lived in opposition to war and to religion for form's sake; *The Praise of Folly (Moriae encomium,* 1509), a satire attacking superstition and Catholic traditions, which is his best-known work; and *The Education of a Christian Prince (Institutio principis Christiani,* 1516), a treatise admonishing rulers to strive to be loved by governing justly, kindly, and wisely. A critic of the excesses of Roman Catholicism, he opposed Lutheranism as well. A man who preached compassion and compromise, Erasmus lived during intemperate times, and he spent his last years embroiled in bitter controversy with those who reviled him for failing to side wholeheartedly with either theological side. His legacy would be fully recognized only much later. The toleration that would come to characterize Dutch social and intellectual life in modern times can be traced, in part, to its beginnings in the writings of Erasmus. The university in Rotterdam is named in his honor.

Albrecht Dürer, Portrait of Erasmus *(1526). Ink on paper/engraving, 29.9 × 19.3 cm* (Collection Rijksmuseum Amsterdam)

recoiled from both because he hated the violence that would inevitably ensue with religious discord and because he feared that the reformers would ultimately suffer defeat by the forces of the powerful status quo, which would spell the end of his beloved humanism.

But defeat would not come. Martin Luther's impact proved enormous in the Netherlands, sweeping over a country in which the Roman Catholic faith, though not widely organized ecclesiastically—most of the northern Netherlands lay within only the bishoprics of Utrecht and Liège—counted numerous wealthy monasteries and abbeys and a religious body that numbered about 15,000 in the early 16th century, or between 1 and 2 percent of the population.

Luther posted his Ninety-five Theses on October 31, 1517, and his denunciation both of church doctrines (for example, the role of penance and prayers for the dead) and of church practices (the celibate clergy and, most especially, the sale of indulgences as payment for sins) met a receptive audience in the Netherlands. His writings began to be preached in pulpits everywhere, most prominently by Luther's fellow Augustinian monks. By the mid-1520s Martin Luther had become a household name. In that same decade, the literate public obtained a more direct access to spiritual readings with the first full translation of the New Testament into Dutch in 1522 followed, four years later, by the complete vernacular Bible.

Demand for sermons based on the Scriptures soared, accompanied by a marked drop in the practice of, and respect for, Roman Catholic tenets. Devotions to the Virgin Mary and belief in the miraculous power of relics declined. Priests were jeered at in the streets, monks and nuns left—or were driven out of—religious houses, and townspeople closed their windows and doors to express their disbelief as religious processions passed by. Religious dissidents, at first confined to the theologically learned, spread to include craftsmen in the major towns.

Roman Catholics fought back. An early Dutch defender sat on the papal throne itself. Pope Adrian VI (1459–1523), born Adriaan Florenszoon Boeyens in Utrecht, was one of few pontiffs after the church's early years to use his baptismal name. A tutor of Charles V who was elected pope in 1522, Adrian was expected to be a pliant tool of the Habsburgs, but he proved surprisingly independent during his short reign. Although he acknowledged past abuses, which reformers gleefully took as proof of the correctness of their cause, Adrian struggled to battle the wave of rebellious sentiments just then breaking over Europe. He proposed reforms but met a hostile response from the curia in Rome.

Adrian Pietersz van de Venne, Fishing for Souls *(1614). Oil on panel, 98 × 189 cm. The painting depicts Protestant and Catholic fishermen vying to win people's souls.* (Collection Rijksmuseum Amsterdam)

Saddled with debts left by his profligate predecessor, confronted with corruption at the papal court, and unable to unite Christendom to face the rising power of the Ottoman Empire invading Europe from the east, Adrian succumbed on September 14, 1523. He died shortly after the fall of Rhodes to the Turks, which reputedly hastened his death, the last non-Italian elected to the papacy until the 20th century.

In 1520–22 Franciscans and Dominicans launched a wave of sermons across the country denouncing the new doctrines. In 1521 Charles V banned Luther's writings and, in 1525, forbade the mention of his name in public preaching. His adherents were declared to be criminals. Jan de Bakker, the pastor at Woerden, Holland, was burned as a heretic at The Hague (September 1525), the first Protestant martyr in the northern Netherlands. Fines, beatings, and banishment followed as the usual punishment imposed by the authorities until 1531 when a law decreed death as the penalty for heresy. These measures and methods, in effect, brought the tools of the Spanish Inquisition (established 1478) into the country. Dissenters were now forced into hiding.

Official proscription could not stop sentiment for reform from spreading, however, and, once begun, doctrinal offshoots soon swirled through Dutch society, espoused by new recruits. Anabaptists preached the necessity of adult baptism and early leaders included the Germans Thomas Münzer (c. 1489–1525), who called for violent overthrow of the social order, and Melchior Hoffman (c. 1495–c. 1544), who proclaimed the end of the world to be near at hand. In 1534 Haarlem baker Jan Mattys (d. 1534) and Jan Bockelson (John of Leiden, 1509–36), militant preachers of Christ's second coming (millenarianism), led 1,700 men and 6,000 women and children to the German city of Münster, where they converted the mayor, took over the city council, and established a religion-based regime. Thousands more traveling to Germany were captured and returned to the Netherlands. At Münster, a pentacostal revival atmosphere prevailed. A communist-style regime was installed in which guildsmen worked for no wages and food was declared public property. Bockelson tore down the church steeples, chose 16 wives, and had coins minted depicting his image and the words "The Word Was Made Flesh." By spring 1535, the inhabitants—besieged by Catholic forces and beset by bickering—began to starve. Women and children were sent out of the city but, refused safe conduct through the lines, they succumbed to famine under the city walls. In June, after a daylong struggle, the city fell and most of the remaining residents were massacred.

After the fiasco at Münster, Dutch Anabaptists found their greatest spokesman in Menno Simons (c. 1496–1561). An early convert to Lutheranism and outwardly a Catholic priest in Friesland for a decade, Simons wrote his principal work, *The Foundation of Christian Doctrine* (*Fondament-Boeck*, 1539), a paean to pacifism, and then preached in Amsterdam and across the northeast Netherlands. Advocating non-participation in government and avoiding judgment of the religious sentiments of others, Menno's followers, dubbed Mennonites, rejected doctrinal strictures and formal church organization. Consequently, they split into many groups, united by little more than a shared rejection of infant baptism.

A major contribution to the theological currents streaming through Europe was made by Cornelis Hoen, a jurist at the court of Holland, who set forth the first formal rejection of the doctrine of transubstantiation—the belief that the bread and wine of the Eucharist are, in fact, the body and blood of Christ—in favor of their symbolic presence only. Hoen's little treatise *Epistola christiana* (1525), while denounced by Luther as blasphemous, found favor among Swiss reformers, most notably Geneva theologian John Calvin (1509–64). Calvin made denial of transubstantiation his own, adding it and other standard Protestant tenets, such as faith alone was sufficient for salvation (justification by faith), to his own preeminent contribution, namely, that God's elect are preordained for salvation (predestination). Calvin's clear, straightforward principles found especially fertile ground in the Netherlands and within a decade, beginning in the 1550s, they had eclipsed all other Protestant strands in the country. The drafting of the *Netherlands Confession of Faith* (*Confessio Belgica*) in 1561 by Guy de Brès, a Calvinist preacher, gave what were now being called "Reformed" congregations a nationwide text for worship. By the mid-1500s, organized communities were gathering in secret. Their numbers grew steadily, aided by the impact of the *Confession* and by Calvinist gains in surrounding countries.

Increasing numbers of dissenters inflamed religious passions, threatening public order in the towns. Civil authorities worried about outbreaks of street brawling, and their concerns were not without foundation. As early as 1526, the arrest of a suspected heretic set off a full-scale riot in s'Hertogenbosch. As religious divisions hardened through midcentury, the ability to maintain the civil peace while at the same time permitting the exercise of both Catholic and Reformed faiths strained the patience and resources of urban officials. Religious tensions smoldered, adding to the general sense of unease.

Philip II

The ruler of the biggest empire the world had yet seen, Charles handed control of the Netherlands; Spain; the overseas Spanish possessions in the Caribbean, Mexico, and Peru; and Milan, Naples, and Sicily to his son Philip in 1555 and retired to a monastery in Spain. The Habsburg possessions in Germany later went to Charles's brother Ferdinand I. Though always a staunch defender of Catholicism and of his princely powers, Charles was respected as a wise ruler and, having been raised in the Netherlands and spent much of his time there, he was genuinely liked. Philip II (1527–98) never was. Short-sighted, austere, rigidly Roman Catholic, and always considered a foreigner—he was raised in Spain and spoke neither French nor Dutch—Philip followed the same policies as his father, but with so unbending a purpose that the forces of opposition, gathering under his predecessor, speedily assembled.

Charles had left the coffers of state largely empty, making Philip II heavily dependent for approval of monies on the States General, a body little inclined to consent to their release. The transfer of power found the country at war with France (1551–59) as well, which further frayed tempers between a monarch needing funds and a public weary from seemingly never-ending financial demands. The nobility begrudged paying for a war fought, they affirmed, not in the interests of the Netherlands but to give Spain a solid stake in Italy.

The conclusion of peace in April 1559 brought a hardening of religious policy. To better combat heresy, three new archbishoprics and

14 new bishoprics were created, the clerics to be nominated now by the crown, not by the collegiate churches, so as to make them loyal retainers of the secular power, and to be paid out of revenues from historic, independent abbeys. The loss of appointment privileges and finances by the abbots and canons raised a storm of protest by these religious figures and by secular elites. The magnates feared that this latest move to concentrate power in the hands of the central authorities would require greater and greater diminution of local prerogatives. Disaffection with a regime seen as hostile to local rights of self-governance, disinclined to rely on local elites to staff the state administration, greedy for ever more resources, and fanatically intolerant in religious matters now coalesced into open opposition, launched by the nobility.

Philip II returned to Spain, the pivot of his policies and his home base, having designated his illegitimate half sister Margaret of Parma (r. 1559–67) as regent. Knowing she lacked political skill, he entrusted policymaking to Cardinal Granvelle (1517–86), Margaret's chief adviser, in consultation with the Council of State. Granvelle proved irascible, intent above all on wiping out heresy, relying on no one but himself to give counsel to the king, and so paying little heed to the voices of great magnates who, as stadholders, held seats on the council.

William of Orange was the wealthiest, most astute, and most eloquent of the appointed stadholders. In charge of Holland, Zeeland, and Utrecht, he emerged as Granvelle's chief rival, a rivalry brought into sharp relief by his marriage to the Protestant Anna of Saxony in 1561, which revealed on which side of the religious divide he stood. Persecutions proceeded apace, alienating civil magistracies forced to endure meddlesome inquisitors in their midst, but they failed to stem the tide of change. By the mid-1560s Protestantism permeated the country and Philip II was forced to recall Granvelle (1564). Disenchanted noblemen, both Protestants and Roman Catholics, met at Breda in 1566, and, putting aside their differences, they signed a compromise (Compromise of the Nobility) pledging to resist curtailment of their liberties. On April 5, 1566, some 400 among the lesser nobles from across the country marched in solemn procession to the ducal palace in Brussels to present a petition to Margaret asking that, among other measures, the heresy laws be suspended, in effect ending the Inquisition. Trying to calm the frayed nerves of a tearful Margaret, alarmed and frightened by so large a gathering, Charles, count of Berlaymont, one of her councilors, said: "What Madame, afraid of these beggars?" The request was subsequently denied and the denial

WILLIAM OF ORANGE

William I of Orange-Nassau (April 24, 1533–July 10, 1584) was born at Dillingham on ancestral land in Nassau (now in Germany), and he became prince of Orange, a small territory in the south of France in 1544, the year he moved from Dillingham to the family estate at Breda. A favorite page of Emperor Charles V, William was educated at the French-speaking court in Brussels from the age of 11. Reared a Roman Catholic and instructed in Lutheranism, he developed a tolerant attitude toward religion. Stadholder of Holland, Zeeland, and Utrecht from 1553 until 1567, William was one of many leading nobles to oppose King Philip II's oppressive policies. A committed Protestant following his second marriage, he fled to Nassau on the arrival of the duke of Alva in 1567. Emerging in 1568 as the leader of armed resistance, William financed the Sea Beggars and raised an army, which he led in an invasion of the southern Netherlands. He entered Brussels in 1577, but the moderate policies he advocated failed to prevail. Hoping to unite all the provinces under a tolerant regime, he at first opposed the Union of Utrecht, but finally gave the agreement his support on May 3, 1579. Reappointed by the provinces as stadholder in 1572, as well as of Friesland (1580–84), he directed continued resistance as captain-general of the United Provinces. Four times married and the father of 14 children, he was politically astute and personally incorruptible.

was memorialized in the courtier's scornful reference to "beggars" (*gueux*), a word adopted as a badge of honor and a battle cry by those who saw themselves oppressed.

Open Revolt

Religious restraint now dissolved. Open-air Calvinist mass meetings, many preached by exiles returned from abroad, were held outside towns in the relative safety of the countryside in the summer of 1566. Small mobs, inspired by anti-Catholic rhetoric, rampaged through churches, smashing statues and defacing paintings in an iconoclastic fury (*beeldenstorm*) that was accompanied by assaults, and sometimes murder, of priests and nuns. Protestant congregations were established everywhere and Calvinists even seized power in s'Hertogenbosch and several other towns. Civil militias rarely intervened.

Declared an outlaw by Philip in 1580, William was assassinated at Delft by Balthasar Gérard, a French Catholic fanatic. His last recorded words were: "My God, my God, have pity on me and on this poor people." He is buried in the New Church at Delft.

William is popularly known as "the Silent" (Willem de Zwijger), reputedly not because he was shy—he was not—but because he would not say what he thought. William is also known as "Father of the Fatherland." The flag of the Netherlands is derived from his family flag—three vertical stripes of blue, white, and orange—and orange is the patriotic color of popular choice today. The country's coat of arms and motto (*Je maintiendrai*, French for "I will maintain") are also based on those of his family.

Adriaen Thomas Key, William I [1533–1584], Prince of Orange, Called William the Silent *(c. 1579). Oil on panel, 48 × 35 cm* (Collection Rijksmuseum Amsterdam)

The nobility split three ways, some for rebellion, some for repression, and some, such as William of Orange, for compromise. In the end, their divisions proved irrelevant as the government succeeded in suppressing the dissidents. With Catholicism restored, officialdom moved to make sure the threat to crown and church would appear no more.

Don Fernando Álvarez de Toledo, third duke of Alva ([or Alba] 1507–82), arrived in August 1567 at the head of 10,000 German and Neapolitan troops. A fanatic Catholic from Castile, rigidly royalist and coldly autocratic, Alva harbored a barely veiled contempt for the people of the Netherlands and their leaders, a contempt immediately expressed with the arrest of suspected traitors. He set up a Council of Troubles to try suspected troublemakers. In the end, the council sentenced some 9,000 persons and executed some 1,000, which earned it the title of the Council of Blood. Outraged, Margaret of Parma resigned, leaving Alva as governor-general in name now as well as in fact.

In the northern provinces, unlike the southern, a majority of leading nobles had opted for rebellion in 1567, and now they fled, along with prominent citizens. They rallied around William of Orange, in exile in Nassau, from where he launched an invasion in 1568. The rebels were defeated, and incarcerated nobles, whose petition was blamed for starting the turmoil, were executed, most memorably the counts of Egmont and Hoorn, who were beheaded in Brussels before appalled crowds. Public opinion hardened against the regime, incensed further by a demand from Alva that the populace pay a 10 percent sales tax, the hated "Tenth Penny" (*tiende penning*). Blood and taxes proved too much and rebellion ripened into open revolt. Hostilities at Heiligerlee on May 23, 1568, are generally recognized to be the opening battle. The conflict with Spain would rage for eight decades. The Eighty Years' War began as a revolt that spread to become a rebellion; from local battles waged by partisans in all the 17 provinces, the rebellion evolved to a civil war pitting Protestants in power in the northern provinces against Catholics allied with Spain in the southern provinces.

William of Orange possessed impressive resources in an army of exiled recruits, significant sums of money, and support from neighboring sovereigns, but, from 1568 to 1572, he managed to mount only small, sporadic attacks. A breakthrough, when it arrived, came by sea. On April 1, 1572, a fleet of some 300 ships, financed by William and manned by 600 so-called Sea Beggars (*watergeuzen*), a ragtag band of Protestant seamen battling under their motto "Better the Turk than the Pope," captured the town of Brill (Brielle), a feat that opened the way for rebellious forces to secure control of most of Holland and Zeeland in the summer of 1572. The Estates of these two provinces as well as Utrecht, meeting illegally, appointed William stadholder on July 20, 1572; this act constituted a direct act of defiance in ascribing to themselves a power reserved to the prince. Spanish forces subsequently counterattacked, defeating William's army and forcing him to flee. Spanish troops reentered many cities.

The few pitched battles that occurred gave way to prolonged sieges because most cities were protected by large defensive works and the boggy ground made large military maneuvers difficult. The Spanish seized Zutphen, where they massacred the inhabitants, and Haarlem succumbed in July 1573 after having tenaciously resisted a seven-month-long assault. From his base in Amsterdam, Alva struck north to besiege Dutch rebels in Alkmaar, but they were driven off in October 1573. The first of the major occupied towns in the northern

THE DUTCH FLAG

The Dutch flag of three equal horizontal stripes of red, white, and dark blue derives from the flag flown by the Sea Beggars, which was known as the "Prince's Flag," probably because it was based on the colors of the livery of William, prince of Orange, namely, orange, white, and blue. Red is first mentioned as a replacement for orange in 1596, and the former became more common as the 17th century progressed, until, by 1660, red was in standard use. The impermanence of orange dyes available at the time may have encouraged substitution of red, then a more stable and brilliant color than orange. Red may also have been adopted to symbolize the political importance of the States General, whose flag was red with a gold lion.

Netherlands to successfully resist Spanish attackers, Alkmaar marked a significant victory. The following month Alva was replaced as governor by Luis de Zúñiga y Requesens (1528–76). More docile in temperament, he strove to pursue a more conciliatory policy, but limited financial resources kept him preoccupied in ensuring the loyalty of Spanish troops. After a siege of two years, on February 19, 1574, rebels took Middelburg, the last major Spanish fortress-town in Zeeland. The costliest, most persistent, and most significant siege took place at Leiden. If the town had fallen, The Hague and Delft would likely have followed, leaving the revolt in jeopardy. Defended largely by a citizens' militia, the city withstood royalist attacks from December 1573 until October 1574, when the townsmen, starving behind their breastworks, broke the dikes in desperation and, on October 3, put the enemy to flight. In recognition of its resistance, Leiden was the site chosen to host Holland's first university, which was founded the following year. Dutch rebels were in firm control throughout Holland and much of Zeeland by the mid-1570s. On May 28, 1578, Protestant supporters of the prince of Orange arrested Catholic town council members and took control in Amsterdam (the *Alteratie*), the last major city in Holland to switch sides.

Although seizure by the Spanish of Zierikzee in Zeeland in 1576 marked a victory of strategic significance, within hours of the takeover the Spanish troops mutinied over pay arrears. Widespread mutinies by Spanish soldiers unpaid by an empty royal treasury—the state had declared bankruptcy in 1575—followed, most spectacularly at

Otto van Veen, Distribution of Herring and White Bread at the Relief of Leiden, 3 October 1574 *(1574). Oil on panel, 40 × 59.5 cm* (Collection Rijksmuseum Amsterdam)

Antwerp in November 1576 when, over the course of several days, the city was sacked. A third of the town was burned and an estimated 8,000 citizens were killed in an orgy of brutality justly remembered in history as the Spanish Fury. The fall in Spanish fortunes provided an opportunity to reach an all-party settlement among the Dutch. The Estates General took control of the whole country. The Pacification of Ghent was signed between Calvinists and Catholics on November 8, 1576, which aimed to unite the rebels and make peace based on compromise and religious toleration. The first major expression of Netherlands's national consciousness, the document called for expulsion of Spanish troops, an end to persecution of Calvinists, and a restoration of provincial and local liberties. But in the same month, Philip II's brother, Don Juan (John) of Austria (1547–78) arrived as the new governor-general intent on restoring royal authority. In response, from 1579 to 1580 Calvinist rebels, in violation of the terms of the Pacification of Ghent, took control of many cities, including Brussels, Antwerp, and Mechelen in the South. Catholic populations here resented the actions, a sentiment that helped to cement the polarization of North and South that would now be made manifest in two separate unions.

The Union of Utrecht, 1579

The hopes of moderate rebels to effect a reconciliation were forever dashed with the failure of Matthias, archduke of Austria (1557–1619), whom the Estates General brought to the Netherlands to counter the Spanish appointee Don Juan, to establish his authority. In 1579 the battle lines were clearly defined when the southern provinces, now united against Calvinist radicals, formed the Union of Arras (January 6) to uphold royal authority and the Catholic faith while the provincial Estates of Holland and Zeeland joined with Utrecht, Friesland, Gelderland, and the lands around Groningen—the city itself remained loyal to the Habsburgs—to form the Union of Utrecht (January 23), a formal pledge to pool their efforts to carry on the struggle.

The Union of Utrecht formed the constitutional foundation of the emerging state, although the governing institutions that would eventually evolve would differ markedly from the loose league of sovereign states envisaged by the union's creators. The pact's birth represented the triumph of the policies pursued by Holland, the province that stood at the core of the revolt, where Protestants had early taken over town councils, with the notable exception of Amsterdam, and where authorities had joined with their compatriots in Zeeland to create a forerunner of the union in June 1575.

Religions too now sorted themselves out. Catholicism reigned supreme in the South, and the provinces there, having remained loyal to Spain, became the Spanish Netherlands (present-day Belgium). Protestant refugees from these areas fled north to the rebellious provinces that, under the Union of Utrecht, now called themselves the United Provinces. Wherever the rebels triumphed, the old faith was swept away or scurried underground. Calvinism emerged as the state-sanctioned creed. Catholic practices were steadily disallowed; Haarlem was the last place that witnessed public worship. Only in war-weary Overijssel did the Catholic mass persist, but the authorities there, caught between opposition to Spanish rule and dislike for the hegemony of Holland, were compelled in the end to opt for union with the six other insurrectionary provinces.

Under the terms of the Union, the Estates of the seven provinces in the North did not explicitly renounce Spanish sovereignty, but, having resolved to persist in their resistance, they now searched for a ruler. They settled on Francis, duke of Anjou and Alençon (1555–84), the brother of King Henry III of France, who accepted their offer in 1580. And having chosen a ruler, they formally declared the deposition of Philip II in the Act of Abjuration (July 1581).

THE ACT OF ABJURATION, 1581

The Dutch declaration of independence, proclaimed by the States General at The Hague on July 21, 1581, sets down in simple but eloquent terms the economic, political, and religious motivations of those in rebellion against King Philip II. The document stands as a bold act of courage and, as an assertion of the reasons for renouncing allegiance, represents a precedent-setting statement in defense of liberty, one that would serve as a model for Americans and others in the centuries to come. An excerpt follows:

As is apparent to all that a prince is constituted by God to be ruler of a people, to defend them from oppression and violence as the shepherd his sheep; and whereas God did not create the people slaves to their prince to obey his commands, whether right or wrong, but rather the prince for the sake of his subjects (without which he could not be prince) to govern them according to equity ... and even at the hazard of life to defend and preserve them. And when he does not behave thus, but, on the contrary, oppresses them, seeking opportunities to infringe on their ancient customs and privileges, exacting from them slavish compliance, then he is no longer a prince but a tyrant and the subjects are to regard him in no other way. And particularly when this is done deliberately, unauthorized by the States, they may not only disallow his authority but legally proceed to the choice of another prince for their defence. This is the only method left for subjects whose humble petitions and remonstrances could never soften their prince ... and this is what the law of nature dictates for the defence of liberty, which we ought to transmit to posterity, even at the hazard of our lives.

Source: F. Gunther Eyck, *The Benelux Countries: An Historical Survey* (Princeton, N.J.: Van Nostrand, 1959,) pp. 130–135.

In revolt against one autocrat, the Estates had no intention of abetting another and were careful therefore to place limits on their new lord's powers. Arriving in the country in February 1582, Francis soon chafed at the restrictions. In January 1583 he attempted a coup at Antwerp, where he met violent resistance (the "French fury"), and he left the country in June, discredited. The provinces came to realize that retaining the high degree of autonomy, which, over time, they had come to possess, would serve them best in arranging a government of union. They established a ruling body, a States General of all the provinces, to meet at The Hague, Holland's seat of government since the days when the counts ruled, whose delegates would decide matters of common concern but who would still have to refer back to their provincial Estates (now styled "States") before voting. No longer a lord lieutenant of the king, the stadholder was made executive officer in each of the provinces. William of Orange was delegated executive powers as stadholder of Holland and Zeeland.

The United Provinces had formed a republic under a unique form of government never before seen in contemporary Europe. But its mettle to endure had yet to be tested.

De Facto Independence, 1579–1609

Territorially compact and endowed with the trappings of political authority, the Dutch Republic set out to secure its status as a sovereign state, a struggle that would continue until 1648. The southern provinces, including the cities where Calvinists held sway, were systematically subdued by forces under Alessandro Farnese, the duke of Parma (1545–92), King Philip's new governor-general, whose armies then pushed on to the north to take towns in Gelderland, Overijssel, and Groningen. In 1579 the Spanish captured Maastricht from the Dutch rebels, who surrendered after a siege of four months. The Spanish massacred 8,000 inhabitants in retaliation for 4,000 casualties incurred by them. Under William of Orange, appointed captain-general of the union by the States General to direct military affairs, Dutch forces clung to their northwestern coastal base, where they fought essentially a holding action.

The assassination of William in 1584 marked a low point in the struggle. The act shocked the Dutch and deprived them of their leader, but it gave their cause a martyr. In the end, William's death proved to be only a momentary setback as Parma's offensive ground to a halt after 1585, his sovereign's attention and resources now focused on launching the Armada against England (1588) and intervening in the wars of religion in France (1562–98).

As an anti-Catholic power, England under Elizabeth I (r. 1558–1603) saw a natural advantage in making common cause with the Protestant Dutch rebels, and the queen duly made an alliance in 1586. The United Provinces, in turn, extended to her an offer of limited sovereignty, which she declined, but she did agree to send an expeditionary force under the command of her favorite, Robert Dudley, earl of Leicester (c. 1530–88), who would serve as governor-general and captain-general.

The Revolt of the Netherlands, 1579–1648

——— Frontier of 1579

·········· Approximate linguistic frontier

United Provinces (The Dutch Republic, from 1648)

Spanish Netherlands, 1648–1713; Austrian Netherlands, 1713–94

Archbishopric of Liège

Territories ceded by Spain to France under Louis XIV (1667–1713)

North Sea

West Frisian Is.

Groningen
Groningen
Friesland
Drenthe
Holland
Haarlem
Amsterdam
Overijssel
Leiden
The Hague
Utrecht
Gelderland
Rotterdam
Brill
Rhine R.
Zeeland
Breda
The Generality
Ostend
Antwerp
Dunkirk
Bruges
Ghent
Brabant
Liège
Maastricht
HOLY
Flanders
Brussels
Limburg
ROMAN
Dutch
Walloon
Liège
EMPIRE
Lille
Namur
Artois
Hainaut
Arras
Cambrai
Cambrai
Luxembourg
Luxembourg
German
French
FRANCE
N

0   50 miles
0   50 km

© Infobase Publishing

Flamboyant, tactless, and impulsive, Dudley proved a disaster, and he departed in 1587. Replaced by Maurits of Nassau (1567–1625), the second son of William of Orange, the republic now found a leader to match his illustrious father. Appointed stadholder in all the provinces save Friesland in 1589, Maurits won major successes in taking Bergen op Zoom in 1588, Breda in 1590, and Nijmegen and Zutphen in 1591. Further campaigns led to the recovery of all the lands lost in the 1580s. Occupation of Zeeland meant that the Dutch were able to close the Scheldt estuary, preventing ships from reaching the port of Antwerp. Together with his nephew William Louis (r. 1584–1620), stadholder of Friesland, Maurits took the city of Groningen—the territory around it was already in Dutch hands—in 1594, and the last royalist garrison in the northern Netherlands was reduced in 1597.

Volunteers from England, Scotland, and France flocked to join the Dutch, and the United Provinces, propelled by success and now joined in a general European war, moved to take the fight to Spanish soil by invading Flanders. The rival armies clashed in the dunes on the North Sea coast near Nieuwpoort on July 2, 1600, in a battle in which both sides claimed victory, although the Dutch held the field at day's end.

Tensions smoldered and hostilities sputtered on. In 1607 a Dutch fleet under Admiral Jacob van Heemskerck (1567–1607) defeated the Spanish at Gibraltar. The ability of the Dutch to take the fight to Spanish home waters demonstrated the growth in their military prowess, a feat that contributed to a willingness by Spain, albeit reluctantly, to treat with the rebels. By now the Spanish royal treasury was drained, but the Dutch too found themselves deeply in debt. Both sides sought, if not an end to the war, at least a respite from the fighting. They could not agree to make peace, but they did settle for a Twelve Years' Truce,

"WILHELMUS"

William of Orange, scion
Of an old Germanic line
I dedicate undying
Faith to this land of mine.

These are the opening lines to the "Wilhelmus," the national anthem of the Netherlands. The complete text totals 15 stanzas that were written between 1568 and 1572 in honor of William of Orange. Long a popular tune of the people, it was not chosen as the national anthem when the Kingdom of the Netherlands was established in 1815 because of its close connection to the House of Orange-Nassau. Finally recognized as the official national hymn on May 10, 1932, it is considered the oldest anthem in the world.

Hendrick Cornelisz Vroom, Dutch Ships Ramming Spanish Galleys off the Flemish Coast in October 1602 *(1617). Oil on canvas, 117.5 × 146 cm* (Collection Rijksmuseum Amsterdam)

which was ratified in 1609. Under the agreement, King Philip III (r. 1598–1621), Philip II's son and his successor to the Spanish throne, consented to treat the Dutch Republic "as if" it were, indeed, a sovereign state. Catholics in the United Provinces, although not free to worship, were freed from fear of persecution under a guarantee of the king of France.

To Europe's general surprise, rebellious residents of the northern Netherlands, few in number and living in a scattering of tiny territories, had stood their own against the power of the Continent's mightiest empire. They had not only survived, they had increasingly thrived. Under terms of the truce, direct trade between the Dutch and Spain's overseas possessions was tolerated. It was a concession that the Spanish had been compelled to grant out of necessity. By now, the merchants of Holland and Zeeland—comfortably secure from the fighting that in the 1590s was waged in border areas—were busily engaged in making the Dutch Republic the major commercial power in Europe.

4

RESPLENDENT REPUBLIC
(1609–1702)

When the representatives of the United Provinces left Antwerp for home after signing, amid pomp and pageantry, the Twelve Years' Truce on April 9, 1609, they returned to a country that had been transformed over the course of 30 years of war. A disparate group of provinces had banded together and made themselves into a sovereign state, and, forged by war, a nascent sense of Netherlands "nationality" began to emerge. The Dutch had succeeded in creating a politically viable and economically powerful polity that would soon be the envy of Europe. In an age characterized by great monarchs, from Elizabeth Tudor to Louis XIV, the Dutch crafted a republic, an entity entirely out of place in Europe. Nevertheless, during the 17th century, the Dutch Republic would occupy Europe's center stage. Treaties ending the century's wars would be signed in a host of Dutch cities.

By 1609 the business of trade on which unprecedented wealth would be made was well under way. Fleets of merchantmen and men-of-war were already plying the world's oceans. A dynamic society emerged, fueled by a degree of political and religious toleration remarkable for its time. Dissidents, malcontents, and outcasts arrived from throughout Europe to further enrich the economic, social, and intellectual fabric. The revolution in thought that would stem from tolerant tempers, which replaced divine authority with a human-willed drive to experience and experiment, would be nurtured in an urban beehive of commerce and a cultural melting pot unrivalled elsewhere in Europe. Dutch printing presses produced many of the great books that gave expression to the new ideas. Bourgeois democratic capitalism, born in the Netherlands in the 17th century, would, for the first time, be given visible expression here in an artistic flourishing that made the era a "Golden Age" of Dutch painting, one of the most spectacular bursts of creative brilliance in history.

Dirck van Delen, The Great Hall of the Binnenhof, The Hague, during the Great Assembly of the States General in 1651 *(1651). Oil on panel, copper, 52 × 66 cm* (Collection Rijksmuseum Amsterdam)

Political Institutions

Beginning in 1593, on almost every day including Sundays, between 11 A.M. and 1 P.M. about 30 men would gather around a table in a small room in the Knight's Hall (or Great Hall) of the Binnenhof in The Hague. Each man served as a member of one of the delegations from the seven provinces of the Dutch Republic. They constituted collectively the States General of the United Provinces, and together they were addressed with all the respect due to their station as "High Mightinesses" (Hooge Moogende).

The States General (Staten Generaal) emerged from a body that met only occasionally in the 1580s to become the country's central governing institution. From an entity established to better direct and finance the war with Spain, to discuss foreign relations arising from the struggle, and to perform other functions, such as the grant of charters to trading companies, the States General came to control foreign and military affairs. Each province could send as many delegates as it wished, and each week the provinces would take turns presiding as

60

president. But each province had only one vote and all seven votes had to be unanimous for policy to proceed.

Every province had its own assembly of "States" and all were constituted differently. The maritime provinces were dominated by representatives from the towns, while in the inland provinces local landed nobility wielded more equal power. In Holland, 18 towns sent delegations to the provincial States at The Hague, each with one vote, along with the nobility (*ridderschap*), which had one vote. The States of each province appointed a permanent official—the Pensionary (*raadspensionaris*)—who, as the chief administrator, provided information, carried on correspondence, and implemented decisions. Pensionaries served as the leading civil servant of their respective States. The official of the largest and richest of the provinces, Holland's Pensionary always attended the sessions of the States General with his province's representatives. He acquired the title of Grand Pensionary to indicate his status as the country's informal prime minister, whose opinions carried great weight and whose expertise made him indispensable in reaching decisions. Yet he had to tread carefully because the United Provinces were, in essence, a federation, each of the provinces complete master in its own house and each jealous of its rights.

Revenues were raised by each of the provinces on the basis of quotas assigned to each, but, if one should fail to pay, there was no way to compel receipt of monies. Taxes were gathered through various means, primarily as excise levies on a wide range of commodities, and they were collected by tax-farmers (*pachters*), who were everywhere detested. Uniformity prevailed nowhere. Each province printed its own currency and each maintained its own system of courts, with no codification of varying local laws and provincial customs.

The stadholder survived from royal times, but he was now appointed in each of the provinces by the States. There was thus no stadholder for the country as a whole, but unity was achieved because most of the provinces usually appointed the same man. Any disagreements between the stadholders would be resolved in the States General. It was natural both that descendants of the House of Orange should aspire to the post and that the memory of Prince William as the man who had given his life for the country should dispose public opinion in favor of their claims. The stadholder had ill-defined duties, largely advisory in nature, but as captain-general and admiral-general of the Union, or commander in chief of the army and navy respectively, he provided real direction in martial matters. Finally, the Council of State, a powerful organ of central government from 1585 to 1587 when it directed much of the war effort, evolved to become an important bureaucratic body, administering the army and newly acquired territories. Twelve councilors sat on the council—three from Holland and one or two from the other provinces—plus the stadholders, the treasurer-general (superintendent of finances), and the clerk of the States General. Councilors administered the army and newly acquired territories and set annual military budgets, which they sent on to the States General. The States General then forwarded petitions for the funds to the provincial States. Holland always paid more than half the sums.

The system could in no way be called a democracy because, although Dutch urban dwellers were perhaps the most literate and best informed in Europe, none of the political institutions was based on participation by popular elections. It could more correctly be defined as an oligarchy because members of the States General, provincial States, and town councils were drawn exclusively from the regents (*regenten*), namely, the wealthiest merchants, with a few from the nobility.

The governing arrangement was not an efficient one. The provinces—and the major towns within them—regarded themselves as more or less sovereign. Before decisions could be reached, constant consultations took place among the States General, the provincial States, and the town councils. Policymaking could be agonizingly slow and the process was fraught with tension. The provincial elites, zealous to maintain their prerogatives and anxious to expand their wealth, promoted local autonomy and pacifist policies, whereas the prince of Orange and his backers, concerned for the state's security, stressed centralization of power at the national level and military readiness. Politics amounted to a seesaw between the two parties, with each alternating in ascendancy. But the process made for open government, and, because no one party was ever able to secure an all-powerful grip on power, the division of interests made possible the high degree of toleration that so characterized the country. In the end, the system survived virtually unchanged until the fall of the Republic in 1795.

Religion Riles the Republic

At the same time that the Dutch stood united in fashioning a government and striving to secure their political independence, they were battling among themselves over faith-based issues. Calvinism predominated as the preferred creed of the ruling elites but its institutional embodiment, the Dutch Reformed Church, was established only in 1619 and only after the outbreak of religion-driven hostilities near to civil war. Disputes arose in the early 1600s that revolved around the core Calvinist conviction that salvation could be gained solely through divine grace dispensed by a gracious God to souls predestined to eternal bliss. Others were predestined to eternal damnation, and the utter depravity of the human condition precluded any attempt by men and women to affect the outcome. Jacobus Arminius (1560–1609), who became professor of theology at Leiden in 1603, modified that view in allowing that individuals held the power to choose God's offer of salvation. Franciscus Gomarist (1568–1641), a refugee from Bruges and also a teacher at Leiden, retorted, on the contrary, that a strict orthodoxy must prevail.

Arminians and Gomarists soon drew up sides and verbal sparring from the pulpits spread to fighting in the streets. In the minority, Arminians drafted a remonstrance in 1610 setting out their views, and they appealed to the States of Holland for protection. The regents were inclined to sympathize with the Arminians (now called Remonstrants) but maintenance of public order came first and, when a crowd of Gomarists (now called Counter-Remonstrants) attacked a Remonstrant congregation in Amsterdam in 1617, religious differences spilled over into politics.

The Grand Pensionary, Johan van Oldenbarnevelt (1547–1619) wielded considerable power as the leading official of Holland and he enjoyed enormous prestige throughout the country. Appointed in March 1586, he had opposed the earl of Leicester's dictatorial pretensions, kept the rebellious provinces united after the earl's departure, helped Maurits of Nassau concentrate the nation's military power, and negotiated the Twelve Years' Truce with Spain. In 1617, under his leadership, the States of Holland passed the "Sharp Resolution" (August 4) empowering the province's towns to raise special troops (*waardgelders*) to keep public order and declaring that regular army units owed their primary allegiance to the provincial States rather than to the States General. Holland's assertion that ultimate sovereignty rested with the provinces and not the central government enraged the Counter-Remonstrants. They proclaimed themselves the true patriots and defenders of Calvinist orthodoxy and they intimated that their opponents collaborated clandestinely with Spain. Civil war in Holland loomed as Counter-Remonstrant towns—Amsterdam, Dordrecht, Edam, and Schiedam—faced off against Remonstrants—Rotterdam, Leiden, Haarlem, and Gouda.

Prince Maurits, on the other hand, openly endorsed the Counter-Remonstrants. He garnered support to undermine Oldenbarnevelt, under whose leadership he had long chafed. Purging town councils of Remonstrants where he could, he worked to isolate Holland in the States General. In July 1618, over the objections of Holland and its ally Utrecht, the States General voted to disband the *waardgelders*. Maurits led troops into Utrecht to enforce the decision. With Holland itself divided, Oldenbarnevelt abandoned the struggle and the special troops dispersed in August. Arrested and charged with treason, the Grand Pensionary went to the block at The Hague in May 1619. The stadholder and his party replaced the States of Holland in controlling the reins of government.

In the same month that Oldenbarnevelt met his fate, a national synod of the Dutch Reformed Church concluded six months of deliberations at Dordrecht (Synod of Dort) in condemning Arminian theology. Remonstrant preachers were banned. Roman Catholics and all Protestants but Calvinists were excluded from holding office in church and state. A professor of theology at Utrecht and a Counter-Remonstrant, Gijsbrecht Voetius (1589–1671), developed a Calvinist scholasticism that became academic orthodoxy throughout much of Protestant Europe. An influential voice in shaping Dutch culture, he affirmed that doctrines must be actively practiced and he called for strict observance of the Sabbath and a sober personal morality.

Calvinist ministers (*predikanten*) served both as central pillars of society, exhorting, admonishing, and warning their congregations to follow the teachings of the Scriptures, and as major props of the state, which, they believed, Calvinists had created with God's blessing and aid. The Dutch Reformed Church enjoyed a special status as the officially sanctioned creed. However, although ministers had a greater influence in the affairs of the Republic after the Synod of Dort, they remained subject to rule by the regent-oligarchs. Their request, for example, to remove all remaining pictures and interior decorations from Calvinist churches was granted, but the regents disallowed removal of organs. Ministers were forbidden to serve on town councils or in the provincial States.

Calvinism extolled virtues of sobriety, thrift, and hard work, and it was the practice of these, many believed, that contributed to a considerable degree to the Dutch commercial expansion and cultural flowering of the 17th century.

Independence from Spain

The religious disputes that wracked the Republic played out during the 12 years' respite from fighting from 1609 to 1621. The battles over religion reflected the atmosphere of tension that prevailed in a country whose citizens' right to be free from foreign rule had still to be definitively settled. The Dutch awaited the renewal of hostilities while busily building up their economic wealth and maintaining their military machine. The army and navy were kept in prime readiness thanks to measures first put in place in the 1590s that established orderliness and discipline in the ranks and mandated regular payment of troops, reforms necessitated in part by the building of a defensive ring of fortifications around the country's periphery.

Better defenses put in place before 1609 were badly needed because, with the expiration of the Twelve Years' Truce, the country found itself besieged by Spanish armies, isolated diplomatically, and reeling economically following the reimposition of Spanish embargoes. Plague raged in Amsterdam, Delft, Leiden, and elsewhere in 1624. New taxes on butter provoked riots, but a stamp duty imposed on legal and other documents marked an innovation in European taxation as a measure to tax the wealthy and not the poor. Prince Maurits's death in April 1625 and the fall in June of Breda, under siege for almost a year, found fortunes at their lowest ebb.

Frederick Henry (1584–1647), Maurits's younger half brother, who was made captain-general and then stadholder, led an energetic drive to revive the states' fortunes. Stylish, culturally refined, and a statesman who sought compromise where he could, Frederick Henry profited from Spain's overextension in fighting France in Italy and from England's entry into the contest as a Dutch ally. An alliance with France was also concluded (1635). Spanish forces contracted while Dutch armies grew. Spain's supply lines on the lower Rhine were severed and Frederick Henry, dubbed the "forcer of cities" (*stedendwinger*), commenced a conquering campaign. The garrison at s'Hertogenbosch was the first to surrender in 1629, North Brabant was won between 1629 and 1637, and parts of Limburg were taken. The besieged fortress city of Maastricht fell in 1632. The city would be ruled jointly by the United Provinces and the prince-bishop of Liège until 1795.

Negotiations for a settlement began in the 1630s; in the 1640's these merged with those under way to end the Thirty Years' War (1618–48), the conflict over territory and religion fought among all of Europe's major powers that had enmeshed the Dutch struggle. It took three years (1643–46) for the provinces to reach agreement on the composition and powers of the Dutch delegation to the international conference at Münster. By 1648 all the provinces save Zeeland were willing to make peace. It was arranged, with the agreement of Zeeland's representative, that a settlement would be signed "unanimously by those present" while he was out of the room. Under terms of the Treaty of Westphalia (October 24, 1648), the United Provinces won not only formal recognition as an independent state but also territorial gains in the south and southeast, including the northern strip of Flanders on the southern bank of the Scheldt (Zeeland-Flanders), Maastricht and the area around it, and the present-day province of North Brabant. These lands of the so-called Generality were ruled directly by the Council of State as a conquered territory, in part because of the perceived threat posed by a population that was overwhelmingly Roman Catholic. The Dutch secured a major concession with the agreement to keep the Scheldt River closed to commerce, a lock that put a stop to the once lucrative trade in Antwerp, the Spanish Netherlands, and opened a key to the continued prosperity of the northern Netherlands.

Once the threat to national survival subsided following battlefield victories in the 1620s, religious toleration returned as well. By 1630 there were Remonstrant churches in Amsterdam and Rotterdam. A state-sanctioned Bible finally appeared in 1637. The writers who transcribed the Bible borrowed from various Dutch dialects, but they used primarily those spoken in the urban centers of Holland, thus contributing to the emergence of a standard modern Dutch language.

Roman Catholics still totaled about a third of the population in the mid-17th century. Pockets of Catholics existed everywhere, especially among the lower middle class, and they constituted a majority in Limburg and notably in newly conquered North Brabant, where the Counter-Reformation had been in place for 50 years and whose population stiffly resisted vigorous protestantizing policies. For more than 150 years after militant Calvinism emerged relatively triumphant at the Synod of Dort, Catholics could not legally worship in public or in private. The buying and selling of Catholic devotional literature, the celebration of Catholic feast days, and the wearing of crucifixes and other Roman Catholic insignia were all strictly forbidden. Catholics were not allowed to give their children a Roman Catholic education or even send them abroad to receive one there. Many among Dutch Protestants viewed them as actual or potential traitors liable to give aid, from 1568 to 1648, to Spain and, from 1648 to 1748, to France.

Catholics were bitterly disappointed that the peace signed at Münster included no recognition of their rights to practice their religion, but, in fact, the laws in place against their faith were never fully enforced, and they became easier to evade by the late 17th and into the 18th centuries. Underground networks of pious women (*klopjes*) supported church activities and the Mass could be heard in safehouses located, at first, in attics and warehouses and, later, in houses adapted as chapels (*schuilkerken*). Protests by Protestants met a tepid response, authorities often agreeing to allow clandestine services in return for a gift of money.

Orthodox Calvinist attitudes toward other Protestant sects were less hostile than toward Catholics. Grudging toleration was accorded to these denominations, which practiced under differing legal rights and met varying degrees of social acceptance. Mennonites won full citizenship rights in 1672. Religious dissenters of varied stripes from across Europe found refuge throughout the century—from French Huguenots to Scottish Presbyterians to English Brownists and Baptists, including, most famously, the Pilgrims, who began to arrive in Leiden in 1607.

RELIGIOUS TOLERANCE IN THE DUTCH COLONIES

The religious toleration that made the Dutch Republic unique in 17th-century Europe also characterized its far-flung possessions. In a letter dated April 13, 1663, the Dutch West India Company admonished its director-general at New Netherland, Peter Stuyvesant (1612–72), not to carry out his request to expel Quakers from the colony. The company drew reference to the beneficial effects brought by tolerance to the city of Amsterdam, effects that were reproduced in New Netherland and New Amsterdam and that would continue under the same policy, after 1664, in the colony and city of New York. The company directors wrote from Amsterdam:

> The consciences of men, at least, ought ever to remain free and unshackled. Let every one be unmolested as long as he is modest; as long as his conduct in a political sense is irreproachable; as long as he does not disturb others or oppose the government. This maxim of moderation has always been the guide of the magistrates of this city, and the consequence has been that, from every land people have flocked to this asylum. Tread thus in these steps, and, we doubt not, you will be blessed.

Source: Anton Phelps Stokes, *Church and State in the United States*, Vol. I (New York: Harper and Brothers, 1950), p. 152.

Jewish exiles from Spain and Portugal settled in urban areas, notably Amsterdam, where Jews congregated in the district around the Breestraat, later renamed the Jodenbreestraat (Broad Street of the Jews) and where the Portuguese Synagogue, founded in 1675, remains today an enduring monument to their presence. Jewish merchants there became active early on in the sugar and slave trades. Jews were tolerated on condition they not intermarry with Christians, refrain from proselytizing, and provide for their own poor. In 1657 the States General recognized Jews as nationals of the Republic, although full citizenship rights were not awarded until 1796.

Toleration remained the key feature of the Dutch creedal scene. The Union of Utrecht enshrined a non-meddlesome approach toward issues of conscience, which endured. An English visitor to Amsterdam observed: "I believe in this street where I lodge there be well near as many religions as there be houses: for one neighbour knows not, nor cares not much what religion the other is" (Howell 1753:26).

At the Center of Global Trade

The Dutch Republic can be characterized as Europe's earliest modern economy, in that during the 17th century capital amassed through commerce there was first invested in large amounts in widely diversified economic sectors to produce high productivity in industry, trade, fishing, and farming. Investment brought organizational and technical improvements, reflected in lower costs and higher quality. By the standards of the time, the large proportion of the population serving in formal apprenticeships and enrolled in higher education attests to a high investment in human capital formation.

Maritime Trade

Ringside witnesses to the age of exploration opened by their Spanish overlords a century before, the Dutch had never stopped their waterborne commerce during the conflict-laden late 16th century. By 1600 they had become the Continent's premier pilots, sailors, shipbuilders, and maritime merchants. During the 16th century, the focus of Dutch trade gradually moved from the inland waterways to the ocean ports. By the end of the century, the Dutch had secured a dominant position in Baltic Sea shipping, the "mother trade" (*moedernegotie*) of the Republic since the late Middle Ages, in perfecting a new kind of cargo ship to ply the relatively short runs of the Baltic and North seas trades. The famous *fluyt*, "flute" or "flyboat," first developed probably in Hoorn about 1590, comprised not much more than a closed hold. Long and flat-bottomed with a shallow draft and masts spread far apart for maximum cargo space, the *fluyt* was the first ship designed to fit its function. Cheap to build, with few or no guns and the sparest possible rigging, it needed a smaller crew and proved so economical to run that the Dutch could charge freight rates a third to a half lower than their English competitors. Wherever it sailed, the *fluyt* reigned supreme, carrying timber, grain, and naval stores.

Timber imports were indispensable to economic growth. In 1647 alone 387 ships sailed back and forth between Dutch ports and Norway bringing the wood for constructing ships, wharves, and the very bedrock for buildings. Large planks driven into the marshy ground provided the firm foundation needed for Amsterdam's building boom. By the mid-17th century, the products of Dutch shipwrights were in demand throughout Europe, and it is estimated a quarter of a million men were serving on Dutch merchant and military vessels.

The fishing fleet followed the herring, haddock, and cod, sailing in June and returning in September thanks to a system whereby, having stored salt onboard, crews were able to transship the barreled catch to other craft. A central prop of the economy in the 16th and 17th centuries, the fishing trade operated out of all of the ports in Holland and Zeeland, the fleet at Enzhuizen being the largest. Salt refining was centered in and around Zierikzee and Dordrecht.

That the merchants and mariners of Holland operated their ships more efficiently than their competitors also stemmed from the manner in which they managed their commercial activities. Starting in the 16th century there emerged in the northern Netherlands a highly flexible form of business organization known as the *rederij*, a cooperative business enterprise in which individuals (*reders*) would contribute capital in varying amounts to buy, build, and charter a ship and its cargo. Often the skipper himself was a part owner with a direct interest in the success of the venture. Operating a business this way helped to spread investment in shipping, giving more and more people a stake in making money and helping to further integrate the maritime and mercantile communities.

The United Provinces emerged from their struggle for independence the richest country in Europe. By the middle of the 17th century, the Dutch had become the exporters, importers, and carriers of goods from the Baltic to the Mediterranean seas and from Russia to England.

The urge to make and spend money drove the Dutch to expand their commercial activities worldwide. In the course of the 17th century, traveling outward from their northern waters, they built trading networks in spices, silks, coffee, tea, sugar, and slaves from the Mediterranean to North Africa, from the Arctic North to North America, and from the East Indies to the West Indies. Dutch seamen led the way as pioneering wayfarers exploring the world's farthest reaches. As early as the 1590s Willem Barentsz (c. 1550–97) captained several expeditions into northern seas beyond where Dutch whaling fleets were active in an effort to find a northeast passage to China. Forced to spend a harrowing winter on Novaya Zemlya, on what was later named the Barents Sea, he and his crews failed to find one, but they won for the Dutch access to the Russian trade in furs and timber.

In 1580 Spain acquired control of Portugal and closed its capital, Lisbon, to Dutch traders, the port from which the Dutch had long secured Asian goods for resale throughout Europe. In 1595 a book appeared in Amsterdam that created a sensation. Jan Huyghen van Linschoten (1563–1611), who had spent 13 years in the Far East, published a volume, *Itinerario,* describing not only Portuguese commercial methods in Asia but also the shaky foundations of their rule there. Desperate to retain their lucrative trade, Dutch merchants fitted out their cargo ships and set their sights on the Orient. The first Dutch expedition to reach what is now Indonesia arrived in 1596 and what they found there confirmed their expectations—a treasure trove of spices ready for the taking. A second Dutch fleet of 22 ships fitted out by five rival trading companies left in 1598. One company sailed west around South America and through the Pacific to make the first Dutch trip around the world. A second group of four companies sailed their ships through the Indian Ocean, laying claim to the island of Mauritius, which they named for Prince Maurits and where the Dutch remained until they abandoned the outpost in 1710. Four of these vessels returned in July 1599 and the wealth they brought exceeded the wildest expectations of backers and public alike. Amsterdammers rang their church bells in delight. "For as long as Holland has been Holland, there have never arrived ships as richly laden as these," noted an anonymous observer of the cargoes that contained 600,000 pounds of pepper and 250,000 pounds of cloves, nutmeg, and mace (Haley 1972, 24).

To maximize their competitive advantage, the government persuaded the many competing trading companies to pool their financial assets to create the United Netherlands Chartered East India Company (Verenigde Oost-Indische Compagnie, VOC) in 1602. Under the charter granted by the States General to the VOC, the company was granted monopoly rights to trade and navigation for 21 years over the vast reaches east of the Cape of Good Hope and west of the Straits of Magellan. The company consisted of chambers (*kamers*) in six port cities—Amsterdam, Rotterdam, Delft, Enkhuizen, Middelburg, and Hoorn—made up of individuals chosen from the community of wealthy merchants and bankers. The chambers assigned from their members delegates to sit on the central board of 17 directors (Heeren XVII), the number allotted each chamber based on the regional representation of capital in shares contributed. Amsterdam held the largest number of seats at eight. The company was given the power to conclude treaties of alliance and peace, to wage defensive war, and to build forts and trading posts.

Backed by the government's blessing, the VOC constituted the world's first trading company based on permanent shares of capital. Fitted out with gunpowder and cannonballs, fleets were dispatched to the East Indies—more than a year's journey away—to take Portuguese military/trading posts by force. In 1605 armed merchantmen captured the Portuguese fort at Amboina, in the Moluccan Islands, which the VOC then established as its first secure base in the Indies. In the midst of declaring dazzling dividends that jumped from 50 percent in 1606 to 329 percent in 1609, the company soon emerged as master of the spice trade. The Dutch seized Jakarta in 1619, renaming it Batavia and making it the administrative center of the Netherlands East Indies.

Andries Beeckman, The Castle at Batavia, Seen from West Kali Besar *(c. 1656–58). Oil on canvas, 108 × 151.5 cm* (Collection Rijksmuseum Amsterdam)

Model of the Prins Willem *(1651). Oak and limewood, 103 cm. The East Indiaman* Prins Willem *was named for Prince William II. Built in Middelburg, it was launched on January 1, 1650.* (Collection Rijksmuseum Amsterdam)

Interloping English traders on Amboina were massacred in 1623. By the mid-17th century, the company operated as a virtual state within a state, the distance from the homeland and the wealth its ships brought home compelling the States General to leave the firm alone and give it virtually a free hand in the East Indies. The richest private company in the world, in 1670 the VOC counted 150 merchant ships, 40 warships, a private army, and 50,000 employees.

Employing ruthless methods to push their competitors aside, the company moved beyond the Indies to drive the Portuguese systematically from the trading posts they had held for a century in Ceylon (Sri Lanka) and on the South Asian subcontinent. By 1658 they held all of coastal Ceylon and, a decade later, they occupied isolated trading stations on the southern coasts of India. Moving farther afield, they founded Fort Zeelandia on Formosa (now Taiwan) in 1624, drove the Portuguese out of southern bases on the island and, in 1641, pushed the Spanish from northern holdings, before the Dutch in turn were expelled by Chinese arriving from the mainland in 1662. Regular trading relations were also established with Japan. From 1641 to 1854 the Dutch were the only Europeans permitted to trade there, exchanging European goods for Japanese gold, silver, and lacquerware from their isolated island post of Deshima in Nagasaki Bay.

Within only a few short decades, East Indiamen ships had won fame for the seemingly irrepressible daring of their captains and crews. South and east of Batavia they pressed on to within sight of western Australia's barren shore and Abel Tasman (1603–59) sailed beyond the continent's east coast to discover Tasmania, Fiji, and New Zealand. Jacob Le Maire (c. 1585–1616) and Willem Schouten (c. 1567–1625) sailed two vessels from Texel in 1615 west across the Atlantic, discovering a new route to the East Indies through Cape Horn, rounded for the first time on January 29, 1616, and which Schouten named for his birthplace. They sailed in search of gold, but they found none, leaving instead a legacy in new island discoveries, including the Admiralty Islands and the Schouten Islands in the southwest Pacific.

Enticed east by spices, the Dutch traveled west in search of salt, their sources in Portugal closed by Spain in 1621. The Dutch West India Company (Geoctroyeerde West-Indische Compagnie, WIC) was chartered that year, under a central governing board of 19 members (Heeren XIX), to finance incursions into the Spanish and Portuguese Americas, where the Venezuelan coastal pans in particular furnished a fine natural salt with which to preserve the fishing fleets' catch. Caribbean waters offered added benefits in goods from contraband trading with Spanish settlements and in booty seized from preying on Spanish ships. The capture by Piet Heyn (1577–1629) of the Spanish silver fleet in 1628 assumed mythic status in the Dutch historical memory.

Anxious to secure trading depots on Caribbean islands, the WIC occupied Curaçao, the largest of the Leeward Islands and one that had long been abandoned by the Spanish, in 1634. Aruba was seized in 1636 and the Dutch, together with the French, drove the Spanish from Sint Maarten, which they divided between them in 1648. Sint Eustatius (Statia) was colonized by the company in 1636 with settlers from Zeeland, and Saba with those from Sint Eustatius in about 1640. Colonies were founded in Guyana (1625–1803), Brazil (1630–54), Suriname (1667–1975), and Demarara (1667–1814). The WIC under

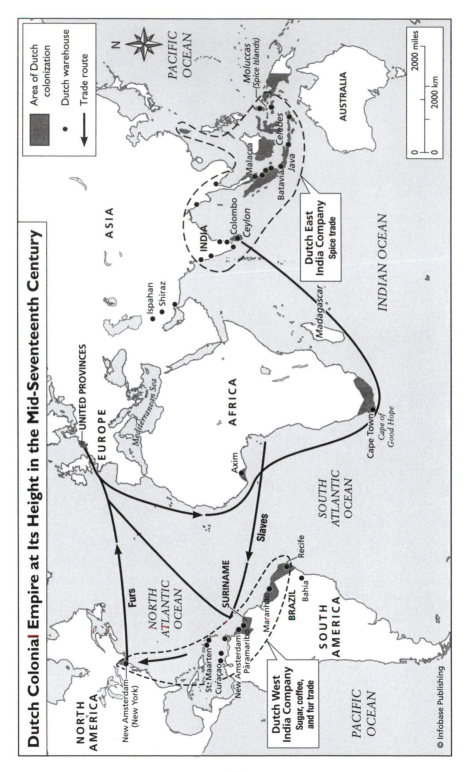

Dutch Colonial Empire at Its Height in the Mid-Seventeenth Century

Legend:
- Area of Dutch colonization
- Dutch warehouse
- Trade route

N

2000 miles
2000 km

PACIFIC OCEAN

Moluccas (Spice Islands)

Celebes
Malacca
Batavia
Java

ASIA

Colombo
Ceylon
INDIA

Dutch East India Company
Spice trade

Ispahan
Shiraz

EUROPE

UNITED PROVINCES

Mediterranean Sea

AFRICA

Madagascar

INDIAN OCEAN

AUSTRALIA

Cape Town
Cape of Good Hope

Axim

Slaves

SOUTH ATLANTIC OCEAN

Recife
Maranhão
BRAZIL
Bahia

Dutch West India Company
Sugar, coffee, and fur trade

SURINAME
Paramaribo
New Amsterdam
Curaçao
St. Maarten

Furs

NORTH ATLANTIC OCEAN

New Amsterdam (New York)

NORTH AMERICA

SOUTH AMERICA

PACIFIC OCEAN

© Infobase Publishing

its governor-general John Maurits of Nassau-Siegen (1604–79) made an especially vigorous effort to occupy northeastern coastal areas of Brazil. The Dutch transformed the region into a profitable colony, largely through sugar production, and Jewish merchants arrived to set up operations at Recife before Dutch colonizers were ousted by the Portuguese, the discoverers of the country, who returned in force in 1654.

Colonists on Sint Eustatius first planted tobacco but soon switched to sugar, and sugar plantations established throughout the Dutch Caribbean islands furnished the bulk of Europe's supply in the 17th century. On Sint Eustatius as well as on Curaçao, the largest of the Leeward Islands, the WIC established slave depots for trade with the continental Americas.

A fashion fad in Europe for furs drew the Dutch north. In Dutch service, Englishman Henry Hudson (1565–1611) in 1609 sailed his *De Halve Maan* (*The Half Moon*), a brand-new ship with a crew of eight Englishmen and eight Dutchmen, up the river later named for him and, in doing so, laid claim to one of the most strategically significant slices of the North American mainland. The first permanent settlement of Fort Orange (just south of present-day Albany, New York) was founded in 1614 to trade directly with Native Americans for beaver pelts even before the settlement of New Amsterdam was made in 1626 on Manhattan island, famously purchased by Governor Peter Minuit (1580–1638) for 60 guilders ($24) worth of goods. Unlike elsewhere in their empire where the Dutch preferred not to plant settlements but rather to set up military trading posts at strategic spots to which the native inhabitants would come to trade, their North American territory became a real colony. Not only soldiers and WIC employees came but also ordinary settlers, who arrived intending to stay. Its history short (1614–64) and tempestuous, marked by wars with Native American tribes, threats from intruding Swedes and English, and, above all, neglect by a ruling company—wholly engrossed in the struggle against Spain—more intent on privateering and profitmaking than attracting emigrants, New Netherland managed, nevertheless, to bequeath a scattering of settlements from western Long Island up the Hudson and Mohawk rivers as far as present-day Schenectady, New York, that has left an enduring legacy in place-names, folklore, and English-language loanwords.

Under the auspices of the VOC, Jan van Riebeeck (1619–77) founded Cape Town, southern Africa's oldest settlement, in 1652. At first a watering place for ships bound to and from the Far East, the Cape Colony saw settlers start to arrive by the end of the 17th century. By then a series

The Stadthuys (City Hall) of New York in 1679. Buildings with Dutch-style gables survived in New Amsterdam for many decades after the English takeover. They vanished in time until revived in lower Manhattan in the early 20th century. (City Museum of New York)

of forts and trading posts dotted the West African coast, first serving as watering stations but soon also operating as slave markets to meet the constant need of Dutch New World plantations for such labor. Curaçao, in particular, grew wealthy on the trade. In 1637 the Dutch wrested Elmina from the Portuguese, their strongest fortification on the Guinea coast. They also sold captive labor to other nations, bringing the first 19 slaves, captured from a Spanish slave ship, to Virginia in 1619, and, from 1663 to 1701, Dutch traders held the state contract (*asiento*) for transport of African slaves to Spain's American colonies. Global trading ties gave a cosmopolitan character to the major cities, especially those in Holland, that was probably unmatched in Europe. The Dutch acquired a flair for foreign languages that they have retained ever since. A traveler remarked: "There is no Part of Europe so haunted with all sorts of foreigners as the Netherlands, which makes the Inhabitants as well Women as Men, so well versed in all sorts of Languages, so that, in Exchange-time, one may hear 7 or 8 sorts of Tongues spoken. . . ." (Howell 1753, 103).

Wealth at Home

The Dutch Republic lived by trade, and it was commerce carried on largely in the maritime provinces of Holland and Zeeland that produced unprecedented levels of prosperity in the 17th century. The integration of specialized industry and agriculture with the expanding mercantile activities in the port cities combined to energize the economy. Commerce was spurred by the existence of a relatively large class of people with the money to invest. The population grew everywhere, but Holland and Friesland experienced a demographic explosion between 1500 and 1650, the number of inhabitants increasing threefold, from 350,000 to 1 million. Urban growth proved the most rapid—as early as the first decade of the 17th century 45 percent of the population lived in cities; this percentage was the highest in Europe. Municipalities across the country grew but nowhere more so than in Holland, where 61 percent of the population lived in urban areas in 1675. Protestant immigrants, evicted from the Catholic South, notably from Antwerp after its fall to the Spanish in 1585, proved a boon to the Republic. They brought capital, connections, and skills.

Antwerp's loss proved to be Amsterdam's gain. A predominantly Catholic city when Calvinists took control in 1578, Amsterdam adapted quickly to the change of regime. The influx of newcomers arrived with funds to spend and to lend that soon made it the commercial and financial center of northern Europe. Awash with money and with the population soaring to 105,000 in the 1620s and double that a mere 20 years later, Amsterdam's planners approved one of the earliest and most extensive real estate schemes. Three concentric canals were mapped out to arc around the city. Closest to the city center, the Herengracht (Gentlemen's canal) was designed to be—and it remains today—the choicest of the new waterways. Rows of gabled townhouses made of brick—long and narrow and packed tightly together to accommodate the maximum number of residents—lined newly built canals, and a monumental new town hall—now the royal palace—built between 1648 and 1655 manifested municipal wealth and self-confidence. It was at this time that the city first earned its title "Venice of the North" in reference both to the watery configuration and to the economic wealth that it shared with the Italian city-state. Born in Utrecht, sculptor and architect Hendrick de Keyser (1565–1621) moved to Amsterdam, where he was named city architect. A prolific artist, de Keyser designed a profusion of houses and churches and singlehandedly gave birth to a style subsequently known as Amsterdam Renaissance in which classical elements, such as cornices and pilasters, were used lavishly but

THE GOLDEN AGE OF AMSTERDAM

Peter Mundy, a member of a merchant family from Cornwall, England, visited Amsterdam in April 1639. The following is an excerpt from his description of the city during the Golden Age.

At Amsterdam, when building a house, they must drive in certain timbers 42 or 43 feet before they meet any solid foundation: these timbers are said to last hundreds of years as long as they lie in moist earth....The canals and streets so long, so straight: the buildings so fair and uniform: ranks of trees on each side of the canal....

They strive to adorn their houses especially the outer or street room, with costly pieces. Blacksmiths and cobblers will often have a painting by their forge or in their Stall. Also their other furniture and ornaments costly and curious. Rich cupboards and porcelain, costly fine cages with birds commonly to be found in houses of the lower class. Few carts or sleds used but great quantities of commodities are brought by water in lighters to their warehouse doors.

For their shipping, traffic and commerce by sea, I conceive no place in the world comes near it. Whilst I was there 26 ships came into the Texel.... By means of their shipping they are plentifully supplied with what the earth affords for the use of man, as corn, pitch, tar, flax, hemp from Danzig and the Baltic Sea; masts, timber and fish from Norway; cattle from Denmark.

Their hospitals for orphans, sick persons, lame soldiers, old people, mad people, etc. are fairly built, wonderfully well furnished and cleanly kept.

chiefly as decorative elements. Works of his that survive include the Zuiderkerk (1603–11), with its accompanying tower (1614), and the Westerkerk (1620–31), as well as the town hall in Delft (1618–20).

The Bank of Amsterdam (Amsterdamsche Wisselbank), founded in 1609, formalized the direct bank transfer, which made the bank's future in giving it an enduring reputation for sterling stability and helped make the Dutch Republic a highly monetized economy in the 17th century. But it was not uniformly monetized. The Dutch retained from Habsburg days the guilder as the unit of account but there were no less than 14 mints, including two in Holland and one in each of the other six provinces, actively minting coins. The government established a Generality

Amsterdam townhouses (The Netherlands Board of Tourism and Conventions)

Source: Peter Mundy, *The Travels of Peter Mundy 1597–1667,* edited by John Keast (Redruth, England: Dyllansow Truran, 1984), pp. 62, 64.

Mint Chamber to implement a unified monetary policy, but it failed to stem the independence of the mints. Coins of all types, including many foreign coins, circulated widely, debasing the money supply. The Bank of Amsterdam accepted deposits of all types and values of coins, assessed the gold and silver contents, and allowed depositors to withdraw equivalent values at rates of exchange, which it set in gold florins. By 1701 it boasted 2,698 depositors, who banked more than 16 million florins. In doing so, the bank made it easier for merchants to operate and helped reduce monetary confusion by supplying mints with coins, furnished by depositors. The Amsterdam Bank van Lening (lending bank) extended individual and business credit and the two banks together produced an expanding fund of credit and the lowest interest rates in Europe. The government's control over coinage came with edicts in 1691 and 1694 closing six of the mints and, of the eight remaining, mandating that most of the metal for minting be given to only two (Dordrecht and Utrecht). In conjunction with the city's commercial growth, they grew to become the clearinghouse of world trade, implementing capital transfers and settling international debts. German emperors borrowed here, both sides in the English civil war sought credit here, and rulers sent subsidies to other rulers by way of Amsterdam, which remained Europe's financial capital until the French Revolution.

The Amsterdam Stock Exchange (*beurs*), founded in 1602 by the Dutch East India Company to conduct business in its printed stocks and bonds, began trading shares of long-term joint-stock companies, another financial innovation, in 1613. Speculation started with commodities and grew to include futures. Developed and perfected here,

TULIP MANIA

Tulips arrived in the Netherlands from Ottoman Turkey around 1570. The flowers were scarce at first, but demand grew as gardeners strove to acquire bulbs, which they would crossbreed to produce ever more brilliantly colored blooms. By the 1630s some 500 different varieties were grown. A class of brokers arose in all the major towns engaged in buying and selling, which soon progressed from trading for flowers they actually possessed to dealing in bulbs still in the ground. The creation of a futures market transformed tulips from blossoms treasured by connoisseurs for their beauty to abstractions valued by dealers only for their profits. By 1636 tulip trading had turned to tulip mania. The most famous bulb—the *Semper Augustus*—sold for 6,000 guilders (when average yearly income was 150 guilders), and tulips were also

Although not native to the Netherlands, tulips are the country's most famous flower. (The Netherlands Board of Tourism and Conventions)

such trading could produce both booms and busts in the market; nevertheless, the Amsterdam bourse became the foremost commodity market on the Continent. Its price lists were consulted across western Europe.

Trade in Polish and Baltic grain that began in earnest in the late 15th century made Amsterdam Europe's leading storage center by the turn of the 17th century. By then, not only wheat from these areas but also Russian timber, American tobacco, Spanish wool, Brazilian sugar, and East Indian spices poured into Amsterdam's warehouses, some of it to be reexported and some to serve as source materials for domestic industries. Diamond cutters from Antwerp brought their craft to Amsterdam, where it joined shipbuilding, tobacco curing, beer brewing, glass blowing, and a host of other trades. The VOC's shipyards in the city—Europe's largest—served as the lodestone for those intent on learning the latest in shipbuilding designs and nautical expertise, drawing no less an illustrious visitor than Czar Peter the Great of Russia (1672–1725), who spent

exchanged for land, livestock, and houses. Prices even for popular kinds rose to record highs—from 60 guilders per pound in January 1636 to 1,400 guilders in February.

However, demand for these ordinary, commonplace tulips, which were sold in bulk by the pound, was largely nonexistent. Gardeners—the only people interested in actually planting and growing flowers—did not want them. Ill at ease with a market increasingly perceived to be out of control, brokers began to sell their holdings without reinvesting profits in yet more bulbs. Too many sellers for too few buyers led to a fall in the market, beginning in Haarlem on February 1, 1637, that produced panicked selling nationwide within a few days.

Tulip mania (alternatively tulipomania) is used metaphorically today to refer to any large economic bubble in which stock market speculation causes prices of commodities and assets to increase astronomically, leading to an eventual crash that oftentimes produces serious economic and social dislocations.

Tulip growing did survive. Worldwide demand soared in the 19th century, and sites just west of Haarlem expanded to newly drained areas to the south, where the huge tulip fields of tourist fame appeared. The majority of bulbs are grown in North Holland today. Dutch farmers introduced many different species, and techniques to keep bulbs at low temperatures in a state of suspended animation now make it possible to grow tulips year-round.

four months in 1697 in Amsterdam and Zaandam studying carpentry and naval science as well as soliciting skilled craftsmen whom he engaged to return with him to assist in his efforts to build a modern navy.

The Dutch were the first to import Chinese and Japanese porcelain on a large scale into northern Europe, and, as early as 1614, sky blue–colored, tin-glazed pottery began to be produced in Delft as an imitation of Chinese porcelain. Production techniques improved so that, by the last quarter of the 17th century, Delftware had become refined enough to be sold in China. Leeuwarden became a center for gold- and silversmiths. By the middle of the century Leiden led Europe in the weaving of woolens and Haarlem led it in production of linen.

When not invested in trade, funds were used to finance land reclamation. New polders appeared from 1597 to 1647 as deep lakes—many formed by peat digging—that pockmarked the landscape in northern Holland. They were drained by means of more efficiently built windmills. The Beemster (1608–12) to the northwest of Amsterdam—the first large-scale polder reclaimed from a lake—was the first to feature a detailed plan to follow the reclamation. A strict rectangular pattern of land division was implemented based on a grid of squares superimposed on the landscape, and this rational scheme was followed in future land reclamation projects.

The newly drained regions added 1,400 farms that further fueled the growth of market gardening to supply nearby towns. Cheese and butter became widely available and more beef entered diets as cattle bred in Scandinavia were shipped to the Netherlands to be fattened for slaughter. Holland and Friesland became famous for their cows, while wheat was grown predominantly in Zeeland and Groningen provinces. Rural society in the west became increasingly commercialized and mobile, while in the east it remained traditional and settled. An agricultural depression set in during the 1660s, induced by a rise in English grain and dairy imports and a drop in exports, but even the poorest of the country's rural residents—the peasant tenant-farmers of Drenthe—experienced an improvement in living standards over the course of the century.

Society and Intellectual Life

The total population of the Republic at its zenith in the 1650s is estimated at about 1.9 million, less than the population of England and far less than that of France. Refugees from the southern Netherlands joined emigrants from the countryside to swell the ranks of town dwellers, and, comfortable in their prospering, tolerant homeland, the Dutch felt little urge to emigrate to their overseas colonies. Even though the Dutch people were at war for most of the century, they were not subject to lengthy invasions or occupations and the civil wars that wracked England, France, and Germany were absent. Bandits and highwaymen were minor nuisances.

Too small to feed its own populace, the country relied on Baltic grain imports. The country's short distances and many waterways gave it an efficient system of distribution that ensured the Dutch did not starve. However, outbreaks of plague periodically recurred, especially in the vulnerable seaports.

The United Provinces were rich, but the imposing wealth of the regents and the nobles, reflected, as the century progressed, in their grand townhouses and country estates, represented the fortunes of only the few. For those engaged in practical trades, whom the Dutch called the artisan class, hours were long—14-hour days were normal—and wages low. Taxes were the bane of the working classes because practically every necessity of life required payment of an impost. Wood, salt, soap, peat, meat, bread, butter, and beans were taxed. Duties were levied to register a house and on land, horses, cows, and various kinds of fruit. A payment was demanded to enter a walled town at its gate and tolls were charged over bridges and at canal crossings.

Carpenters, cobblers, weavers, bakers, blacksmiths, and others lived in cramped, one- and two-bedroom houses; because they were in short supply, the rents for these houses were high. Their diets varied little and consisted of a typical midday meal of cod, herring, or a meat stew (*hutespot*) made of chopped mutton, vinegar, parsnips, and prunes boiled in fat, which was eaten with a sticky black bread and washed down with beer, a healthier beverage than the fouled water that was all too common. The popularity of tobacco endured, and the pipe-smoking Dutchman became pervasive in European imagery.

The Dutch, both rich and poor, dressed simply. The family formed the centerpiece of society. Dutch families were unique in Europe at the time in being relatively small—averaging three to four children—and largely nuclear—relatives such as grandparents rarely shared the home. The Dutch hugged and spoiled their children in an age when most Europeans believed the young should be subdued and held to strict parental submission, and the young often stayed at home until their mid- to late twenties (Montias and Loughman 2001, 13). They took great pride in furnishing their residences and would bequeath to later ages the notion of home as an intimate, private place. Dutch men and women—whether merchant or milkmaid—wielded brooms and mops with such vigor that tidiness and cleanliness became national trade-marks. An English traveler observed:

> No people in Europe are so neat in their houses; the meanest sort being extremely nice in setting them out to best advantage. The women spend the greater amount of their time in washing, rubbing, and scouring. . . . The floors of their lower rooms are commonly chequered with black and white marble, and the walls and chimneys covered with a kind of painted tile; their upper rooms are often washed and sprinkled with sand, to hinder any moisture from staining the boards. You had almost as good spit in a Dutch woman's face as on her floors, and therefore there are little pots and pans to spit in. (Veryard 1701, 212)

Dutch women benefited in being treated at law more generously than women elsewhere in Europe—they could engage in business transactions, enter into contracts, and bequeath their dowry to whomever they wished.

Although life could be harsh, the Dutch came to believe that through hard work, thrift, investment, and a little luck it could become better. A new social attitude, unmatched anywhere else in Europe, emerged in conjunction with nascent capitalism. Upward mobility came to be seen as a national birthright. By saving and investing, one could acquire a minute share in a burgeoning business or in a ship setting out to trade and, in time, by reinvesting the profits earned, work one's way up to become an owner. Such success could be had because the Dutch could see it happening all around them.

Poverty was not as pervasive as in many other places, but still it could be real enough. The commercial and industrial nature of the Dutch economy meant that the seasonally employed—fishermen, sailors, and others in ancillary trades—and those working in industries that experienced periodic slumps would suffer. Poor relief remained the preserve of the church. Much church and monastic property confiscated at the time of the revolt was devoted to educational and charitable purposes, and each Dutch Reformed parish was governed by a consistory (church council) with a board of deacons responsible for poor relief. Their work was supplemented by extensive charity carried out by urban officials, who dispensed money and set up almshouses run by regents. Unlike in other countries, the chief focus of relief was not on providing basic sustenance at moments of crisis but rather on distributing bread, peat for fuel, and cash on an ongoing basis. Begging was prohibited, and punitive workhouses (tuchthuizen) were maintained for convicted beggars and other criminals.

Dutch cities abounded with sources of information and Amsterdam saw the early arrival of newspapers—the *Amsterdamsche Courant* first appeared in 1618. In 1656 the *Weecklijke Courante van Europa* was founded, and it remained in publication until World War II as the *Oprechte Haarlemsche Courant*. French-language papers such as the *Gazette d'Amsterdam* drew an international readership. The city became Europe's greatest book market. Amsterdam publishers Willem Blaeu (1571–1638) and his son Joan (1596–1673) earned fame for their exquisite maps and atlases depicting the new geographic discoveries while, in Leiden, Lodewijk Elsevier (c. 1540–1617) founded a publishing house in 1581 that produced some of the 17th century's major masterpieces. The firm was liquidated in 1681 but a company founded in 1880 carries on the name. By the late 17th century, more than 270 publishers in the country were printing tracts in many languages.

The Republic earned renown for its five major universities, and the academic culture they spawned drew students from all over Protestant Europe. The University of Leiden was among the first in Europe where professors made use of instruments in imparting lessons and gave practical demonstrations in teaching physics and medicine. Overseas trade aroused an intense interest among the elites for collecting and classifying flora, fauna, fossils, and minerals from around the globe. Amsterdam artist-inventor Jan van der Heyden (1637–1712) invented a glass and metal street lamp with shielded air holes to allow smoke out and keep wind from getting in. By January 1670, Amsterdam was lit by as many as 1,600 public lanterns affixed to posts and walls. Van der Heyden wrote and illustrated one of the world's first books on firefighting, invented a usable fire hose, and, in 1685, organized Amsterdam's first fire brigade.

The greatest 17th-century Dutch scientist was Christiaan Huygens (1629–95), the son of Stadholder Frederick Henry's secretary Constantijn Huygens. A mathematician, he was also an astronomer and famous for making and perfecting microscopes and telescopes. Using a giant 12-foot (3.66 m) telescope, he discovered the rings and one of the moons around the planet Saturn. Anthoni van Leeuwenhoek of Delft (1632–1723) was, like Huygens, highly skilled at working with lenses. A self-taught researcher largely ignorant of any language but Dutch, which unfortunately isolated him from wider scientific circles, he relied on his skill in mathematics, his keen eyesight, and his superb hand-to-eye coordination to make major advances in botany, entomology, and anatomy using microscopes, of which he constructed about 520, with lenses ground to achieve the highest known level of magnification. In

1676 Leeuwenhoek discovered bacteria and, in the following year, the structure of human sperm; in 1683 he observed blood capillaries and in 1684 he viewed red blood cells.

Leeuwenhoek and others carried out their work by applying a Cartesian method to scientific investigation that stressed a skeptical, open-minded approach and in-depth examination and systematic categorization of evidence as prescribed by René Descartes, who lived from 1628 to 1649 in Amsterdam, a city where, he said, the people were too busy making money to disturb the solitude he needed in order to think.

Order and precision were bywords of the times, during which a dynamic Dutch culture emerged, shaped in part by the fragmentation of religion and the quest for some degree of social order with which to counter that fact. Justus Lipsius (1547–1606) propounded a way out of the confessional divide in advancing a neo-Stoic, non-Christian view of ethics and politics in his principal work *De Constantia* (1584). However, he counseled outward conformity to the established church for the sake of the public peace, a call made also by Simon Stevins (1548–1620). Stevins, a Flemish immigrant and protégé of Prince Maurits, was the early Republic's leading scientist, mathematician, and engineer. In his *De Thiende* (1585), Stevins called for adoption of the decimal, which he affirmed would be useful for improved precision in hydraulic engineering, land surveying, and building construction.

Hugo Grotius (1583–1645), acclaimed as one of the fathers of international law, argued for freedom of the seas (*Mare Liberum,* 1609) and greater order in the relations of nations based on natural law, to which he contributed in drawing up rules for a just war (*De Jure Belli ac Pacis,* 1625). His writings reflected the practical concerns both of a man of politics, who was himself imprisoned in 1618 as a partisan of the regents' party, and of a citizen of a nation that, because its lifeblood was trade, valued peace for the profits it brought.

Grotius also published pioneering religious criticism, an interest shared by Benedict (Baruch) de Spinoza (1632–77). An Amsterdam Jew expelled from his faith for expressing heretical opinions and one of Europe's finest lens makers, Spinoza was also an enormously powerful thinker. A devotee of Cartesian philosophy, he championed criticism of revealed religion in a major work *Tractatus Theologica Politicus* (1670). Spinoza sought to liberate society from the superstitious fear bred by the churches, which he said had perverted religion so that "faith has become a mere compound of credulity and prejudice" (Spinoza, *Tractatus,* 54). Denying the divine truth of every biblical passage and even the existence of Satan and devils, he affirmed that scriptures should be studied using human reason as the enlightening tool. The *Tractatus* caused a sensation. Spinoza's books were banned by the States of Holland after his death, but they continued to be read, and his ideas proved influential in helping to shape modern secular notions of freedom and rational inquiry.

The Dutch Golden Age in Art and Architecture

The flourishing economy generated the resources to engender a massive outpouring of pictorial art that in quantity, quality, and variety remains unsurpassed. The era stands in marked contrast to the immediate past when, during the years 1566–90, there was no money to spare for investing in art and when, during the iconoclastic fury from 1566 to 1580, images, sculptures, and paintings suffered wide-scale destruction. Greater stability in the 1590s saw the start of a renaissance in art. Refugee artists, who arrived in large numbers after 1585, brought with them masterly skills acquired in the centuries-old art centers of Bruges, Antwerp, and Ghent, and they made the art of the Dutch Golden Age, like the finances brought by expatriate merchants, the product of both native northerners and immigrants from the southern Netherlands.

During the 1590s, the regents of Holland, Zeeland, and Utrecht began to commission works of public art, and output escalated rapidly in urban areas. It was accompanied by a large-scale building boom that witnessed construction of town halls, schools, military barracks, and, for the first time, imposing new elite merchant residences, including the grandest of all, those along Amsterdam's stately Herengracht.

Nowhere else and never before or since has so much art been produced in so short a time as in the United Provinces—chiefly Holland and Utrecht—in the first three-quarters of the 17th century. By 1650 it is estimated that about 2.5 million paintings existed in Holland alone, most reproductions or inferior works, but including about 10 percent quality pieces. Mirroring the Republic's economic status as the repository of world trade, art captured the entire cultural, social, and physical milieu of the prosperous, stolid Dutch citizen. Dutch Golden Age art is renowned for its depictions of everyday life and objects, and paintings and prints could be found hanging on walls everywhere. For the first time in history, art was produced in great amounts for a wealthy, secular clientele. Everyone who could afford it wanted their portrait preserved for posterity, and their faces, framed in white lace collars and high-topped black hats, remain to tell us who it was that built this vibrant society.

Rembrandt Harmensz van Rijn, The Company of Frans Banning Cocq and Willem van Ruytenburck, *known as the "Night Watch" (1642). Oil on canvas, 363 × 437 cm. Arguably Rembrandt's most celebrated work, this is the most famous painting in the Rijksmuseum.* (Collection Rijksmuseum Amsterdam)

The man who tells this most visually is Frans Hals (c. 1580–1666), Haarlem's most celebrated painter, whose ability to capture the fleeting moment in his portraits was unrivaled. Haarlem also witnessed the birth of both realistic landscape painting, first developed about 1614 by Esias van de Velde (1587–1630), and the "Merry Company," group pictures of extravagantly dressed revelers. Such scenes abound in the work of Jan Steen (1626–79), a prolific painter whose pictures feature disorganized households filled with cheerful carousers and whose *Sinterklaas* (or *The Feast of St. Nicolas*) portrays the beloved Christmas-time characters of Dutch folklore. Pieter de Hoogh (1629–83) painted guardroom scenes, and portraits of groups of all sorts are depicted, none more skillfully than in the work of Rembrandt van Rijn, indisputably the outstanding genius of the period. Rembrandt reigns supreme in his ability to convey psychological insight in his paintings. Carel Fabritius (1622–54), a pupil of Rembrandt, developed a unique style of his own. Some portraits exhibit techniques characteristic of those of his master, but others evince features that are the reverse. In these, subjects are displayed in darker hues on a light background, in contrast to Rembrandt's method of placing the central action under a spotlight and giving a gloomy cast to the setting behind. Fabritius died at 32 in the explosion of a Delft powder magazine, a tragedy that horrified the Dutch public, and few of his paintings survive.

Painters portrayed the Dutch countryside with an accuracy and attention to detail that continue to inspire and that others have emulated. Aelbert Cuyp (1620–91) of Dordrecht depicted peaceful pasturelands, Paulus Potter (1625–54) specialized in painting animals, and Herman Saftleven (1609–85) sunny, forest vistas. Jacob van Ruisdael (c. 1628–82), perhaps the greatest of all the landscape artists, painted the dunes, the low horizons and sweep of cloud-studded sky, and the bucolic patches of woodland that timelessly identify his homeland.

Jacob van Ruisdael, The Mill at Wijk bij Duurstede *(c. 1670). Oil on canvas, 83 × 101 cm* (Collection Rijksmuseum Amsterdam)

89

REMBRANDT HARMENSZOON VAN RIJN

Rembrandt Harmensz van Rijn, Rembrandt Drawing at a Window *(1648). Ink on paper, etching and engraving, 16 × 13 cm* (Collection Rijksmuseum Amsterdam)

Rembrandt van Rijn (July 15, 1606 or 1607–October 4, 1669) was born either in 1606, or, more likely, in 1607 in Leiden, in a mill on the Old Rhine River, and his family name is taken from the river. His father was a fairly well-to-do miller, which afforded the family the means to send the boy to Latin School and then to Leiden University, which he soon left to apprentice with Leiden painter Jacob van Swanenbergh. Rembrandt opened a studio in 1625. His early works, painted in rich details, dealt especially with allegorical and religious themes, often drawn from the Old Testament. He won the attention of poet and statesman Constantijn Huygens and, by 1631, he had moved to Amsterdam,

The subjects of Golden Age art vary widely and they include portraits, still lifes, church interiors, festive occasions, rural domestic scenes, and, perhaps most famously because they occur for the first time ever, the comfortable domestic interiors and views of everyday life (genre) of the middle class. Jan Steen (c. 1626–79) of Leiden draws on Dutch proverbs and literature in showing scenes of daily life, often humorous and lively and always colorful, that carry instructive insights. Johannes Vermeer (1632–75) never left Delft, seeking only the tranquility of his native town in which to paint. His quiet interiors all depict rooms in his own beloved home. Dark subjects on a light background are a distinguishing feature of his canvasses. Vermeer evinced a passion for light, mirroring in his art the new world of observation being opened up by the microscope and telescope. Determined like the scientists to record

where his painting *The Anatomy Lesson of Dr. Nicolaes Tulp* (1632) created a sensation, and he began to receive numerous commissions
for portraits. He painted many landscapes as well. Rembrandt lived
lavishly, marrying Saskia van Uylenberg in 1634 and, after her death
in 1642, Hendrickje Stoffels, a much younger woman who had been
his maidservant. Forced into bankruptcy in 1656, he moved from an
elegant home on the Jodenbreestraat, in the Jewish Quarter, to a
more modest dwelling on the Rozengracht. Advancing age, financial
misfortune, and personal tragedy are reflected in his works beginning in the 1640s, when the exuberance on display in large, earlier
canvasses was replaced by smaller paintings depicting New Testament
themes and quiet rural scenes. Larger works, painted with rich colors that he applied in strong brush strokes, reappeared in the 1650s.
Excellent self-portraits define his career in his last years. They display
the sorrow occasioned by the loss of both his wives and three of
his children. Rembrandt died grief-stricken shortly after the death
of his beloved only son Titus. He lies in an unmarked grave in the
Westerkerk.

Rembrandt's ability to render with subtle skill the intense, inner
emotions of the human spirit remains unequaled. His distinctive use of
light and shadow (chiaroscuro), the animated presentation he gives to
his subjects, eschewing the rigid formality characteristic of many of his
contemporaries, and the ability to convey compassion that is so evident
on his canvasses are hallmarks of his artistry. Rembrandt produced
more than 600 paintings, 300 etchings, and 2,000 drawings, and his
works have never gone out of fashion.

exactly what he saw, Vermeer painted so meticulously that he makes
the viewer actually feel the movement of light. The preoccupation with
composition and light that would thereafter characterize traditional
Dutch painting dates from this period.

In the written arts, in Joost den Vondel (1587–1679) the Republic
found its greatest poet and playwright. Born in Cologne, his parents
Anabaptist refugees from Antwerp, Vondel became a Catholic in 1639.
While working as a clerk at the Bank van Lening he penned plays that,
because their characters express clear Catholic sentiments (*Gijsbrecht
van Aemstel*, 1637) or portray biblical figures (*Lucifer*, 1653), incurred
official displeasure. He was forced into hiding following the performance of *Pallamedes* (1625), an attack on the late Oldenbarnevelt's
enemies masquerading as an adaptation of an episode from Homer. The

Johannes Vermeer, View of Houses in Delft, known as "The Little Street" *(c. 1658). Oil on canvas, 54.3 × 44 cm* (Collection Rijksmuseum Amsterdam)

popularity of his plays exemplified the shift under way in the mid-17th century from the dramas presented by amateur rhetoricians toward professional theatrical productions. The Leidse Schouwburg (Leiden Theater) would open in 1705, the first theater in the Netherlands.

Daniel Heinsius (1580–1655), a professor first of poetry and then of Greek and history and concurrently a librarian at the University of

Leiden, wrote elegant orations and published annotated editions of classical authors. Jacob Cats (1577–1660), a jurist who became Grand Pensionary, outsold all other authors, his collections of poems instructing in manners and morals proving immensely popular.

Recurrent Wars, 1652–1702

During the peace negotiations at Münster the Dutch sat at the table as one of Europe's major players. Economic wealth and military success had brought international recognition and engendered rivalry from the surrounding powers. Just four years after the conclusion of general peace in Europe in 1648, the Dutch Republic found itself at war with a trading rival that challenged—and would ultimately usurp—its place as the Continent's major maritime power. In this, the first of six wars the Dutch would fight with England, they would do so without the leadership of a stadholder for the first time since the foundation of the Republic.

Frederick Henry died in 1647 and was succeeded as stadholder of five provinces and captain- and admiral-general of the union by his 20-year-old son William II (1626–50). Tensions had long simmered between the regents of Holland, anxious to preserve provincial autonomy and, with it, the peaceful pursuit of trade, and the prince of Orange and his supporters, zealous to advance a strong central government essential to national defense. Peace having been reached, Holland demanded that the army be reduced from 35,000 to 26,000 men. The prince of Orange countered that more, not less, troops were needed to defend the country's expanded borders.

Holland claimed the right to disband that portion of the army for which it paid, thus, with haunting overtones of the crisis of 1618, raising the issue to a constitutional question of who controlled the Republic. Haughty and stubborn, William II won support in the States General from other provinces, always jealous of Holland's power. He staged a coup, arresting and imprisoning six regents at Loevestein castle, which silenced Holland's opposition. The Orangists celebrated, but their joy was short-lived. William died of smallpox in October 1650.

Determined to be rid of overbearing princes, the States of Holland bypassed the States General and met at a Grand Assembly in The Hague where they agreed to keep the constitution intact, but with two exceptions—command of the army would be delegated to the provincial States, thus giving the country seven local forces, and a stadholder would no longer be appointed. The States of Zeeland, Utrecht,

Gelderland, and Overijssel—where William also held the post—agreed to follow Holland's lead in also seeking greater local control. Friesland was the one notable exception. A junior branch of the Nassau line, which had occupied the stadholderate since the 1590s, would continue to do so through the 18th century.

During the previous year England had deposed its Stuart king, Charles I (r. 1625–1649), following a civil war between the king's supporters and supporters of the Parliament. The military dictatorship of Oliver Cromwell proposed a union of the two Protestant republics, but the Dutch swiftly rejected the offer. Rebuffed as an ally, the English struck back with a Navigation Act (1651), which stipulated that foreign goods could be imported to England only in English ships or in ships of the nation where goods originated. A measure aimed directly at Dutch supremacy in the international carrying trade, it could lead only to war, which broke out in 1652 in the Channel between an English fleet and a Dutch convoy commanded by Maarten Tromp (1598–1653), an iron-willed officer who affixed a broom to the bowsprit of his ship in announcing his intention to sweep the Republic's enemies from the seas.

Managed by five boards of admiralty and made up of ships built with skill equal to that of Dutch merchantmen, the Dutch navy was superbly led by adroit admirals such as Tromp and Michiel de Ruyter (1607–76). The Dutch relied on the navy to ensure the country's trade lifeline, but during the first year of the first Anglo-Dutch war (1652–54), the fleet could not match greater English firepower and massed strength. Serious defeats in the summer of 1653 saw riots break out in Rotterdam, The Hague, and elsewhere by advocates for the House of Orange who supported the return of a unified command under an admiral-general. Trade began to plummet.

The Dutch drove the English from the Mediterranean (Battle of Leghorn, March 13, 1653), but the victory earned them nothing, as Tromp's defeat at Portland in February–March led to a blockade of the Dutch coast, which severed the country's sea route lifeline. Tromp's death at the Battle of Scheveningen (August 10, 1653) dented Dutch morale, but the English were compelled to end the blockade. By now both sides were exhausted. In 1653 Johan de Witt (1625–72) succeeded Jacob Cats as Grand Pensionary of Holland. A skilled negotiator, he secured terms in the Treaty of Westminster (1654) that ensured the Dutch their trade in return for agreement to keep the deposed Stuarts out of the Republic and the prince of Orange out of the government.

Dutch prosperity rebounded but the peace amounted only to a truce. Hostilities resumed a decade later, spawned again by friction over trade.

English harassment of Dutch shipping and colonies had reached such a point that by 1664 skirmishing began. In September the English seized New Netherland even before fighting officially commenced in March 1665. In the second Anglo-Dutch war (1665–67) the Dutch, having refurbished the fleet, had a larger standing navy than before, but ideological tensions left over from the last round of bickering between backers of the prince of Orange and supporters of the States General riddled the ranks. And the English navy was larger still.

The English won the opening battle off Lowestoft (June 3, 1665) and setbacks for the Republic mounted with the country under invasion on land by forces of the bishop of Münster, an English ally. By 1667, however, the Dutch had rallied. Blockading southeast England, Admiral de Ruyter made his famous raid up the Medway in June, burning installations and scuttling and capturing 16 vessels, even towing away the *Royal Charles,* the English flagship. The daring deed sufficed to turn the tide in a war fought essentially to a draw, and, by terms of the Treaty of Breda (July 31, 1667), the Republic triumphed merely by making no concessions. Trading New Netherland, where New Amsterdam became New York, for Guiana (present-day Suriname and Guyana), they kept their commerce intact.

However, for the third time in less than 30 years, the respite from fighting again proved brief. France's king Louis XIV, the Sun King (r. 1643–1715), took control of affairs of state in 1661 and he lost no time in assuming an activist role in European power politics. De Witt and his supporters found a French-Dutch treaty negotiated in 1662 advantageous as a counterweight to Orangist sympathizers at home and abroad, but tensions between the two countries persisted. A vigorous French monarch busily raising Europe's largest army gave the Dutch cause for concern, and rivalry over commerce and colonies added further strains. In addition, a vacuum of power had emerged in the southern Netherlands following Spain's withdrawal of most of its forces, which had served to counter French expansionism. The French lost no time in taking territories there in 1667–68.

Johan de Witt sought to retain government control under the leadership of Holland's regents, but, with fears of war mounting, he faced growing pressures from allies of the House of Orange for a return of the stadholderate. The provinces were reluctant to do so; however, with Holland's grudging consent, they did agree to the appointment of young prince William III (1650–1702) as captain-general in February 1672.

The move came none too soon. A month later, the English launched a surprise attack on a returning Dutch convoy. In 1672, its armies undermanned, its frontier fortifications in disrepair, and without allies, the Republic endured the most traumatic year in its history (*Rampjaar*). Assailed by allied English and French forces, joined by several German states, the Dutch held their own at sea, where Admiral de Ruyter again scored several victories. On land, however, disaster struck. French and German forces overran the eastern provinces and occupied Utrecht, Zwolle, and Kampen. Holland was saved, at first, by sheer luck, and then, in the time-honored way, by opening the dikes and inundating the terrain from the Zuider Zee to the Waal.

Defeatism swept Leiden, Gouda, and other towns closest to the front lines. Desperate to stiffen resolve by injecting new leadership, Zeeland appointed the 22-year-old William stadholder in July 1672 and Holland soon followed. Public blame for the debacle fell on Johan de Witt as the architect of a ruling arrangement that had failed the country. He was caught with his brother Cornelis during rioting in The Hague on August 20 and both men were beaten, stabbed, and shot to death, their mutilated corpses strung from a gibbet and parts of their bodies roasted and eaten by the frenzied mob.

The States of Holland empowered William to compel changes in town councils to curb the power of the regents and restore the independence of the civic militias, which had been subordinated to the will of local government during the stadholderless period.

Unknown artist, The Bodies of the de Witt Brothers, Hanged at Groene Zoodje on the Vijverberg in The Hague *(c. 1672–1702). Oil on canvas, 69.5 × 56 cm* (Collection Rijksmuseum Amsterdam)

William III was declared stadholder of Utrecht in 1674 and of Gelderland and Overijssel the following year. His assumption of the post marked the reestablishment of the stadholder as the dominant player in the politics of the Republic. William wielded greater political power than any stadholder before him, possibly excepting Maurits, and he used it to secure firm control domestically and unify command of the war effort. Autocratic and aristocratic, William's monarchical pretensions were plainly evident in his residence, a grand palace and garden built for him in the manner of Versailles beginning in 1584 on the site of the former hunting lodge of the medieval dukes of Gelderland at Loo, outside Apeldoorn. Firmly ensconced in power, William saw to it that regents were purged from town councils and princely favorites placed in municipal and provincial posts.

The war went on. A French army, laying siege to Maastricht, took the city on June 30, 1673. In the naval war, de Ruyter beat a combined English-French fleet in a thunderous, 11-hour engagement off Texel on August 11, while Dutch privateers swept English vessels from the sea, capturing more than 550. New Netherland was retaken and held for a year (1673–74). Its seaborne commerce paralyzed, England made peace in signing a second Treaty of Westminster on February 19, 1674. The third Anglo-Dutch war ended with the colonial status quo of 1667 restored.

In alliance now with Spain, Brandenburg, and the Holy Roman Empire, the Republic sent its armies into the Rhineland and took Bonn, the logistical link between the French and their German allies. The blow led the French to negotiate peace terms, which were signed at Nijmegen in 1679. The French evacuated Maastricht and granted tariff reductions favorable to Dutch traders.

The war left Louis XIV implacably hostile to the Dutch, who had consistently opposed his aims to secure French territorial and economic gains. By the late 1680s he revived high French tariffs to stifle Dutch commerce—the life's blood of the Republic. By then, the country had forged closer ties to England, with which it had signed a treaty of alliance in 1678.

The alliance followed the marriage the year before of William III to Mary (1662–94), the Protestant daughter of England's unpopular Catholic king James II (1633–1701). In 1688 disgruntled English politicians turned to Mary, who as a Stuart guaranteed the stability of the succession and as a Protestant kept the throne safely in the hands of the established religion, and William, who as leader of the Dutch added his country's economic and military muscle to English resources. Invited by Parliament to assume the English throne, William sailed across the North Sea aided by a "Protestant wind," bringing with him an army that included more than 14,000 Dutch mercenary troops. The prince of Orange landed from a massive 500-vessel armada at Torbay, near Brixham, in southeast England, on November 5, 1688. The next month James fled. Mary returned in February 1789, accompanied by a prominent political refugee, the philosopher John Locke (1632–1704), who had fled to the Republic in 1683 on suspicion (never proven) that he assisted in a plot against King James. During his years in the Republic, Locke had reworked his *An Essay Concerning Human Understanding* (1690) and written *A Letter Concerning Toleration* (1689), seminal works in laying the foundation for empiricism and in arguing for religious pluralism, respectively. William and Mary were crowned as joint monarchs on February 13, 1689.

Slight in build and asthmatic, William's physical stature belied an iron will and a shrewd intellect. Resolute and resilient, he shaped his international policies keeping his homeland's geopolitical position always in mind. He was a true match for Louis XIV, the absolutist ruler of France. James's efforts to regain the English crown compelled the stadholder-king to keep a large part of his army in England and Ireland from 1689 to 1691. To compensate for the diversion of Dutch men and material, William forged an international coalition of states to balance French power. He held Louis to a draw throughout the Nine Years' War (War of the League of Augsburg; War of the Grand Alliance, 1688–97). The treaty signed at Rijswijk, just outside The Hague, while leaving France in possession of territories in the Spanish Netherlands, won for the Republic the right to garrison a line of "barrier" forts in towns in the southern Netherlands from which to keep watch over French intentions and, if necessary, ward off any future aggressions.

The Dutch had entered the war prosperous and powerful. The economy expanded, trade flourished, and urbanization intensified in the 1680s. During the 1690s, however, wages and living standards began to fall a bit and a slight drop in urban populations set in. It was an ominous portent.

5

DYNAMO IN DECLINE
(1702–1795)

William III died at Hampton Court Palace, in England, on March 19, 1702. Church bells tolled throughout the United Provinces to mournfully mark his passing. The last stadholder in the direct line of the House of Orange-Nassau, William had forged a commanding presence, and no one followed to match his stature. His departure marked a major change in the Republic's government. Another period of rule without a stadholder began and the regents once again held full control. In 1702 they governed a country that was still a great power. By 1780, however, when a restored stadholder held court at The Hague, the Dutch Republic had lost its place as one of Europe's major economic, diplomatic, and intellectual players.

Change swept through the United Provinces swiftly and bewilderingly in the years from 1780 to 1795. The struggle waged on behalf of liberty and democracy in North America found ready support in a country rooted in republican traditions, and the Dutch Republic became the first place in Europe where such sentiments found a home in helping to launch a thoroughly revolutionary movement. The Republic, economically prostrate and socially moribund, was fatally weakened politically when its leaders opposed the new ideas. Any lingering popular enthusiasm for the old order waned when the regime proved unable to regain its authority without outside aid: The Dutch Republic fell at last to the forces of France, the power that it had successfully held at bay for more than a century past.

Rule by the Regents, 1702–1747

Six days after William III's death, the Grand Pensionary, Anthonie Heinsius (1641–1720), announced that the States of Holland had decided to leave the stadholderate vacant despite the stadholder-king's stated wish, made in his will, that he be succeeded by Johan William Friso (1687–1711), who had followed his father Hendrik Casimir as stadholder of Friesland in 1696. The power of the provincial elites, ascendant in the first stadholderless period from 1650 to 1672, waxed again. The regents who ran the States General ruled the country without restraint, although the Orange-appointed officeholders in Zeeland, Utrecht, Gelderland, and Overijssel that also discarded their stadholders put up a stiff resistance in protests, riots, and boycotts from 1702 to 1707, which was broken only after a determined effort spearheaded by Holland.

The disturbances proved troublesome and inconvenient as the country found itself simultaneously engaged in the War of the Spanish Succession (1701–13). The war arose after the death of the last Spanish Habsburg king, Charles II (r. 1665–1700). Charles bequeathed all his possessions to Louis XIV's grandson Philip, duke of Anjou, of the House of Bourbon. As king of Spain, Philip stood in line of succession to the French throne, a union of Bourbon monarchies too powerful for surrounding rulers to permit. French forces occupied parts of the Spanish Netherlands already. The Dutch Republic's geopolitical policies remained the same as those in place under William III, namely, to check the threat of French hegemony. Heinsius easily secured the assent of the States General to declare war on France and Spain on May 8, 1702. Declarations followed quickly by the Austrian Habsburg emperor, Leopold I, who was fighting to protect his dynasty's claim to Spain, and by England (Britain after 1707), Prussia, and Portugal.

England shared the Republic's concerns about the French menace and the two maritime powers, closely tied during 13 years of joint rule by the king-stadholder, joined forces together. Fielding their largest army ever—more than 100,000 men—the Dutch placed their troops under the joint command of John Churchill, the first duke of Marlborough (1650–1722). Together they won victory after victory, defeating French forces that had invaded the Spanish Netherlands and Germany in battles at Blenheim (1704), Ramillies (1706), and Oudenarde (1708). Bourbon forces were driven out of most of the Spanish Netherlands.

English and Dutch navies swept the Mediterranean of enemy fleets. The two powers signed a secret treaty (First Barrier Treaty) in 1709, granting the Dutch the right to hold and garrison a number of towns in the Spanish Netherlands to give them a forward line of defense against French attack. However, by 1710 the war—the world's first truly global conflict—had exhausted all of its participants. Never bested but badly bloodied—at Malplaquet (1709) the English and Dutch secured a victory but at the cost of 20,000 casualties, twice the number of French losses—the Dutch had overreached themselves. The provincial States incurred heavy debt in financing the large troop levies. To pay for the increase in the army, the government had diverted funds away from the navy, sacrificing its strength. The inland provinces had paid nothing toward the navy's upkeep for most of the war and, by 1713, the five provincial admiralties were deeply in debt. The prolonged hostilities led to the collapse of trade with France, Spain, and Spanish-American markets. The strain proved enough for the British to respond to French overtures for peace, and a congress was convened in January 1712 at Utrecht.

Although public debates went on at Utrecht, the real terms were thrashed out secretly between Britain and France. Without having been consulted, the Dutch found to their surprise that they had been side-lined. Anti-British riots erupted at The Hague. The French and British concluded an armistice and the Dutch, fighting with the Austrians, were disastrously defeated at Denain in the Spanish Netherlands in July. The Republic's ruling regents, their resources sapped, realized they could not fight on deprived of British help. A new defensive and offensive treaty of alliance with Britain, including a Second Barrier Treaty, was signed in January 1713. The Peace of Utrecht signed on April 11, 1713, left France in possession of most of her conquests and left Philip V as king of Spain on condition he renounce his rights of succession to the French throne. The Spanish Netherlands were awarded to Austria. The Dutch surrendered portions of Upper Gelderland to Prussia and acquired the towns of Venlo and Roermond. They won agreement to keep the Scheldt River closed to all but Dutch shipping. The Republic held the Spanish Netherlands in trust for Charles VI (r. 1711–40), emperor of Austria and Holy Roman Emperor, until the latter reached an agreement on a new barrier treaty. The Third Barrier Treaty was duly signed at Antwerp in November 1715 under which the Dutch were given the right to garrison a maximum of 35,000 men in towns in the Austrian Netherlands, two-fifths of the cost of which the Austrians agreed to pay. The pact was made stronger in being backed by Great Britain, which emerged from the war in a position to become, in the course of the 18th century, Europe's major maritime power.

Reduction of troop strength from 130,000 in 1712 to 40,000 in 1715 and the army's return to garrison duties along the borders paralleled the patterns followed in previous wars, but whereas before, the Republic had fielded one of Europe's largest and best-trained armies in both peace and war, now the precipitous drop in numbers while neighboring countries increased their forces meant that the United Provinces assumed the status of a lesser power.

The regents of Holland ran the country largely problem-free until the mid-1720s, when stresses began to mount. Sentiment in favor of a return of the House of Orange began to grow, fueled by rising international tensions and a gradual crumbling of the overseas trading system. In 1729, the prince of Orange, William Friso of Nassau-Dietz (1711–51), a descendant of William of Orange's brother John, was duly declared stadholder by Friesland, Groningen, and Gelderland. Concerned to curb his ascending course, the patricians of Holland barred him from the Council of State. They could not, however, stifle growing public opinion blaming them for the increasingly self-evident economic decline.

Economic Decline

It was the Dutch overseas trading system that spawned and sustained the Golden Age and, equally, it was the weakening and, ultimately, the collapse of the Republic's global commercial primacy that brought economic decline. Trade slackened slowly and spottily after expansion peaked about 1688. The Mediterranean, African, and Spanish-American traffic declined disastrously as the 18th century progressed, but the Asian trade of the Dutch East India Company (VOC) remained steady through most of the century.

The VOC became a territorial colonial power in the 18th century. It constituted the governing power in the East Indies, and its resources remained impressive. The company employed thousands of workers, and it maintained posts, in addition to those in the Indies, on the coast of India, in Ceylon, and at Nagasaki, Japan. In the Indies, it continued to secure its dominant commercial position by making treaties with coastal sultans on Sumatra and Celebes, but on Java, in contrast, the company began a campaign of conquest, starting in 1677 when the company's governor-general reluctantly intervened in a succession dispute of a local prince.

Trading went on, although the company's sea power declined noticeably in the course of the century, most especially in the number of ships traveling between ports in Asia. The five to 10 East Indiamen that sailed between Batavia and Nagasaki in the late 17th century had dropped to only one or two a century later. Smuggling and piracy, provoked by the stranglehold on trade the company tried to uphold, challenged its primacy. Ships returned to Europe as richly laden as ever, though the cargo holds packed with spices and cotton in the 17th century held porcelain, coffee, and tea in the 18th. Tea became the fashionable drink of the rich and its medicinal qualities were touted—Amsterdam's famous physician Dr. Nicholas Tulp recommended it as a cure for virtually all ills. The VOC encouraged consumption, and, after 1750, tea became the most valuable commodity in westbound cargoes, the company thus playing a part in bringing about lasting changes in European social habits.

Shares of the initial working capital of the VOC had been held by all classes of society, although from the beginning the rich held the most. By the 18th century, the larger holders had bought out small investors. Shareholders of the Amsterdam chamber came to predominate by the 1670s, and the rich private merchants who occupied chairs as directors in the 1700s had been largely displaced by town magistrates in the 18th century. Vacancies were filled by consultation and cooptation between the councilmen of the towns where the chambers met and directors of the chamber. A burgomaster of Amsterdam almost always sat as a director.

The West India Company prospered less than its eastern counterpart. Intended from the start as a weapon to strike at Spanish power in the Americas, the WIC expended funds on naval and military expenditures, primarily in efforts to conquer all or part of Brazil in the 1650s, that far exceeded revenues earned from the sale of sugar and other exports from its Caribbean island possessions. The company declared bankruptcy in 1674. A new one was set up in its place the same year organized in the same way as the old and, like the VOC, Amsterdam money held sway here as well. In the 18th century the company survived largely on the export of slaves assembled at its forts in West Africa and shipped to the West Indies, especially Curaçao, which also operated as a major base for contraband trade with Spanish America. In the WIC, as in the VOC, a close connection existed between the companies' management and the country's governing elites.

Shipbuilding remained significant in the first quarter of the century, declined in the middle decades, and then plummeted by the 1790s, the drop-off caused largely by a lack of naval stores. Naval power foundered with a heavily indebted state unable to secure sufficient funds to maintain a fleet, once numbered among Europe's largest. The four inland provinces had always considered it proper that the maritime provinces of Holland and Zeeland should fund the building and upkeep of the fleet from the profits of their seaborne trade, and the refusal of Utrecht, Overijssel, Gelderland, and Groningen to contribute monies—a fundamental problem that plagued the republic from its founding—now proved ruinous, given the straitened economic circumstances.

Dutch maritime power declined technologically as well. Manned by top-heavy crews whose captains used outdated charts and maps, the ships of the late 18th century were no longer the efficient engines of world commerce of 100 years before. A Swedish traveler observed: "The Dutch also have occasion for a greater number of men to work their ships than other nations, as their rigging is made after the old fashion with large blocks and thick cordage, heavy and clumsy in every respect" (Thunberg 1795, 115).

Although the volume of Dutch maritime commerce was not insignificant as late as 1780, it paled in comparison with gains made by Britain and France. And although changes in European dietary habits helped spark downturns in many once-strong industries—consumer tastes for herring and cod declined in the 18th century—the rising economic power in neighboring countries stands as a root cause of the country's reduced fortunes.

The Dutch economy failed because it fell victim both to competition from expanding manufacturing activity in Britain, France, and the Austrian Netherlands and to widespread protectionism implemented under theories of mercantilism in vogue in northern Europe after the mid-18th century. Driven to draw wealth to themselves, nations put in place high tariffs and outright prohibitions on imports of goods from other countries, which shut the Dutch out of markets where they had often dominated. France placed an embargo on importation of Dutch herring in 1751, followed by the Austrian Netherlands, Denmark, and Prussia. Merchants lost the important export market to Britain in linen and sail-canvas, Rotterdam's entrepôt trade in French wine fell by one-third, and Prussia excluded almost all textile imports. Tobacco processing and sugar refining, which continued to grow into the early 1700s, stopped doing so thereafter.

In addition, local tolls and tariffs and fragmented town and provincial economies contrasted with the larger, and increasingly more centrally knit, economies of Britain and France. France and Britain, with their larger populations and growing colonial empires, which could serve as sources of raw materials and outlets for the mother country's manufactures, could compete much more effectively than the Dutch, who lacked fast-growing colonies populated by European settlers that could take up the slack in compensating for lost markets in Europe.

Only overseas trade in imports and reexports of sugar, tobacco, tea, coffee, spices, and cacao from Asia and the Americas expanded, fueled by an increase in domestic and European consumption of these products. But here, too, considerable volumes of these commodities came to be carried in British, French, and other foreign vessels. And only a few specialized crafts bucked the downward trend, most notably tile making in Delft, which remained buoyant throughout the century. Even in Delft, however, during the years the industry grew the greatest—between 1680 and 1735—the population dropped from 24,000 to about 15,000, the city losing residents to Rotterdam, a larger city that enjoyed wider commercial advantages, and to The Hague, which, as the seat of the national government, offered administrative and service-related work. And even the famed Delft earthenware saw its markets contract in the last years of the century in the face of competition from cheap and resilient chinaware from Stoke-on-Trent in England. The Dutch met the threat by increasing production of high-quality porcelain, which was manufactured in factories in the Amsterdam area at Weesp, Loosdrecht, and Amstel.

The agricultural depression that set in during the 1660s continued into the early 18th century and deepened in the mid-1700s. Natural disasters in storm-caused flooding and an outbreak of cattle plague (rinderpest) ravaged the countryside, and an unusually severe winter in 1739–40 caused widespread hardship. During the late 18th century a moderate recovery occurred with an expansion in output of basic foodstuffs such as rye; the introduction of potatoes, which replaced Baltic grain imports; and the cultivation of tobacco, although much of the latter was shipped abroad in the wake of the collapse of the domestic processing industry. Dairy farming remained important throughout the century, its strength sustained by steady increases in reclaimed polderland. Cheese and butter were major exports, although the latter had to meet severe competition from Irish butter between 1666 and 1757 when the English government banned imports of the latter, leading Irish farmers to look for markets in continental Europe.

With the decline in trade and industry, the urbanization of the Netherlands, a process that had continued uninterrupted for centuries, came to an end. Inland manufacturing towns such as Leiden, Delft, and Haarlem and smaller port cities such as Hoorn, Enkhuizen, and Middelburg fared the worst while the three largest cities—Amsterdam, Rotterdam, and The Hague—managed to maintain, if not grow, their populations in attracting newcomers moving out of places severely affected by economic malaise. The urban proportion of the population fell from just over a third in 1730 to just under a third a short 25 years later. Decaying cities brought social dislocation. Unemployment mounted and beggars appeared on streets. The artisan class contracted as shops closed, their customers having moved elsewhere. Breweries went out of business as consumer tastes switched to tea, coffee, and gin.

Decreasing manufacturing and maritime activity meant wealth came to depend increasingly on investment property, government bonds, and shares in the VOC. Monies also flowed outward to profitable foreign ventures that brought high-yield returns, which fueled growth abroad, not at home. In essence, Dutch society in the 18th century lived off the past. Drawing on their investments in nonproductive sources, wealthy regents and nobles no longer engaged in business pursuits. Dressed in their powdered wigs and silk knee-breeches and luxuriating in elegant townhouses and fine country villas, they serve to aptly epitomize the economic malaise of a time Dutch historians define as the *Pruikentijd* (the Periwig Era).

The Dutch Enlightenment

The fine clothes and manners of the regent-oligarchs and those who aped them reflected the trappings of a class that grew more exclusive in the 18th century. The ruling class emerged almost as a separate caste distant from the mass of the population. Its distinguishing character-istic became a slavish adoption of French culture, which, although it had never been absent, now came to dominate among the ruling circles almost to the exclusion of their own. French language and styles of fashion were preferred and Dutch literature was not read. Unsupported by society's elites and subject to the effects of a country growing steadily poorer, Dutch cultural life in the 18th century no longer set European standards.

But adoption of French culture did not extend to a ready acceptance of elements of the new ideological currents emanating from France by midcentury. Anticlerical attacks on the institutional church that so characterized French Enlightenment thinkers such as Voltaire and Rousseau found no ready audience in a country without an all-powerful church and absolute monarch and where a relaxed religious atmosphere had long been practiced. During the 18th century, the United Provinces became the major publishing center for European Enlightenment authors, but, although the writings circulated throughout the country and their ideas percolated through fashionable circles, they made no deep impact. Neither ruling regents nor Calvinist ministers coun-tenanced attacks on the established order. At the request of church authorities, both Rousseau's *Contrat Social* (1762) and Voltaire's *Traité sur la Tolérance* (1763) were banned, although the proscription proved largely unenforceable.

BOSWELL DESCRIBES THE PERIWIG ERA

English lawyer, author, and diarist James Boswell (1740–95) lived an active social life and earned fame for his perceptions and observations of people and places. *Boswell, Boswellian,* and *Boswellism* have passed into the language in defining traits of a good conversationalist, a keen observer, and a cherished companion. Intending to continue his legal studies at the University of Utrecht, Boswell spent the years from 1763 to 1766 touring the European continent instead. In a letter from Utrecht dated June 17, 1764, to his lifelong correspondent William Johnson Temple (1739–96), he made the following observations on conditions in the country:

Most of their principal towns are sadly decayed, and instead of finding every mortal employed, you meet with multitudes of poor creatures who are starving in idleness. Utrecht is remarkably ruined. There are whole lanes of wretches who have no other subsistence than potatoes, gin, and stuff which they call tea and coffee....The Hague is a beautiful and elegant place. It is, however, by no means a Dutch town; the simplicity and plain honesty of the old Hollanders has given way to the show and politeness of the French, with this difference, that a Frenchman is (truly at) ease, whereas the Dutchman is (as yet) but a painful imitator....Were Sir William Temple to revisit these Provinces, he would scarcely believe the amazing alteration which they have undergone. The Magistrates' places in most of the towns, which in his time were filled up by worthy, substantial citizens who were burgomasters for honour and not for profit, are now filled up by hungry fellows who take them for bread and squeeze as much as they can from the inhabitants....The universities here are much fallen. In short, the Seven Provinces would require the powers of all the politicians that they ever had to set them right again.

Source: James Boswell, *Boswell in Holland 1763–1764 including His Correspondance with Belle de Zuylen (Zélide),* edited by Frederick A. Pottle (New York: McGraw-Hill, 1952), pp. 288–289.

In any case, characteristic features that marked the 18th-century Enlightenment in Europe, namely, the growth in religious toleration and empirical examination and classification of knowledge, were already well under way in the Dutch Republic in the late 17th century.

The attack on revealed religion so spectacularly launched by Spinoza continued. Balthasar Bekker (1634–98), a Reformed theologian, sustained Spinoza's denial of the existence of Satan, devils, and angels in arguing in *The World Bewitched* (*De betoverde wereld,* 1691) that scriptural references to these beings amounted to no more than figurative allegories both of sin and sinfulness and of God's omnipotence.

Spinoza found a critic in Pierre Bayle (1647–1706), a French Huguenot émigré, whose *Historical and Critical Dictionary* (*Dictionnaire historique et critique,* 1696) broke new ground in laying the foundation for innovative study and debate in the early Enlightenment. The works of French Protestant writers, who arrived in the Netherlands after the revocation of the Edict of Nantes (1685), were avidly read by Dutch theologians and thinkers, even though French intellectuals, having no knowledge of Dutch, worked apart. Much influenced by Huguenot refugees, Justus van Effen (1684–1735) of Utrecht wrote in French. However, he also introduced the magazine format to Dutch readers by publishing the Dutch *Hollandsche Spectator* (*Dutch spectator*) beginning in 1731. The magazine was modeled after the *Tatler* and *Spectator* periodicals he had seen on a visit to London, and helped keep alive an interest in, and an audience for, Dutch literature in a period that witnessed a diminution in quality and a dissolution in style. Effen was a leading figure in promoting the spread of English ideas in philosophy and natural science among the better-educated classes of Dutch society.

Dutch observers of Europe's intellectual scene championed toleration at the same time as they strove to show that the new scientific and philosophical thinking was not antireligious. They sought, as did Bayle, to combine a pious, tolerant nonconfessional belief in God with a passion for empirical investigation. In doing so, Dutch attitudes aligned more closely with the views of leading thinkers of the German Enlightenment (*Aufklärung*), who provided a serious moral content to their works. German philosopher and mathematician Christian von Wolff (or Wolf) (1679–1754) popularized the ideas of his predecessor Gottfried Wilhelm Leibniz (1646–1711) in arguing for a consistent rational universe emerging according to a divine plan. Wolff's insistence on clarity and precision and his belief that philosophy and science, guided by reason, should serve to buttress rather than question established religion proved popular in the Netherlands.

More than religion, science—especially applied and theoretical science and technology—interested Dutch Enlightenment (*Verlichting*) thinkers. Willem Jacob van s'Gravesande (1688–1742) was, before Voltaire, continental Europe's preeminent popularizer of the ideas of

Sir Isaac Newton (1642–1727), the English physicist and mathematician whose *Principia* had a profound impact on the development of the science of physics. Nicolaas Hartsoeker (1656–1725) carried out microscopic and telescopic observations in the tradition of Huygens and van Leeuwenhoek, and Herman Boerhaave (1668–1738) published a celebrated catalogue of 3,700 plant species. A professor of medicine, Boerhaave was, by the 1720s, Europe's most famous medical teacher. An avid Newtonian, he stressed empirical demonstrations in anatomy, botany, and chemistry. In advocating this approach, he exemplified the mainstream Dutch Enlightenment, which abandoned Cartesian deductive reasoning in favor of a passion for scientific classification.

After the mid-18th century, Dutch scientific and intellectual contributions to the Enlightenment no longer occupied a central place in European developments. The universities lost their path-breaking place in Europe as municipal and provincial authorities lacked the financial resources to invest in staff, laboratories, and equipment. Fewer foreign students attended lectures. However, philosophical and scientific societies flourished in the second half of the century. Groups such as the Holland Society of Sciences in Haarlem (1752) and the Zeeland Society of Sciences in Flushing (1765) arranged lectures and published treatises, even if the topics about which they spoke and wrote failed to set any trends.

Paralleling the socioeconomic decay so much in evidence, Dutch art dropped from the sublime heights it had occupied a century before. The market for paintings dried up and almost all 18th-century artists held closely to the techniques of the Golden Age. Willem van Mieris (1662–1747) at Leiden produced refined genre paintings and Jan van Huysum (1682–1749) of Amsterdam painted exquisite floral arrangements, the only still-life specialty from the 17th century to survive. Cornelis Troost (1697–1750) displayed considerable innovation in his theatrically depicted street and interior scenes. Theater too fell into decline after the death of Vondel. Led by Andries Pels (d. 1681); most Dutch playwrights produced works modeled after those written by great French authors, notably Molière and Corneille.

Just as foreign influences were felt in culture, science, and philosophy, creative trends at work elsewhere in western Europe made an impact in the written arts. In this case, Britain served as the source of inspiration. The novel, specifically the novel as a morality tale, introduced by the English writers Samuel Richardson (1689–1761) and Henry Fielding (1707–54) found echoes in the Netherlands, where they served to inspire, most prominently poet and author Elizabeth "Betje"

Wolff (1738–1804), an Amsterdam widow who is widely considered the first important Dutch novelist. In her first and most famous work, *History of Miss Sara Burgerhart* (*Historie van mejuffrouw Sara Burgerhart*, 1782), which she coauthored with Agatha "Aagje" Deken (1741–1804), a poor governess with whom she lived for almost 30 years, Betje recounts the story of a young woman forced to flee from her family's cruel treatment. Told in a novel-in-letters format that proved enduringly popular well into the 19th century, the book presents a restrained but very real analysis of human emotions. At the same time, the authors impart their attitudes toward the philosophical issues of the day. The book conveys their rejection of both the deism and materialism of the French Enlightenment and the strict Calvinism so prominent in Dutch theological tradition.

The House of Orange Returns, 1747–1780

In the 1700s intellectual currents swirled freely past borders, but the geopolitical realities of the century led to a near constant march of armies crossing and recrossing Europe's frontiers. Saddled with debts, the United Provinces could ill afford to do battle, and thus the outbreak of a war launched by Prussia, backed by its ally France, to secure territorial gains at the expense of Empress Maria Theresa (r. 1740–80), newly arrived on the throne of Austria, found the Republic anxious to remain neutral. Treaty obligations, however, trumped economic considerations. An ally of Britain, which supported Austria, and compelled by diplomatic commitments to defend the Austrian Netherlands against France, the country perforce became embroiled in the War of the Austrian Succession (1740–48). The French marched north into the Austrian Netherlands in 1744 to meet a joint Dutch-Anglo-Austrian army at Fontenoy (May 11, 1745), where a French victory led the British to blame the Dutch for the defeat. Occupying all of the Austrian Netherlands and sweeping past the Dutch-manned barrier fortresses, a small French force advanced into the United Provinces to seize Bergen op Zoom (September 1747) and several towns in the extreme southwest in mainland Zeeland (Dutch Flanders), which the French held as a warning to the Republic to cease its support of Britain and Austria. The invasion proved to be the spark that ignited a popular uprising.

French penetration of the border made starkly real the humiliating weakness of the country, with its economy contracting, its cities decaying, and its army retreating. Town councils closest to the French in Zeeland demanded a restoration of the stadholder, who, as in the crisis of 1672, was seen as a savior during a time of military peril. In April 1747 the States of Zeeland obliged. William Friso, already stadholder of Friesland and Groningen, was recognized as such in Zeeland. Demands grew that Holland do likewise, and soon Orange ribbons and cockades appeared all over the province. A huge Orange banner was unfurled from the Amsterdam town hall. Agitation proved unstoppable and William Friso was proclaimed William IV, stadholder of Holland, Utrecht, and Overijssel, by popular request in a spontaneous burst of mass appeal against a demoralized regent class that amounted to a virtual revolution, the only one to occur in Europe in the mid-18th century.

The French threat remained along the southern frontier and a French army advanced to take Maastricht in May 1748. Only the conclusion of general European peace at Aix-la-Chapelle (October 18, 1748) put an end to the French menace with the withdrawal of the occupying forces.

Unrest persisted, however, the war having laid bare underlying social tensions. Riots broke out against tax-farmers, whose houses were plundered by rampaging mobs. Civic militias refused to intervene. A democratic tenor emerged in calls made in Amsterdam that the militia be removed from regent control and that citizens be granted the right to appoint the burgomasters from among the town councilors as well as the directors of the Amsterdam chambers of the VOC and WIC. William IV purged councilors and burgomasters, but the populace remained recalcitrant. Turmoil reached such a point in Leiden that municipal officials pleaded for troops to quell the unrest, and the stadholder obliged. Civil disturbances throughout the country subsequently subsided.

Order having been restored, the States General declared that, to ensure that calm conditions persisted, the positions of stadholder and captain- and admiral-general would henceforth be held as hereditary offices by members of the House of Orange.

These posts passed to William V (1748–1806) in 1751. For the first time in the Republic's history, the same stadholder served in all the provinces. The prince's party predominated nationwide while regents and nobles remained thoroughly cowed. Placid times prevailed, but a vague sense of unease set in by the late 1770s. In the States General, the provinces and the stadholder locked horns over issues of military spending. Inland provinces refused to vote funds for the navy's upkeep. Even Zeeland declined to do so. Stadholders by tradition placed great stress on safeguarding the country's land frontiers, and William sided with the inland provinces. They would agree to the funds only on condition the army received higher allotments. Holland flatly refused,

William failed to broker a compromise, and political deadlock ensued, neither branch receiving the monies.

It was clearly evident by now that the country was poorer, and, although shipping and the colonial trade remained impressive, the rise of Britain to global preeminence threatened even these sectors. During the Seven Years' War (1756–63), fought by Great Britain and Prussia against France and Austria, the United Provinces profited as neutrals but the British acted with impunity in interfering with Dutch seaborne trade. Anxiety over the naval threat posed by Britain joined with fears of Austria and Prussia, two rising continental powers with which the Republic shared land borders. Weak-willed and vacillating, William V headed a country characterized, in 1780, by a stalemated government, a stagnant economy, and a vulnerable geostrategic position. Held in little esteem by large segments of urban public opinion, the regime was ill-prepared to meet the shock waves to come.

The Patriot Revolution, 1780–1787

Popular opinion in favor of democratic change evident in the riots of 1747–51 simmered through the succeeding years. The outbreak of the American Revolution in 1776 was greeted with sympathy by many among the Dutch public. The Dutch took great pride in having won their independence in defense of local liberties, and writers drew a parallel between the battle fought by their rebellious forebears and the struggle waged by British North American colonials, whose virtues they extolled. Joan Dirk van der Capellen tot den Poll (1741–84), an Orangist noble, translated Richard Price's *Observations on Civil Liberty* (1776), a work that drew on John Locke's writings in support of American democratic contentions. Opinions were bolstered by anti-British feelings among the merchant class, embittered by loss of markets to British merchants and tightened constraints by London on the Republic's trade, which was now vastly eclipsed by that of Britain.

American revolutionaries secured a considerable amount of weaponry and munitions from the Dutch. Most of the supplies were acquired indirectly by smuggling from the West Indies, especially from the island of Sint Eustatius, where, in November 1776, the governor-general, acting on his own authority, ordered an 11-gun salute to a visiting American warship, the first in the world to do so. The British government pressed the States General to put a stop to this activity, even taking direct action in occasionally boarding and seizing Dutch vessels on the high seas. Stadholder William V and his allies strongly supported the British, but they could do nothing to stop the smuggling. Britain began regular interceptions and seizures, which revealed the full extent of assistance given by Amsterdam merchants and financiers to American rebels. The Dutch of all classes resented the British actions, which they saw as an ungrateful return for Dutch loyalty to the British alliance of 20 years before. The States General, skeptical that Britain, already at war against the Americans and their allies France and Spain, would add another enemy to their list, considered joining the League of Armed Neutrality, an alliance of Russia, Denmark, and Sweden formed in March 1780 by which these powers threatened joint retaliation for any of their vessels seized by the belligerents. But the British viewed the move as one more unfriendly act by the irksome Dutch.

Having declared its independence in 1776, the newly minted United States found itself engaged in a war for its very life and looked for support—in men or money or both—wherever it could find it. Fully cognizant of the considerable wealth still controlled by Dutch financiers, in October 1779 the U.S. Congress appointed its former president, Henry Laurens (1724–92), as its plenipotentiary to the Netherlands, charged with obtaining a loan. Laurens sailed in October 1780 but his ship was intercepted by a British naval vessel. Laurens attempted to throw his papers overboard, but British seamen reclaimed the documents, which included a proposed draft treaty between the United Provinces and the United States. Imprisoned in the Tower of London, Laurens was later released in a prisoner-of-war exchange.

The incident strained Dutch-British relations to the breaking point and war was declared by Britain on December 20, 1780. The outbreak of the fourth Anglo-Dutch war (1780–84) allowed those circles within Dutch society sympathetic to American revolutionaries the opportunity to actively aid the latter's cause. Where Laurens had failed, statesman John Adams (1735–1826) succeeded. Adams traveled to Amsterdam from Paris, where he had vainly sought to open peace negotiations. Speaking no Dutch and knowing no one in the country, he achieved remarkable success through a combination of his own tireless efforts and the widespread support long evinced by many in prominent civic and financial positions. The Dutch government officially acknowledged the independence of the United States on April 19, 1782, the second European nation (after France) to do so. On June 11 Dutch bankers extended a $2 million loan to the Americans. Adams's residence became the U.S. embassy following his appointment as ambassador to the Netherlands. In October 1782, he secured for his new country a treaty of amity and commerce, the second such treaty

Published in London in 1782, this print shows William V as a rather obese, mentally deficient, bankrupt ruler. He laments his fortune lost in waging war against Britain. (Library of Congress)

between the United States and a foreign government (following the 1778 treaty with France).

The war proved less fortunate for the Dutch themselves. Much of what was left of the country's naval prowess, which amounted to little more than "twenty-five ships of the line, and thirty frigates, half out of repair" (Ellis 1789, 66), was all but destroyed. No less than 200 Dutch merchant vessels were captured in January 1781, which effectively halted the country's shipping. On February 3, British admiral George Brydges Rodney (1717–92) seized Sint Eustatius, sacking the formerly neutral entrepôt and confiscating the booty gathered there. Dutch outposts around the world fell, ranging from the Dutch West India Company's West African forts (except Elmina) to bases in Ceylon and southern India.

Popular dislike for a regime that had exerted so lukewarm an effort in waging so disastrous a war turned into active revolt. In September 1781 an incendiary tract appeared, titled *To the People of the Netherlands* (*Aan het volk van Nederland*). Published anonymously but written by Baron van der Capellen, it extolled the local liberties once held by town councils, militias, and guilds, which, chosen by and composed of free citizens, had checked the power of provincial rulers. The people had been stripped of their freedom by the Habsburgs and they continued to be suppressed in the early Republic, chiefly by the princes of Orange, claimed van der Capellen, and he called on his fellow citizens to regain their freedom by creating a people's militia and agitating for democratic change.

His broadside appeared everywhere, and everywhere the people responded. Stylizing themselves Patriots, they formed clubs, whose task, they affirmed, was to complete the work begun by the revolt against Spain. At the same time, regents who traditionally opposed Orangist control joined with those who now demanded popular election of town councils and restoration of control by the citizens of provincial and national politics.

By 1782 Patriot militias, called Free Corps, replaced the old civic militias. By the late 18th century, the latter had become largely moribund, their ranks composed mostly of Reformed Church members who by now had grown resentful at perceived neglect by the government. Unlike the militias of old, the new groups were open to all Dutchmen.

The Patriot presence spread quickly. By August 1785 the Free Corps held control in Leiden, Haarlem, Dordrecht, Gouda, and in towns in Gelderland and Overijssel. Sporting black cockades and ribbons tied in a V for "freedom" (*Vrijheid*), they massed in their thousands at Utrecht, their main center, where they adopted an Act of Association calling for the reestablishment of a republican constitution.

Thoroughly alarmed at the growing radicalism, the regents now began to withdraw their support. Voices from among the working classes, feeling threatened by the potential rivalry inherent in Patriot power, also began to speak up in opposition. Street clashes between rival crowds, which began in 1784, grew more frequent by 1786. Viewing developments from Nijmegen, where he had retreated, Stadholder William V could count on the loyalty of the regular army but could never be sure if the troops, together with Orangist backers among the public, would prove sufficient to suppress the Patriots.

By August 1786 Utrecht stood in open rebellion and, in September, the States of Holland suspended the stadholder as captain-general, releasing the province's troops from allegiance to him. On May 9, 1787, the Free Corps killed 80 Orangist supporters at Jutphaas, near Utrecht, a skirmish that marked the opening hostilities in a civil war that would last four months.

In the end, only foreign intervention broke the deadlock between the two sides. Prussia's new king, Friedrich Wilhelm II (r. 1786–97), of the House of Hohenzollern, untried but brash, combined an iron discipline and hatred for democratic ideas with family links to the House

Jonas Zeuner, Exchange of Fire on the Vaartse Rijn near Jutphaas at 10 p.m. 9 May 1787 *(1787). Oil (?) on glass, 27 × 33 cm* (Collection Rijksmuseum Amsterdam)

of Orange: He was the brother of William's wife Wilhelmina. The arrest of the princess by the Gouda Free Corps, who held her in detention for five hours while she traveled to The Hague to address the States General in June 1787, spurred Friedrich Wilhelm to action, backed by British encouragement. To avenge the insult to the Prussian royal house, an army of 26,000 crossed the border at Wesel on September 13, 1787, and marched virtually unopposed to Amsterdam. In advance, as the Prussian army drew near, the Free Corps disappeared. The Patriot Revolution evaporated. William V returned in triumph to The Hague, determined to restore the old regime in its entirety.

The Fall of the Republic, 1787–1795

William wanted restoration without retribution; however, in the end, Patriot clubs and Free Corps were dissolved, political meetings banned, and the press silenced. Thousands of Patriots fled to France.

King Louis XVI (r. 1774–91) welcomed them, but the émigrés did not return the favor, rejoicing in the revolution that swept their place of exile beginning in 1789. Dutch radicals, such as Anacharsis Cloots (1755–94), participated with others from all over Europe—both by word and by act—in upheavals that grew progressively more violent. A Batavian Legion of Dutch troops commanded by Patriot Herman Daendels (1762–1818) joined the French revolutionary armies.

The moderate French constitutional monarchy put in place in 1789 tottered by 1792 as radicals grew increasingly fearful of threats to the revolution posed by domestic opposition and declarations by foreign powers of their intention to intervene should harm befall Louis XVI. War broke out with Austria in April 1792. In September a new government, the National Convention, deposed the monarchy and made export of revolution its stated policy. French armies invading the Austrian Netherlands won a victory at Jemappes (November 6, 1792) and occupied the entire country by winter. Louis XVI went to the guillotine in January 1793, an act that united all Europe against the revolution. On February 1, 1793, the French government declared war on the powers of the First Coalition, an alliance that included the Dutch Republic, Britain, Prussia, and Austria. The defeat of the Austrians at Fleurus (June 26, 1794), in the Austrian Netherlands, exposed the Republic to attack. It was a country in which many remembered and nurtured the radically democratic ideas of the Patriots. Reading societies began to meet in private homes ostensibly to discuss literary topics; in fact, they met to propagate anti-Orangist beliefs, and some were attended by former Free Corps members armed with hidden firearms. A so-called secret committee of the revolution flooded Amsterdam with pamphlets in September 1794 and an attempted uprising in October was suppressed.

Maastricht fell to French armies in 1794. In January 1795 the French under General Charles Pichegru advanced north over the great rivers and reached Utrecht, where they found the streets bedecked in French revolutionary tricolors of red, white, and blue. Ahead of the armies, revolutionary committees took over cities. William V fled to Britain. A feeling of liberation—a sentiment that had been thwarted in 1787—swept the country, popularly expressed in theatrical plays, victory parades, and banquets. The motivating factor that had served to underpin Dutch foreign policy since the days of William III—the dread of French aggression—had met with defeat. But the France of 1795 was not the France of Louis XIV, the Bourbon Sun King. A revolutionary regime in Paris would spark major change in the Netherlands.

6

FROM REPUBLIC TO EMPIRE TO KINGDOM (1795–1839)

The joyous crowds that greeted the arrival of the French were ready for change. A new republic replaced the old. All traces of the stadholderate were gradually erased, and groundbreaking democratic innovations introduced—universal male suffrage, an end to hereditary titles, civil rights for Catholics and Jews. Greater liberty, however, did not entail being left alone. War waged by France never ceased from 1795 to 1815, except for a brief interval in 1802–03, and the Dutch were drawn in, backing the new continental master in battling the British for the fifth and sixth times, respectively. The French demanded from the Dutch more and more—more money to meet wartime expenses, more men to help fill the ranks of French regiments. When the Batavian Republic proved insufficiently cooperative, Napoléon Bonaparte brought his brother Louis in to run a puppet regime. And when Louis himself proved more solicitous of his new subjects' interests than of his imperial brother's wishes, Napoléon removed him and incorporated the country directly into the French Empire. For five years Dutch evasions of French exactions intensified, met by brutal countermeasures, until Napoléon's defeat brought universal relief. Planners of a postwar order set out to create a different form of government and to bring back a familiar old name to head a new kind of ruling house.

Prince William V of Orange, son of the last stadholder, arrived at Scheveningen to be greeted by a joyful reception on the last day of November 1813. He had left the country from the same port 18 years before, sailing away in a humble fishing smack, a junior member of a discredited ruling house. Now he returned, this time aboard a British man of war, and this time as both the head of the House of Orange-Nassau and the soon-to-be king of an entirely new regime. The leader of the dynasty that had played so major a role in the affairs of the country before 1795, William served as the vital link connecting the old Republic with the new kingdom now to be established. In the 16th century, the Dutch had tossed out monarchy as a foreign institution. Now it was foreign power that put it back in place.

The Kingdom of the Netherlands came about by order of Europe's new power brokers. The victors over Napoléon Bonaparte called the new kingdom into being, and it was they who determined the contours of the country in decreeing the reunion of the southern and northern Netherlands. However, the ease with which boundaries were erased on maps could not be matched in eliminating differences that had evolved between the two regions over the intervening 250 years. During that time, the old interregional links—political, economic, religious, cultural—had been decisively severed. In 1789–90 the people in the provinces to the south rose against their Austrian overlords in a revolution waged by rebels who, whether they called for new democratic liberties or old provincial privileges, acquired a distinct consciousness of their being "Belgians." King William I tried hard to make the new arrangement work but, in the end, a union that neither party had actively sought presided over by a ruler who never took kindly to even the slightest bit of censure would prove untenable. And in the end the same powers that had called the new kingdom into existence would be brought back together to decree its dissolution.

The Batavian Republic, 1795–1806

The forces of Revolutionary France entered Amsterdam on January 19, 1795, a day after William V had fled the country. By the terms of The Hague Agreement (May 16, 1795) that ended the war, the name of the country was officially changed from the United Provinces to the "Batavian Republic." The Netherlands became a satellite of France (*état secondaire*) although it remained a sovereign state. As such, the French left the Patriots to do as they would, after imposing a 100 million guilder indemnity on the country and annexing Maastricht and Zeeland Flanders. Orangists were purged and all traces of the stadholderate removed, the United Provinces's last Grand Pensionary, Laurens Pieter van der Spieghel (1736–1800), imprisoned. A new province was carved out of territory in the northeast, Drenthe becoming the eighth province effective January 1, 1796. Burdened with debt from its dual role as trading agent and governing body, the Dutch East India Company joined the Dutch West India Company, which had been dissolved in 1791, in bankruptcy, and it was abolished by decree in 1799. The colonies would henceforth be administered directly by the state. The Bank of Amsterdam, saddled with unpaid loans to the VOC, was forced to suspend payments in 1795, which effectively ended Amsterdam's status as Europe's chief financial center.

Revolutionary committees and militias introduced democratic procedures to local government, but bickering continued among those who favored a centralized state, those who wished to retain some degree of provincial autonomy, and those who wanted a pragmatic compromise.

A Bill of Rights on the French model was introduced (January 31, 1795) and the States General yielded to popular demands for a National Assembly, which convened on March 1, 1796, the first democratically elected national body in the country's history. The members were chosen by all males regardless of religion (except Jews) over the age of 20 in 126 electoral districts, a far more directly representational format than had ever existed in the former republic. One of the first acts of the new Assembly (August 5, 1796) was to detach the Reformed Church from its special status with the state, which, for the first time in 200 years, gave Catholics hope for further gains toward full equality. Jews were accorded full civil rights in an act of September 2, 1796. Constant wrangling beset the Assembly. Enough delegates were elected who favored retaining the federal principles and features of the late regime to produce eventual deadlock, resolved in January 1798 only by a French-backed ejection of federalists by radicals, chiefly Patriots led by Daendels.

A new, unitary constitution—a Netherlands first—was approved by plebiscite on April 23, 1798, and swept away the old structure. Government would be run by five directors, assisted by eight agents, heads of administrative departments. Hereditary titles and rights were ended, and democratic elections put in place. The provinces were replaced by eight departments and given geographical names on the French model. But because the old boundaries remained firmly rooted in the public's consciousness, this last act proved impossible to implement.

In the end, the new government of directors and agents wrestled, like its predecessor, with finding a formula to balance local and national governing powers. In 1801 a new state administration was set up under which the 1798 constitution was disavowed. The old provinces were restored and with them the organization of administration, justice, and taxation by provinces that had been so fundamental for centuries. Members of the regent oligarchy were reappointed to posts of fiscal and judicial authority, working now alongside radicals. Town councils retained control of local administration and militias.

The enthusiasm for revolution that had so gripped the country in 1794–95 evaporated rapidly in the wake of war and economic distress. The Dutch switched sides, as allies now of the French, to battle the British in a fifth Anglo-Dutch war (1795–1802). In October 1797 the Royal Navy's defeat of the Dutch fleet at Camperdown, off Den Helder, spelled the definitive end of the remnant of Dutch naval strength that had survived the losses of 1784. All of the Western Hemisphere colonies, those in South Africa, and the remaining outposts in Ceylon and southern India fell to the British. They would take Java, the key to the East Indies, in 1811.

Encouraged by these successes, Great Britain, backed by the exiled stadholder, made plans in 1798 to restore the old regime. An Anglo-Orangist-Russian invasion force was readied and a 24,000-strong allied army of mostly crack British troops landed under Sir Ralph Abernathy. William V appealed to the people to rise and the Dutch navy mutinied, but popular support remained muted. The invasion army occupied the North Holland peninsula and advanced toward Amsterdam but met defeat by a French-Batavian force at Castricum, near Alkmaar, on October 9, 1799. William beat a hasty retreat. Acknowledging the verdict of the battlefield, he subsequently yielded the Dutch properties of the House of Orange to the Batavian government in return for estates in Germany, where he retired.

Society reeled from the shocks produced by the swirl of events. Defeat, occupation, and ongoing war produced widespread misery. The social fabric was stretched and there was a marked increase in poverty, crime, and alcohol consumption. Nevertheless, public affairs remained remarkably resilient and well ordered as traditional institutions in education, welfare, and religion carried on largely unchanged.

The Kingdom of Holland, 1806–1810

Napoléon Bonaparte's (1769–1821) accession to power on November 9, 1799, shifted the guiding rationale of French continental ambitions from that of securing revolutionary aims to one of pursuing territorial gains. The main architect of French victories in the war of the First Coalition (1792–97), Napoléon took power in the midst of a renewed struggle that broke out only a year after the conclusion of peace, which pitted France against a Second Coalition composed of most of the same powers that had formed the first, including Austria, Great Britain, Russia, Portugal, and others. A man whose ambitions far exceeded those of Louis XIV, Napoléon reorganized the French military to create a superb fighting machine. Setting out to establish French continental dominance, he needed funds to finance his martial schemes, and the Batavian Republic was compelled to contribute 3 million guilders in 1800.

The country was hard-pressed to do so. Every economic sector but agriculture had suffered a decline. Dutch shipping and trade lay in ruins. In 1803 the dockyards and wharves that had once serviced the grand VOC at Rotterdam, Middelburg, and Hoorn were closed. By 1810 Enkhuizen's herring fleet had disappeared. Populations in all of the country's once-thriving cities fell, even in Amsterdam—the only one among Europe's major metropolises to suffer a demographic drop at the time. Manufacturing and food processing slumped, except for the distillation of gin, a gain induced no doubt, in part, by the populace's perceived need to assuage its pain.

After 1800 the Dutch met requisitions of money and men to help fuel the French war machine with increasing reluctance. Napoléon, however, wanted more than a lukewarm associate; he required a reliable ally. To achieve the unified administration and fiscal reforms that would bring closer collaboration and higher monetary flows, he engineered a coup in 1805, installing a dependable helmsman at The Hague.

Rutger Jan Schimmelpenninck (1761–1825), a veteran Patriot and a Batavian ambassador to Paris and London, ran the new regime as a sort of president beginning in February 1805. Appointed Grand Pensionary under a constitution approved by the emperor—and by only 4 percent of eligible voters in April 1805—that created a 19-member legislature and five ministers of state, he presided over a government that removed the final, formal vestiges of the United Provinces. Any lingering debate between unitarists and federal-

Pierre-Paul Proud'hon, Rutger Jan Schimmelpenninck with Wife and Children *(c. 1801–02). Oil on canvas, 263.5 × 200 cm* (Collection Rijksmuseum Amsterdam)

ists ended as provincial and local autonomies were abolished in favor of a strong central government. Progressive general tax laws replaced the old excise levies on foodstuffs. The government broke new ground most especially in the field of education. A new school law regulating school inspections and ensuring teacher competency laid the foundation for reforms well into the 19th century.

From Napoléon's perspective the new arrangement remained flawed because Dutch interests still stubbornly trumped those of the French. Schimmelpenninck's sway thus proved but a brief stop on the road toward complete subordination to France demanded by a regime headed, after 1804, by a self-proclaimed emperor determined to forge his place as Europe's unrivaled ruler.

The greatest challenge to his pretensions came from Great Britain. An opponent of France since 1795, Britain had never been decisively defeated and its power remained undiminished. The Royal Navy reigned supreme across the world's oceans. Napoléon's plan to invade the British Isles in 1803–04 proved unfeasible after the British navy's victory over a combined French and Spanish fleet at Trafalgar (October 21, 1805) and so the emperor struck back with a different kind of attack. Triumphant everywhere on the Continent, having conquered or allied with every major and most minor powers, Napoléon aimed to strangle Britain by cutting off its lifeline—its trade. The Berlin Decree (November 21, 1806) forbade the importation of British goods into continental ports, and the Milan Decree (December 17, 1807) tightened the noose further in establishing a blockade around the British Isles and subjecting neutral ships sailing to and from Britain to search and seizure. The embargo encouraged British merchants to search for new markets outside continental Europe, hurting especially the Netherlands. Dutch traders maintained extensive links to Britain, an important market with its far-flung colonies and, as the birthplace of the Industrial Revolution then underway, its many nascent industries. Smuggling activities across the North Sea began immediately.

Warfare added to Dutch mercantile woes. Allied to France, the country waged a sixth Anglo-Dutch war (1803–14) but it did so only half-heartedly. Squeezed by the pressures of global war between British naval might and Napoléon's continental dominance, the Dutch found little room for independent maneuver. Needing a firmer grip on the country to better battle the British, Napoléon offered Schimmelpenninck his choice of either resigning in favor of a king or acquiescing to the immediate incorporation of the country into the French Empire. The Grand Pensionary preferred the former and departed, the last to hold that title, making way on June 5, 1806, for Louis Bonaparte (1778–1846), Napoléon's younger brother.

Schimmelpenninck's regime had laid the groundwork for a unitary state, which was now fully installed. A monarchy replaced the republic. Local and regional elites wielded no power or influence and the guilds were dissolved. To supersede the Roman Dutch law—a blend of Roman civil law and traditional Germanic customary law—then in place in the old Republic, a legal code consisting of clearly defined rules applicable, for the first time ever, to the entire country was adopted in 1809. The set of laws was based on the French Napoléonic code, drafted in a Dutch version by lawyer and writer Willem Bilderdijk (1756–1831), an Orangist exile who had returned to the country. Every vestige of the old order

Charles Howard Hodges, Louis Bonaparte, King of Holland from 1806 to 1810 *(1809). Oil on canvas, 223 × 147 cm* (Collection Rijksmuseum Amsterdam)

was erased, even to the point of moving the capital to Utrecht in 1807 and then, in 1808, to Amsterdam, where the town hall, the architectural embodiment of the old Republic, became the royal palace.

Louis—"Lodewijk" to the Dutch—tried hard to be a good monarch. Having accepted the throne reluctantly, he determined to make himself, if not beloved, at least accepted and respected. He studied the Dutch language, made efforts to reduce financial flows to Paris, and refused to implement conscription. Louis commissioned a unified code of commerce, which was written by Moses Salomon Asser (1754–1826), the first Jewish member of the Amsterdam law courts. Asser's work symbolized the full achievement of civil liberties by Jews that was first granted under French pressure in 1796. On November 12, 1796, the first Jewish lawyer, Jonas Daniël Meijer (1780–1834), was awarded a diploma.

By his actions, Louis did succeed in winning a degree of popularity among the Dutch, and for three years Napoléon bore patiently the policies pursued by the kin whom he had made king. Amsterdam enjoyed the status and trappings of an imperial capital, but the country's economy benefited little under a regime that kept a high French tariff wall in place until 1812. By 1809 Napoléon's Continental System lay riddled with leaks, sprung most especially in the Netherlands, ruled by a king who looked the other way in allowing large-scale smuggling of British goods. Sullen and grudging in their compliance with imperial dictates, the Dutch seemed to drag their feet at every turn. When they failed to prevent a British attack in Zeeland, the emperor had had enough. Louis was forced to abdicate and, on July 9, 1810, the country was incorporated directly into the French Empire.

The Empire, 1810–1815

Brief but brutal characterized the period of direct rule by France. The Continental System was strictly enforced, conscription introduced, the press censored, and monies in the amount of 100 million guilders a year flowed out of the country. French troops arrived in the Netherlands in force, and the port of Den Helder, the country's main naval base since the early days of the Republic, was fortified in 1811. French imperial overlords oversaw enactment of one major exception to the generally dismal record: The introduction of a civil registrar and a land registry marked a major break with the past and one that would have long-lasting effects.

In the wake of the retreat of Napoléon's Grande Armée from Moscow in 1812 and its defeat at Leipzig in 1813, French power in the country crumbled rapidly. Troops and officials hastily departed, leaving a vacuum that the Dutch looked to fill by, once again, turning to the dynasty that had saved the country in crises past. A movement coalesced around a group of aristocrats and Orangist sympathizers to secure a return of the House of Orange. Gijsbert Karel van Hogendorp (1762–1834), an aristocrat who had occupied a local government post in Rotterdam before 1795 and who now served as one of three officials ruling the country temporarily during the power vacuum left by the French, sent a letter of invitation to Prince William Frederick, elder son of the last stadholder, in Britain. The letter arrived on November 21, 1813, and, a mere nine days later, William stepped ashore at Scheveningen, the little town on the North Sea near The Hague.

The United Kingdom, 1815–1839

William accepted sovereignty at Amsterdam on December 2, 1813, and he acknowledged that he did so by popular acclaim. Nevertheless, having recognized that he owed his throne to the public's will, he harbored no intentions of endowing his government with genuine democratic features. A draft constitution with the king as absolute monarch was approved in 1814, based largely on an outline penned 14 years before by Gijsbert van Hogendorp, but its formal implementation had to await considerable changes to the document that were necessitated by incorporation of the Belgian provinces into the kingdom.

Momentous changes had occurred to the south in the Austrian Netherlands during the years the French dominated the Continent. In 1789–90 insurrectionists had staged a revolution—the Brabant Revolution—in declaring a United States of Belgium. Austrian overlords were briefly ousted before they, in turn, were turned out by French Revolutionary armies in 1794, and the region remained firmly in French hands until 1815. Napoléon's defeat left the provinces there in a political limbo, and their fate awaited the decision of the victorious allied powers assembled at the Congress of Vienna. A scheme to merge the Belgian lands with the Netherlands to form a solid barrier against both France and French revolutionary ideas had first been broached in London in 1798. The idea accorded well with the intentions of the victors at Vienna, and so, urged by British foreign secretary Robert Stewart, Viscount Castlereagh (1769–1822), Austria, Prussia, Russia, and a chastened France joined Britain in signing the Eight Articles of London on June 21, 1814, to put the plan into effect.

Many Belgians were initially hesitant. Catholics eyed the Protestant Dutch king with great suspicion, but fears of reannexation by French anticlericals following Napoléon Bonaparte's return from Elba in March 1815 eased anxieties. The union appeared to work—just as it was getting under way—on the battlefield, where Dutch and Belgians fought fraternally side by side under the leadership of Arthur Wellesley, the duke of Wellington (1769–1852), and of William, who fought bravely and was wounded in the shoulder, at the Battle of Waterloo (June 18, 1815). Napoléon's defeat at this village outside Brussels by allied forces of Britain, the Netherlands, and Prussia put a definitive end to any French threat.

Paralleling territorial rearrangements across Europe, the Netherlands made clarifications to its borders both external and internal in 1815. At the Congress of Vienna, negotiators formalized the Gelderland frontier with Prussia. Lands acquired in the settlement of 1648—North Brabant and Limburg—became the country's ninth and 10th provinces, respectively.

The constitution of 1815 brought back the old institutions of States General and provincial States, but now radically reconfigured. The States General became a bicameral body. The Second Chamber, a body that included 55 seats each for the Netherlands and Belgium, was

WILLIAM I

Born in The Hague, the son of the last stadholder, Prince William V of Orange-Nassau, and Princess Wilhelmina of Prussia, William (August 24, 1772–December 12, 1843) learned early the virtues of discipline and duty, and, through his education, he acquired strong absolutist values. His maternal ties drew him closely to the Prussian royal house, and in 1791 he married Frederika Louisa Wilhelmina, the daughter of King Frederick William, with whom he had three children.

Fleeing with his family to Britain in 1795, William collaborated eagerly with the coalition powers allied against France. He succeeded as prince of Orange on his father's death (1806), and in 1813 he welcomed overtures to come back to the country made by leaders of a provisional government. Returning to a warm reception, he refused the title of king proferred by officials; instead, he preferred to style himself "sovereign prince" and he called for enactment of a "wise constitution" that protected the rights of the people. He accepted the title of king (March 16, 1815) on the urging of the powers gathered at the Congress of Vienna, and he fought bravely at Waterloo.

The first royal monarch of the Netherlands, William ruled under a constitution that suited him perfectly. Granted extensive royal power, he wedded a penchant for personal rule with a stubborn personality. Haughty and arrogant, he brooked little opposition to his plans and proposals. As his reign progressed, he incurred growing displeasure at both the style and the substance of his rule. The loss of Belgium in 1839 left him especially resentful and unreconciled. Feeling that he could no longer remain the sovereign of a people who had forced his hand, and who looked with disfavor on his intention to marry Henriette d'Oultremont (1792–1864), a Belgian Catholic countess, William abdicated in favor of his son on October 7, 1840. Few regretted his departure. It was unlamented by liberals, who now saw a major roadblock removed in efforts to implement democratic reforms, and many conservatives felt that, by his marriage, he had abandoned the staunch Protestantism of Dutch ruling circles. On his death in 1843, Orthodox Calvinists declared it was God's punishment on him.

made up of representatives chosen by the provincial States, themselves elected by, and composed of, males who could afford to pay the most in taxes. The First Chamber consisted of notables appointed by the king to serve for life. The Belgians had wanted a house filled on the basis of

Joseph Paelinck, William I, King of the Netherlands *(1819). Oil on canvas, 227 × 155 cm* (Collection Rijksmuseum Amsterdam)

a hereditary peerage but they met staunch resistance from the Dutch, who rejected the concept as alien to their bourgeois, republican traditions. No one could agree on a single capital for the country, settling on two official seats of government. The court, court ministers, and legislators shuttled back and forth between The Hague and Brussels.

The States General held important legislative and financial powers, but it was not a parliament in the modern sense. Ministers remained responsible to the king, not the States General. Budgetary powers were much reduced since routine expenditures were set for 10-year periods. Royal wishes were never thwarted because final votes to approve or reject legislation were taken in the First Chamber, a body so packed with pliant appointees that observers took to calling it "the king's menagerie."

The new system blended traditional institutions under a moderate monarchical regime that enshrined control by the king with a legislature given sufficient power that if it chose to do so—and it eventually did—could flex considerable political muscle.

Careful to balance the interests of North and South, William was surprised to find the constitution rejected by a plurality of 1,604 Belgian notables chosen by him to vote on the draft. Spearheaded by clerics under the leadership of the bishop of Ghent, Maurice-Jean de Broglie (1766–1821), opponents sought a constitutional provision guaranteeing the Catholic character of the South. The king could not grant such a concession, bound by the Eight Articles to ensure legal equality of all religions in the kingdom. Only a clever manipulation of the vote secured approval in Belgium, but the sour start to the new union left lingering tensions that would contribute to its eventual breakup.

On March 16, 1815, William, who until then had been addressed provisionally as "sovereign-prince," took the title King William I of the Netherlands. Determined to make his realm an economic powerhouse that would restore the glory of the 17th-century Republic, the king could draw on the resources of an enlarged territorial base that included not only Belgium but also both Luxembourg—where William reigned as grand duke under a dual arrangement in which the grand duchy also remained a member of the Germanic Confederation—and all of the Dutch colonies, which were returned in 1816 with the exception of Ceylon, the Cape, and western portions of Guiana (present-day Guyana).

William sought to weld together the economic bases of each of the two regions—Dutch maritime trade and Belgian industry—into a system that would provide mutual advantage to both. Under his plan, the products of Belgian factories would be carried in Dutch ships to the colonies and elsewhere and the ships would sail back laden with wares and goods produced in other places unavailable domestically. Strong support from the central government would back up the economic drive and a number of institutions were created to carry this out. To jump-start the economy, William founded the Bank of the Netherlands (Nederlandsche Bank) in 1814 to serve as the nation's central bank, although operations were largely limited to Amsterdam during its first 40 years in operation. Other institutions included a Fund for the Encouragement of National Industry (1821), a government syndicate for the liquidation of state debt, a Brussels-based Société Générale bank (1822), and, most important, the Netherlands Trading Society (NHM, 1824). The NHM, a mixed public-private enterprise, was designed to steer the economic program by undertaking export-import promotion and research on domestic and foreign economic issues.

The regime's short time in existence proved insufficient to determine the worth of many of these institutions. In the short run, the government syndicate amassed more debts than it liquidated; however, both the Société Générale and the NHM survived, the former becoming so successful that it helped finance the Belgian revolt, whereas the latter evolved into an organization that played a more limited role after 1840 as an East Indian trading organization.

The government also undertook efforts to improve the physical and human infrastructure. Roads were built, canal connections between Amsterdam and the Rhine were upgraded, the approaches to Rotterdam were improved, steamship companies were founded, and railroads began to be built—the first line running from Amsterdam to Haarlem opened on September 20, 1839. The central government took firm control over education, opening new schools in Belgium and absorbing the boards of trustees of the three universities in the North—Leiden, Utrecht, and Groningen—into a state-run system.

Commerce in the North recovered slightly after 1813 but, despite the heightened government efforts, the economy remained based on traditional pursuits in trade, agriculture, fishing, and small-scale manufacturing. Government revenues likewise continued to be derived from the customary activities, namely, taxes levied on goods in transit, revenues from the sale of agricultural produce, and fees for storage and distribution.

Income sources were much more diverse in Belgium, where industry responded well to government incentives. The first area in continental Europe where advanced techniques in mining, metallurgy, and factory operations took root, Belgium followed Britain in adopting the technologies of the Industrial Revolution. By the 1820s industry rivaled agriculture in importance. Textile production, metal smelting, and coal mining intensified, shielded by protective tariffs and fueled by injection of British investment capital, which was actively encouraged by the king.

Paralleling his economic aims, the king sought to win for his newly unified realm greater stature in the arts and sciences. The Royal Academy of Sciences was set up as the successor to the Royal Institute of Science, Literature and Fine Arts that had been created in 1808, and, conscious that artists needed proper training to bring them up to international standards, state funds were extended to those pursuing work in theater, music, science, and the visual arts.

William, his vision clear about the kind of country he aimed to create, would brook no criticism of his methods or measures. In so doing, he helped to spawn the very opposition he could not tolerate. Stubborn and self-righteous, he combined an activist agenda with an autocratic ruling style. No policy could go forward without the stamp of royal approval, his own "royal decree" (*Koninklijk Besluit*). Convinced that he alone knew what was best for the country, he demanded that he be given even greater powers. Backed by a bureaucracy headed by his most powerful minister, Cornelis Felix van Maanen (1769–1846), a man schooled in the centralizing regimes of the Batavian era, William preferred to govern by executive decision rather than through laws, thus bypassing the States General. As a result, when opposition to his policies began to mount in the late 1820s and the king could have used a legislative base from which to draw support, he could not count on any committed backers in the States General. Nor could he look to gain traction from among the general populace, limited by the restrictive franchise to only a tiny, politically active fraction.

The Secession of Belgium, 1830–1831

While the united kingdom found favor with some among the merchants and budding industrialists of Belgium, their Catholic compatriots never felt completely comfortable in a country ruled by a Protestant monarch where Calvinism, although no longer state sanctioned, had long served as the prevailing religious and social ethic. The overwhelming majority of the population in the South and a significant minority in the North as well, Roman Catholics sought greater freedom for their church and resented executive fiats by which nondenominational state schools were opened and limits were placed on the number of religious orders allowed to engage in nursing and elementary education. A state-run institute, the Collegium Philosophicum, established at Leuven in 1825 to supervise the education of priests, drew such strong clerical opposition that William was forced to dissolve it in January 1830. The government implemented a reorganization of the church's administration without the Vatican's approval and when the king did secure a concordat with Rome (1827), he failed to abide by it. Opposition to the regime mounted, most especially in strongly Catholic Flanders.

Anticlericals in Belgium, whose outlooks had been shaped during the period of French Revolutionary and Napoléonic occupation, applauded William's policies toward religion. However, largely French-speaking and particularly prominent in Brussels, they, too, grew disenchanted with the regime largely because of its language legislation. To promote national unity, use of Dutch was encouraged and a law of September 15, 1821, stipulated that, within three years, only Dutch could be used in the law courts and to conduct official business in the Dutch-speaking provinces of northern and western Belgium, which included Brussels. The upper classes here had been speaking French ever since Burgundian days, many knowing only that language, and William underestimated the rancor he raised by his monolingual measures.

Belgian industrialists drawn to laissez-faire principles (the idea that economic systems function best if left alone by governments) then coming into vogue in Britain joined with Dutch trading interests in opposition to the regime's high tariff policies. And democrats in the South added their voices to those in the North in decrying the king's overbearing meddlesomeness, which undercut old traditions of local self-rule and stymied efforts to advance constitutional government.

The South had a larger population (about 3.5 million) than the North (about 2 million) and many Belgians expected that their dynamic society would dominate the kingdom. They rankled at a seemingly omnipresent state run bureaucratically and militarily largely by Dutch speakers from the northern Netherlands, which southerners, in pointing to its immobile society and sluggish economy, characterized as a place mired fast in a glorious but long gone past. The opposition in Belgium acquired real strength when Roman Catholic nobles and clerics joined forces with liberal journalists, lawyers, and other French-speaking elites. They demanded that the king concede powers to the States General by making government ministers responsible to the parliament, expanding legislative oversight, eliminating secretive government, widening the electorate, and granting freedom of the press and education.

Catholic and liberal opposition coalesced in 1828 when both parties came together to create a Union for the Redress of Grievances, established under the leadership of Jean-Baptiste Nothomb (1805–81), a moderate liberal member of the Second Chamber from Luxembourg. The union demanded liberty of instruction and of the press. Tensions crested in the autumn of that year when hundreds of petitions signed by as many as 40,000 people flooded the Second Chamber following defeat of a call for repeal of all restrictions on press freedom made by Charles de Brouckère (1796–1860), a representative from Bruges.

In the end, however, the fuel for a rebellion in Belgium came not from within the kingdom but rather from abroad. In July 1830 a revolution in France brought liberals to power, replacing the restored Bourbon regime with the constitutional monarchy of Louis-Philippe of Orléans (r. 1830–48). Watching the events intently, malcontents in Belgium were stirred, and the flashpoint occurred in Brussels one month later. On the evening of August 25, theatergoers at the opera house La Monnaie listened to *La Muette de Portici* (*The mute girl of Portici*), a new and hitherto banned work by French composer Daniel Auber about a 17th-century anti-Spanish revolt in Naples. Inspired by the ringing words of the aria "Amour sacré de la patrie," they rushed into the streets to join rioting workers in a spontaneous demonstration. The outbreak caught the government completely by surprise. William hesitated while disturbances spread quickly to engulf all of Belgium. Troops under the command of William's second son Prince Frederick (1797–1881) entered Brussels belatedly on September 23 but the ensuing bloodshed only stiffened Belgian resolve. By the end of October 1830 the Dutch army had been driven out of all of present-day Belgium, Luxembourg, and even the Dutch province of Limburg save for the fortified cities of Antwerp, Maastricht, and Luxembourg.

The European powers that had called the kingdom into being expected William to restore order. When he proved unable to do so, emissaries met in London in November 1830 to formulate a protocol, signed in January 1831, in which, following the lead of Britain in accepting the results of the rebellion, they gave recognition to Belgian independence. The Eighteen Articles, a document drafted in June, laid out the terms of the partition between the two countries, including a formal acknowledgment of Leopold of Saxe-Coburg-Gotha (1790–1865) as the new king of the Belgians.

To the surprise of everyone, William refused to accept the articles. He reacted instead by striking back, invading Belgium with an army commanded by his eldest son Prince William of Orange (the future William II, 1792–1849). Dutch opinion rallied behind the monarchy in supporting the Ten Days' Campaign (August 2–12, 1831), the public's patriotism stirred by the idealistic act of Jan C. J. van Speijck (1802–31), a young naval officer who blew up his ship, the enemy, and himself at Antwerp (February 5, 1831) rather than surrender. Dutch armies, led by the prince of Orange, scored initial successes but then fell back on reports of a French army's approach, leaving only the city of Maastricht in the south securely in Dutch hands.

Hostilities ceased after the appearance of a French army under Marshall Gérard (1773–1852) and the abandonment by the Dutch of Antwerp in December 1832, but stalemate persisted. The Belgians would not budge from possession of the towns of Venlo, Roermond, and other parts of Limburg around Maastricht, and William would not surrender Luxembourg, which the Belgians claimed. The king stalled for time, hoping a general European war might erupt in the interim, one in which tiny, new-born Belgium could not survive.

After seven years, the States General tired of this wait-and-see approach. Pressured by parliamentarians and by the five governments that had parleyed the Eighteen Articles, William agreed reluctantly in March 1838 to affix his signature to the documents of partition, which by then had increased to 24. The Treaty of London (Convention of 1839) was signed by the Dutch government, the Belgian government, and the five major European powers—Britain, France, Austria, Prussia, and Russia—on April 19, 1839. By the terms of settlement, the Netherlands recognized Belgian independence. The jagged line that now defines the border between the two countries was set. Southern Limburg, occupied largely by the Belgians, was divided, portions north of and directly around the city of Maastricht remaining Dutch. Two-thirds of Luxembourg went to Belgium, the remnant becoming an independent constitutional grand duchy with William remaining at its head. The Dutch agreed to open the Scheldt River to unfettered navigation but they won the right to charge tolls on the estuary, which they retained until 1863 when a cash payment by Belgium ended the restriction.

The king remained resentful and unreconciled. He abdicated a year later in favor of his son. His people were largely relieved to be rid of both their monarch and their southern countrymen. After almost a decade of unresolved tensions, the Dutch bad their neighbors a decidedly glad farewell.

7

BUILDING THE MODERN NATION-STATE (1839–1914)

The break with Belgium forced the Netherlands to rethink the essence of its domestic and international affairs. In the short run, the rupture proved to bring a measure of economic hardship in the loss of manufacturing and of trade, with reduction in Rhine River traffic, but, in the long run, the country benefited greatly. Shorn of Belgian industries, the Netherlands turned to develop its own, updated industrial base. Endowed with a moderately liberal constitution in 1848, the country acquired a democratic parliamentary system. No longer harboring any illusions about pursuing a return to great power status, the government adopted an aloof, neutral international policy stance and then channeled its efforts into a new foreign relations focus, the prevention of war and the promotion of global legal cooperation.

During the last quarter of the 19th century and the first decade of the 20th, propelled by rapid change, the Netherlands came to resemble other "modern" nations. Mass-based political parties, an advanced capitalist economy, and a secular culture began to develop. At the same time, Dutch society sorted itself out during these years into a confessional structure, organized along strictly separate religious and non-sectarian lines that would emerge fully in the next century. The Dutch participated in new movements sweeping Western society in workers' and women's rights and in efforts to secure early advances in social welfare measures. National pride stirred anew. In the 19th century the glories of the 17th century continued to inspire, but they invoked not a resigned sighing for a bygone past, as in the 18th, but a vigorous striving to build a stable, prosperous future.

The Establishment and Development of Parliamentary Government

Political debate after 1839 centered on devising a new form of government for the kingdom. Before he abdicated in 1840, William I, anxious to retain an authoritarian bias that gave him a direct role in governing, sought minimal change. Reformers wanted to weaken royal control over finances and make ministers fully responsible to parliament. Shorn of its Belgian members, the States General had functioned as a rump from 1830 to 1839. Under the Act of Partition of 1839, William was compelled to alter the number of seats to adjust for the lost territory, which culminated in a new constitution completed on September 21, 1840. The king and his backers largely had their say as constitutional modifications were kept to a minimum. The chief change: Ministers added their signatures to that of the king in being required to cosign all laws and royal decrees. In a major administrative adjustment, the province of Holland was divided into the two new provinces of North Holland and South Holland.

Political parties in the modern sense did not yet exist. Rather, parliament consisted of a collection of individual members who coalesced into largely amorphous groups around a particular issue and then disbanded. Liberals presented the most well-defined program in seeking greater parliamentary powers and, like their counterparts appearing across western Europe, in championing minimal state interference in the economy and maximum opportunity for individual initiative. However, they remained small in number after the departure of the Belgians. Conservatives upheld traditional prerogatives of king and church, and they adhered generally to stances adopted by the Dutch Reformed Church. They, too, were relatively weak because the country, never having had a large nobility, did not serve as fertile ground for a strong conservative party to emerge. Catholics formed a third presence and they could be found usually supporting policies in between those of the other two groups, namely, to the left of conservatives and to the right of liberals.

A Catholic from North Brabant, Lamburtus Dominicus Storm (1772–1859), joined with eight liberals—all of them prominent men, including provincial governors—to form a committee that drafted the "Proposal of the Nine Men" in 1844, calling for constitutional reform, but their proposal failed to even get a hearing before parliament, which continued to be run by conservatives. When it did come, sweeping constitutional change was propelled not by domestic deeds but rather by international developments.

In the early months of 1848 revolutionary movements broke out all across Europe, threatening to overthrow royal regimes from Paris to Vienna. No rumbles of impending upheaval appeared in the Netherlands, but William II—a man every bit as autocratically minded as his father—feared that he too would feel the heat from the hot winds of popular agitation that were buffeting thrones throughout Europe. He transformed himself, in his own words, "from a conservative to a liberal overnight." Bypassing his own ministers, the king gave a green light to change in requesting, on March 17, 1848, that a constitutional reform commission be formed. Headed by the liberal politician Johan Rudolf Thorbecke (1798–1872), the commission of five liberals and one Catholic, with no conservative members to hinder its work, completed a draft document by the end of the year.

Modern parliamentary democracy dates from the constitution of 1848 and the fundamental principles of the Dutch political system promulgated in the constitution remain even today the basis of government in the Netherlands. The constitution enshrines full ministerial responsibility as the foundation of representative government. Parliament continued to consist of two legislative bodies, the more important of which, the Second Chamber (Tweede Kamer) would now, like the provincial States and municipal councils, be directly elected by popular vote. The Second Chamber, which was composed of 76 members apportioned on the basis of population (one seat for every 45,000 inhabitants), was endowed with powers of amendment, inquiry, and oversight. The First Chamber (Eerste Kamer) was given an advisory role; its 39 deputies were appointed by the provincial States for nine-year terms, one-third replaced every three years. Governments could last a maximum of four years before elections had to be called. The constitution guaranteed freedom of education, the press, assembly, and religion. Church and state were strictly separated. Liberals led by Thorbecke formed the first government (1849–53) under the new constitution, and they took important initial steps to give order to the nascent political system. Provincial and municipal laws provided for a balance between the powers of the various lower government levels, the courts were reorganized, the postal system reformed, and trade treaties concluded. An electoral law stipulated that legislators would be chosen on a district by district basis, the districts apportioned by population. The franchise, however, remained restricted to the most prosperous males—those who paid a certain amount of taxes—and the system thus ensured that only about 10 percent of adult men participated in elections to the Second Chamber.

JOHAN RUDOLF THORBECKE

Johan Rudolf Thorbecke (January 14, 1798–June 4, 1872) was born in Zwolle. He read law at the University of Leiden and studied law and history in Germany, where he acquired a thorough grounding in Roman law. In 1824 he returned to the Netherlands and taught at Leiden. In 1830 he entered politics and in 1839 published his *Notes on the Constitution* (*Aanteekeningen op de grondwet*), which thrust him immediately to the forefront as leader of the liberals. Thorbecke sat on the 1844 committee to revise the constitution and chaired the 1848 committee. He drafted the constitution of 1848 almost single-handedly.

In 1849 Thorbecke was elected chairman of the Second Chamber in the States General and minister of the interior, becoming the de facto first prime minister of the Netherlands. With only two fellow liberals in the cabinet, he was not expected to accomplish much. Undaunted, Thorbecke replied to his critics: "Await our deeds," and his government devised important laws on administration and elections. Ousted from power in 1853 by the April Movement, he formed a second government from 1862 to 1866, during which he oversaw the introduction of a new kind of secondary school, the Higher Citizens School, which lessened emphasis on the classics in favor of the sciences and which remained a bastion of Dutch education for a century. Measures were drafted to give greater powers to local governments in public health, regulate child labor in factories, and standardize medical practice by mandating a medical degree for all practitioners. On January 4, 1871, Thorbecke formed his third cabinet. His plans for army and income tax reforms failed, he became ill in December, and he died at his home in The Hague in the spring of 1872. The architect of modern constitutional government, he was mourned by the entire nation.

Johan Heinrich Neuman, Johan Rudolf Thorbecke (1798–1872), Minister of State and Minister of the Interior *(c. 1852). Oil on canvas, 100 × 84 cm* (Collection Rijksmuseum Amsterdam)

Having accomplished their goal of responsible government, liberals now stood for its maintenance and intensification. Conservatives followed no sharply defined program, but they fought the system whenever they could, and, throughout the 1850s and 1860s, they worked to give the king and the ministers he supported as much power as possible. However, they were not helped in their efforts by the new man on the throne. Moody, impulsive, and extremely coarse, William III (1817–90), who succeeded his father in 1849, lacked any political skills.

Most members of parliament held a middle position between liberals and conservatives. Initially opposed to reform, they accepted the changes only grudgingly, but, because they sought above all to ensure well-ordered and financially prudent government, they soon acquired a stake in the new system, which they had no wish to overturn. Later known as conservative-liberals, they afforded constitutional democracy the opportunity to develop.

A firm foundation was laid, but it took time to take root because the precise distribution of powers among parliament, government ministers, and monarch long remained hotly contentious. The king reigned but the degree to which he still ruled remained undefined. During the 1850s William launched several attempts to return the political system to its pre-1848 configuration. In 1866 and again in 1867 he intervened personally in the elections to try to break the power of parliament. He failed. In 1868 the conservative cabinet was forced to resign when the newly elected Second Chamber rejected the cabinet's budget proposals for the third time. William was compelled to ask Thorbecke to form a new government. Henceforth, it became an unwritten rule that cabinets which no longer enjoyed the confidence of parliament would have to resign, and, following that precept, Dutch monarchs assumed an apolitical stance, their policymaking role from then on limited to exercising only informal influence over their ministers.

Thorbecke formed his last government in 1871 and his death a year later brought in a cabinet led by his staunch supporter Gerrit de Vries Abrahamszoon (1818–1900). Liberals held a preponderance of power until 1884, but, by then, still existing as little more than shapeless groups of shifting members, they began to compete with more formally structured political parties organized in response to emerging economic and social issues. They found themselves forced ultimately to follow trends and form more cohesive groups, a development that marked the rise of the modern political party.

The School Conflict and the Rise of Political Parties

The role of religion in the schools of the religiously divided Netherlands evolved into a complicated issue that shaped the political debate in the mid-19th century and helped to define Dutch politics in the century's later years. The school conflict (*schoolstrijd*) was rooted in the Van den Ende Law on Education (April 3, 1806) that created a public school system run by the municipalities, based on Christian principles but favoring no religious denomination. Privately run confessional schools could be established, but only on permission of the municipalities, which was rarely forthcoming. Thus, the state held a virtual monopoly on education.

Catholics led the charge for change. As early as the 1820s, Joachim George le Sage ten Broek (1775–1847), a Calvinist convert to Catholicism, began to demand state recognition be given to what were becoming, in fact, Catholic schools in the country's Catholic majority south. In 1825 Catholic deputy Leopold van Sasse van Ysselt (1778–1844) spoke in parliament demanding freedom of education. After 1848 Catholic strength solidified under the constitutional stipulation of church-state separation, which gave Roman Catholics the freedom to organize their church without government interference. At the same time, however, it deprived them of public support for their organizations, primarily schools.

Catholics had worshipped without resident bishops for three centuries before 1848, when the constitution cut the state's connection to the Dutch Reformed Church in mandating that the government remain neutral in religious matters. Laws directed against Catholics were revoked, and King William II signed legislation allowing Catholic monasteries to again be set up in the country. In 1853 the Vatican created five new bishoprics under the archbishopric of Utrecht (a Protestant stronghold). Reestablishment of a Catholic-controlled church stirred strong protests among Protestants, who collected more than 250,000 signatures in opposition. William III sympathized, though the constitution prevented him from taking sides, and efforts were made in April 1853 to block the move.

In midcentury Catholics constituted 35 to 40 percent of the population, and, although they disagreed often enough among themselves, they stood united publicly. Not so Protestants, however, for whom splits developed that mirrored in many respects the religious divisions of the early 17th century. The approximately 55 percent of the populace who belonged to the Dutch Reformed Church (Nederlands Hervormde Kerk), which became the legal successor to the Calvinistic Reformed Church in 1816, were theologically united initially under the Groningen School.

Adherents sought to counter the enfeebling effects on faith produced in the aftermath of the 18th-century Enlightenment by advocating a return to a theology grounded broadly on the spiritual and moral guidance of the Bible in general and the Gospels in particular.

Because the Groningen School remained nondoctrinal in allowing the faithful much freedom to decide spiritual matters for themselves, it came under attack from some—Orthodox Protestants—who seceded in 1834, and from others who remained in the church to lead a revival drive that stressed a person-based faith and the practice of Christian principles in daily life. Known as the Réveil, the largely aristocratic-led movement was given form and political direction by Guillaume Groen van Prinsterer (1801–76), a historian and archivist in the royal household. Elected a deputy to the Second Chamber, Groen promoted policies reflective of the country's history as a staunchly Protestant power, and he upheld Christian tenets in pursuing what he called an "anti-revolutionary course" against the godless principles of the French Revolution. By the 1850s he emerged as the most formidable opponent of Thorbecke and the liberals.

In 1853 Thorbecke's first government fell before the forces of the April Movement (Aprilbeweging), the Protestant response to the establishment of five new Roman Catholic bishoprics in Utrecht. Backed by their supporters in the States General, radical Protestants rallied around recollections of their martyrs of the 16th century, who had fallen during the fight for independence from Catholic Spain. They burned effigies of the new Catholic bishops in carrying out the most violent religious riots in centuries. Their efforts backfired, however, not only failing to prevent the appointments, but also uniting Catholics with liberals in an uneasy but mutually advantageous alliance. It was an alliance that would fracture over the school controversy.

In the debate over state recognition for confessional schools the Catholics were joined by some Protestants who also wanted their children to be instructed in the tenets and schooled in the moral values of long-cherished doctrines. Both considered the right to choose the type of education their children received to be a basic human one. They were opposed by those who accepted the principles of the Enlightenment in championing modern science and the role of reason in religion. Anxious to promote national over narrow, sectarian interests, liberals sought to establish secular schools that would instill patriotic, progressive precepts in students of all faiths and give them the intellectual moorings to decide for themselves matters of religion.

Prime Minister Justinus J. L. van der Brugghen (1804–63), a moderate Protestant who headed one among a series of short-lived cabinets from 1853 to 1862, favored a public school system that inculcated broad Christian values but did not teach specific Protestant dogma. Following a series of intense parliamentary debates, he managed to secure, with support from the liberals, passage of the Primary Education Act of 1857. While it required that instruction in public schools include instilling in students "Christian and social" values, the law stipulated that there would be no support extended to denominational schools. In essence merely a continuation of the 1806 law, the act changed no minds among the staunchly religious. In 1868 Dutch bishops issued a pastoral letter, backed by the papal encyclical *Quanta Cura* (1864), advising Catholics not to use the public schools. Catholic schools began to be started in earnest, especially in Catholic southern areas.

The issue now centered on state funding for private schools. The Kappeyne Law on Education (1878) raised standards but also costs and so heightened the fierceness of the struggle. A League against the School Law was formed by Protestants, which served as the catalyst of the first nationwide political party, the Anti-Revolutionary Party (Antirevolutionaire Partij, ARP), founded in 1878 under its leader Abraham Kuyper (1837–1920). Orthodox Calvinists proceeded to imitate Catholics in setting up their own independent schools from nursery to postgraduate levels, the latter put in place in 1880 when Kuyper founded the Free University of Amsterdam.

Catholic and Protestant political parties now took shape in opposition both to the liberal state's "neutral" stance, which they saw as indifference, if not outright hostility, to religion; and to the policies of the socialists, which were just now gaining strength, and which they viewed as a threat to the social order. The battle of the schools brought the Anti-Revolutionaries into alliance with the Catholics, and, in coalitions, they managed to control the government for most of the period from 1888 to 1925. Catholics organized politically only slowly because they faced little opposition in elections in the solidly Catholic south. Although Catholic candidates for parliament adopted a common electoral program in 1886, the Roman Catholic State Party (Rooms-Katholieke Staats Partij, RKSP) was not officially founded until 1926.

Since 1848 liberals had exhibited little formal organization, gathering in loose clubs and caucuses, and they now organized to meet the challenge of confessional competition. Divided into progressive (left-wing), centrist, and conservative (right-wing) factions, they united to form the Liberal Union (Liberale Unie) in 1885. In the elections of 1897, 1905, and 1913 the Liberal Union formed the largest party in the Second Chamber. Divisions persisted, however; the progressive wing left to form its own party in 1901—the Freethinking Democratic League (Vrijzinnig-Democratische Bond, VDB). Right-leaning members bolted the party in 1906. Over time, liberal opposition to state educational subsidies softened.

The first Protestant-Catholic coalition, formed under Aeneas Mackay (1838–1909) in 1888, secured an amendment that gave limited state revenues to sectarian schools. Monies were subsequently increased, financial equality for public and private schools was won (1917), and, finally, full state responsibility for funding the education of all children secured in the DeVisser Law on Education (1920), a settlement that has endured. While state funds were provided to all schools, the government mandated the minimum number of pupils that had to attend and, although parents were free to send their children to any school of their choice, if a school failed to attract the minimum number, it lost state funding and was forced to close. Likewise, schools were free to set course content and choose the means of instruction, but they were required to meet state standards as to levels of student competency.

Throughout the 19th century tensions within the Dutch Reformed Church never abated. Another church split (*Doleantie*) occurred in 1886 when Kuyper and his orthodox supporters left the Dutch Reformed Church and, in 1892, merged with the secessionists of 1834 to establish the Reformed Churches of the Netherlands. Concentrated socially in the lower middle classes and geographically in the "Bible belt" that stretched diagonally across the center of the country from Zeeland to Groningen, adherents of the Reformed Churches formed the core of orthodox Protestantism in advocating a return to the doctrines of John Calvin and the Synod of Dort, but they accounted for only 7 to 8 percent of the country's population. In 1906 orthodox Protestants who remained with the Dutch Reformed Church organized themselves into the Reformed Alliance, while Protestant liberals formed the Association of Reformed Liberals in 1913.

Divided by doctrine, Protestants proceeded to break apart politically. Disagreements over Kuyper's leadership and over the need for either strict or loose party discipline and for either more or less social legislation led a group of Anti-Revolutionaries to bolt the party in 1894. In 1908 they merged with others to form the Christian Historical Union (Christelijke-Historisch Unie, CHU). The CHU's electoral base lay almost exclusively with members of the Dutch Reformed Church, while

ARP adherents aligned to the same degree with membership in the Reformed Churches of the Netherlands.

The school conflict and the issues of franchise extension and social legislation framed the political debate from the 1880s to 1914. Elections revolved around essentially a choice between the liberals and the three confessional parties: ARP, CHU, and Catholics. With the widening of the vote in 1887 and 1896 to include lower-middle-class males, socialists began to make inroads among the electorate, and, by 1913, they succeeded in electing 15 members to parliament. The victorious liberals offered them seats in the cabinet, but, after a heated internal debate, the socialists declined, preferring to hold to the line of nonparticipation in "bourgeois" governments, true to their gospel that confrontation, not cooperation, must define their attitude toward the institutions of the capitalist system.

Kuyper believed that human institutions derive their authority from, but exist independent of, the state, a concept he called "sovereignty in one's own circle." The establishment of denominational schools laid the institutional basis for the idea of "pillarization." The concept lends a confessional character to Dutch society in implying that each segment of society exists both separately as its own "pillar," or "column," apart from the others, and collectively as a part of the national "roof," which requires that they work together to sustain the state that is common to them all. Distinctly separate Protestant, Catholic, liberal, and socialist worldviews deepened with time and, by 1914, pillarization had come to characterize Dutch social life.

Industrialization Takes Hold

Shorn of its industrial connections after the loss of Belgium, the Netherlands adopted a policy of enforced industrialization, which, quite literally, gathered steam, for it was steam power tied to the country's traditional economic base in trade that supplied the initial springboard. Steam was used to convert the traditional linen-weaving trade to cotton, and factories using the new source of power appeared at Tilburg by the early 1840s, many built with the help of British engineers. British entrepreneurs arrived also to set up factories, among the first Thomas Wilson (born c. 1780) who opened a cotton printing works in Haarlem in 1833. The new factories gave work to the unemployed, and the hundreds of beggars that could be found in many Dutch towns disappeared.

Steam revolutionized the shipping companies. The Netherlands Steamboat Company, founded in Rotterdam in 1823, was the first

Dutch transportation firm to change from sail to steam, and steamship construction subsequently grew rapidly. Wood gave way to iron and, by the 1890s, iron to steel. The value of the Asian colonies soared in importance after completion of the Suez Canal in 1869 opened up direct steamship service to Europe. Belgian industrialists, shut out of the East Indian market after Dutch-Belgian division in 1839, arrived to set up businesses. Improved means of transportation and links to the Indies led Dutch importers to monopolize the European market for quinine, tin, and indigo—and, for the first time, dairy manufacturers could ship mass cargoes of their products on vessels returning to Asia. The merchant marine became one of the world's largest.

Shipbuilding and servicing produced phenomenal growth in Rotterdam, whose population increased fivefold between 1860 and 1909. Construction of the New Waterway improved links to the sea and creation of the Rotterdam Dock Company in 1872 led to construction of the first oil terminal (1885), the Delftshaven (1886), and the pioneering harbor at Katendrecht (1887). Shipyards began to spread to adjacent villages, which soon developed into industrial suburbs. Massive new wharves and docks at the Maas Harbor, completed in 1905, facilitated swift transshipment of Rhine trafficked goods, and they proved so valuable that similar facilities were built beginning in 1907 along the Waal River. The Haarlemmermeer (Lake Haarlem) was drained, beginning in 1840. Some once sleepy places prospered with the arrival of railroads—Hilversum boomed following rail connections with Amsterdam and Utrecht in 1874. The North Sea Canal was opened in 1876, giving Amsterdam direct access to the open sea and spurring significant development in the last decades of the 19th century. International trade grew and Amsterdam's money market and stock market reemerged as important European centers. Specialty crafts, most famously diamond cutting and polishing, surged.

During this period modern capitalism replaced the formerly dominant trade capitalism in using labor, capital, and materials more intensively than ever before. Old enterprises were transformed into new industries, a trend exemplified by the trading company founded by Hendrik ten Cade of Almelo in 1766. In 1841, under his son Egbert, the firm switched to textile production. New industrial activity was stimulated by expansion of the money supply facilitated by creation of mortgage banks, which allowed limited liability companies to be launched for the first time. The Bank of the Netherlands established branches around the country and the first commercial joint-stock banks were founded, including the Twentsche Bank (1861), the Rotterdamsche

Bank (1863), and the Amsterdamsche Bank (1871). The Netherlands Trading Society began to engage in banking activities in the colonies in the late 1870s. The government founded a postal savings bank—Rijkspostspaarbank—in 1881. Beginning in the late 1890s cooperative agricultural banks spread. Commercial banks built closer ties to trade and industry starting in the early 20th century in extending loan facilities and arranging stock exchange flotations.

New energy sources and communication links appeared. Coal fired the industrial boom. Supplies from new mines in Limburg, where deposits had been known to exist since the 16th century, replaced imports after the mid-1860s until burgeoning demand necessitated reimportation after 1902. By the first decade of the 20th century, when the mines were nationalized, they furnished about 65 percent of the nation's energy needs. Electricity was first supplied at Kinderdijk, near Rotterdam, in 1886. Beginning in midcentury, railroads spread rapidly. Telegraph service began in 1845 between Haarlem and Amsterdam and, in 1869, a standard postal system was put in place. The country's first electric tram ran at Haarlem in 1899.

Of the new industries, highly specialized activities emerged first. Diamond polishing began in earnest in 1822 when a factory was founded at Roeterseiland, near Amsterdam. Now steampower-driven, textile weaving grew in the 1860s, with increasing volumes of finished goods meeting demand from new markets in the East Indies. Powered by electricity, the Philips Company, founded by Gerard L. F. Philips (1858–1942), began production of incandescent light bulbs at Eindhoven in 1891. After 1870 a domestic chemical industry was built and rubber and oil-refining works appeared. Much industrial activity was backed by support from the government, which suspended the law on patents from 1869 to 1912 as part of its drive to catch up with neighboring countries' economies in allowing entrepreneurs to tap into whatever technologies they could acquire.

At the same time that new industries were emerging, traditional activities in international trade and finance and in agriculture remained preeminent. Despite an agrarian crisis in the late 1840s spawned by failure of successive potato harvests, agriculture rebounded. Regionally diversified and highly developed, it boasted strong markets, especially for its dairy products.

However, importation of cheap grain from North America induced a severe agricultural depression from the late 1870s until the 1890s, which drove some rural laborers to emigrate. Altogether, from 1846 to 1932, about 220,000 left the country, most to the United States,

Canada, Australia, and Argentina. The effects of the slump were muted, however, by adoption of highly intensive agricultural methods, by use of abundant supplies of the new chemical fertilizers, and by the growth of cooperative dairies, savings and insurance unions, and state-sponsored educational programs, which offered courses in the cultivation of alternative crops. Unable to compete with North American wheat, Dutch growers switched to concentrating on dairy farming and horticulture. They became Europe's major purveyor of butter and, by the 1890s, condensed milk and margarine joined butter, cheese, and tulips among the products recognized abroad as distinctively Dutch. In 1828 Amsterdam chemist Coenraad J. Van Houten (1801–87) took out a patent for manufacturing milk chocolate in a solid state. Hitherto available only as a thick, foamy drink, Dutch milk chocolate, whether in powdered or solid forms, soon set world quality standards.

Population more than doubled—from 3 million in 1840, numbers grew beyond 6 million in 1914. The pace of wealth creation quickened after 1870, and modernization in industry and agriculture was well advanced by 1900. The years from 1903 to 1914 were especially prosperous. Economic growth occasioned an unprecedented rise in the standard of living among the middle classes, as they did during the 17th century, setting the image of the comfortable Dutch citizen. Increased purchasing power helped fuel, in turn, further economic expansion.

Industrialization raised living standards for the upper and middle classes but, as occurred elsewhere in western Europe in societies undergoing technological transformation, the working classes were usually the last to benefit and then only at lower levels. Urban populations of the major cities swelled in the 19th century. Immigrants from rural areas hard hit by the agrarian crisis of the mid-1800s joined workers in the factories, on the docks, and crowding into tenements in the teeming slums. Laborers earned starvation wages, worked 15-hour days seven days a week, and survived on a monotonous diet of porridge, potatoes, and bread, the last highly taxed. They enjoyed perhaps a single day's holiday every two years and entertainment was nonexistent apart from the popular barrel organs turning out tunes on the streets and in the parks. By the mid-19th century, children under the age of 10 toiled in textile, shoe, and tobacco factories. Industrial hazards, disease, and bad diet produced a life expectancy among the poorest classes of less than 30 years for men and 32 for women in 1850. Set adrift from traditional patterns of work and from sustaining ties to church, community, and kin, adults found diversion in gin and young people in crime-ridden gangs. The abominable conditions gave rise to calls for radical change.

Emancipatory Movements Take Shape

Socialism and Social Welfare

Trade schools appeared in the 1860s offering diversified training opportunities and meeting places where poorer laborers could congregate and mix with better-off artisans such as printers, tailors, and diamond trade workers, who had been forming associations since 1849, at first for social purposes and later to provide mutual aid benefits for unemployment, sickness, and death. Trade unions were created in 1866 in the highly skilled sectors of printing and diamond polishing, and they were succeeded in 1869 by the first socialist general trades union. Founded in Amsterdam by tailor and union activist Hendrik Gerhard (1829–86), the Dutch Workers' Union constituted the Dutch section of the First International. It was followed quickly by other organizations that rejected its advocacy of internationalism and socialism in favor of moderate legislative reforms, including the Catholic group Association of the Companions of St. Joseph (1869), the Protestant and conservative Patriotic Workingmen's Association (1871), and the left-liberal General Dutch Workers' Union (1871). The confessional character of Dutch society that was then developing was reflected in these unions, with, first, socialists and, then, left liberals predominating.

The Marxist tenet that workers' rights would be won by revolutionary action underpinned early socialism. By the 1880s a militant movement had emerged willing enough to organize workers to give them a sense of solidarity and to serve as a tool for mass action tactics—marches, boycotts, strikes—to improve labor's lot, but reluctant to compromise their ultimate goal of ending the capitalist system by working with "bourgeois" elements to secure gains by parliamentary means. They were willing enough also to challenge the governing system from within and, to that end, in 1881 they established the Social Democratic Union (Sociaal-Democratische Bond, SDB), cofounded by their leader Ferdinand Domela Nieuwenhuis (1846–1919). A Lutheran preacher who transferred his religious zeal to a career as a socialist agitator, Nieuwenhuis was a charismatic figure and fiery orator who, elected as the party's first member to parliament in 1888, led the SDB toward increasingly anarchistic positions.

Dominance by radicals favorably disposed to using violence to secure their ends alienated many moderates. In 1893 they bolted the party and formed the Social Democratic Workers' Party (Sociaal Democratische Arbeiders Partij, SDAP), which became the chief party of the democratic left. Led for its first quarter century by Frisian poet and lawyer Pieter Jelles Troelstra (1860–1930), the party affirmed

Strikers in Amsterdam, 1903 (International Institute of Social History)

that socialism should not aim to abolish personal wealth but rather to secure worker ownership of industry. Troelstra called for a new kind of socialist approach that, while not abandoning revolutionary activism entirely, stressed parliamentarian participation, which he practiced as a deputy in the lower house.

Direct action remained the preferred tactic of radicals, however, who generally carried out small-scale strikes and lockouts. They also occasionally staged larger demonstrations, starting with clashes in the Amsterdam working-class district of Jordaan in July 1886, known as the Eel Riots, and later, most spectacularly, with the Great Rail Strike of 1903. Workers struck in January, demanding the right to organize unions and to negotiate a lowering of the 16-hour workday, which the company, hit by a spell of falling profits, refused to grant. The government had conceded the right to strike in the 1870s but, with the country now paralyzed, it stopped the walkout by banning all strikes involving service workers. In defiance, the rank and file went out again in April, backed this time by socialists of every stripe. The action owed much of its early success to support from among the general public;

151

by spring, however, opinion had shifted, the public's patience having worn thin from the prolonged inconveniences occasioned by the transportation tie-up. The strikers were forced to back down. The rail strike marked a watershed in Dutch trade union history. Nieuwenhuis's brand of radical socialism and even Troelstra's more temperate stance were discredited. The internal discord between these competing strands stood exposed, and moderate groups that now came to the fore adopted a more cautious approach in stressing strong organization and the pursuit of gradual reform through parliamentarian means. The new groups merged in 1906 to become the Dutch Alliance of Trade Unions (Nederlandsch Verbond van Vakvereenigingen, NVV), which would become numerically the largest of the socialist unions. Radicals within the SDAP were purged in 1909 and, although they proceeded to form their own Social Democratic Party, orthodox Marxists and far left liberals remained few in number.

The events of 1903 helped give rise to the formation of large trade unions among the confessional groups, which now saw the need to counter the mass actions of the socialists. Rejecting the class struggle, they sought amiable cooperation among the various socioeconomic interests. In 1909 both the Christian National Trade Union Alliance and the Roman Catholic Trade Union appeared, the latter changing its name every 20 years, to become in 1963 the Dutch Catholic Workers' Movement.

Progress in securing social legislation came gradually. Following a government study, industrial employment of children under 12 was banned in 1874 and the Mackay Labor Act the same year limited female employment to a maximum 11 hours a day. A legal reform in 1870 abolished the death penalty for civilians in time of peace. Between 1890 and 1910, a considerable number of measures were enacted, especially under Prime Minister Nicolaas Gerard Pierson (1839–1909). Pierson, a progressive member of the Liberal Union Party, headed a "social justice" cabinet from 1897 to 1901, so called because of his government's commitment to state regulation of social and economic conditions. Under the direction of his home secretary Hendrik Goeman Borgesius (1847–1917), the government enacted measures in worker safety, education, and health, breaking with past traditions in, among other actions, intervening to make vaccinations compulsory and regulating the water supply to combat the outbreak of infectious diseases. Parliament passed a series of factory safety acts to strengthen and expand on demands laid down in the first act, passed in 1895. Local authorities were compelled to establish minimum requirements for safe housing. An act of 1901 made accident insurance mandatory for all industrial workers. The foundations of the welfare state that would emerge in the 20th century were laid at this time.

Poor relief remained largely the preserve of church, family, and private charities. Temperance societies became increasingly active in the 1870s and community health efforts were fostered by groups such as the White Cross (Het Witte Kruis), established in 1875, and, in the 1890s, by the Dutch Association for Child Medicine and the Dutch Union for the Care of the Sick. Major state support came in 1912 with passage of a law providing medical service for the poor.

Pierson's government passed the first compulsory education act in 1901, which mandated a minimum of six years of primary education. A public school reform measure offered students a choice between completing their primary education at the existing Higher Citizens Schools (HBC) or attending the new Grammar Schools (*Gymnasia*), which prepared students for university study. New universities were founded, including the University of Technology at Delft (1905), the country's first advanced polytechnical school, and the School of Economics at Rotterdam (1913).

At the same time the government wrestled with the issue of state funding for schools, it confronted growing demands for widening voter rights. The liberals favored franchise extension and, during Thorbecke's first ministry, the number of voters nearly doubled from 55,000 to 100,000, though these still equaled only 3.5 percent of the adult male population. Socialists waged a strident struggle for universal male suffrage as a tool with which to strengthen their electoral clout. Progress moved incrementally forward in the face of much opposition, which held that opening the vote to all males would invite bribery, violence, and deceit into the political process. Constitutional amendments lowering income and property requirements, together with advances in education and economic wealth, raised the number of voters to 29 percent of the adult male population (1887) and then to 49 percent (1896). Seventy percent of adult males had acquired the right when a constitutional amendment in 1917 authorized universal manhood suffrage. By that date, women too were poised to win the vote. Their victory came following a vigorous campaign that began in a society in which they held few legal rights and no political power.

Feminism

Since the days of the Dutch Republic, women had held a small number of rights; they could enter into contracts and control their own dowries, but up until the mid-19th century they held few legal privileges. Denied the opportunity to own property, study, and participate in political life, they launched a multifaceted drive that won for them wider rights, in opening up the workplace and the schools, and greater equality before the law. The earliest call was made on April 1, 1792, in an address before the French Legislative Assembly by Lubina Johanna Palm (née Aelders, 1743– ?). A Dutch women who found herself in France following a disastrous marriage—her husband had abandoned her—and a succession of fleeting love affairs, she made an impassioned plea for equality of men and women, equal educational opportunities for girls, and the right of women to petition for divorce. She later delivered the same message before the legislature of the Batavian Republic, but she failed in both cases to win a hearing.

Progress would come only when women began entering the workplace in force. Career opportunities began to appear in earnest in midcentury. In 1844 the German Deaconness (Sisters of Mercy) Movement, an organization of Protestant churchwomen, set up a hospital for the poor in Utrecht. The nursing profession, which was largely spawned by their arrival, attracted growing numbers of young, middle-class women. Middle-class women would come to lead the push for rights, and demands accelerated as additional career opportunities appeared. Positions as shop assistants became available with the growth of larger and more varied retail stores. The first department store, de Sinkel, opened in Amsterdam in 1860. In midcentury the kindergarten arrived from Germany and spread rapidly, offering women with young children the opportunity to work and also creating jobs for them as primary-school teachers. To train them for the latter, the government authorized the first girls' middle schools in 1867, which were the first academic schools for females. Until then, instruction had been limited to trade schools for girls, which first appeared in 1846. Women could, if their progress warranted, petition to continue their studies at the all-male HBC schools, but admittance to universities was withheld until 1871, when Prime Minister Thorbecke intervened personally to allow Aletta Jacobs (1854–1929) to study medicine at the University of Groningen, the first Dutch woman to do so.

Jacobs, who supplemented her private practice in Amsterdam with a clinic she operated that provided free medical care to poor women, extended her activities to securing suffrage rights after a letter she posted to the municipal government requesting that her name be added to the voter registration list was denied. Organized efforts did not get under way until 1894, when the Association for Women's Voting Rights was formed. Hopes were roused in 1898 on the accession as queen of

18-year-old Wilhelmina, the country's first female monarch, but no legislation proved forthcoming. Wilhelmina herself did not mention the issue until her speech from the throne in 1913.

Organizations were created to channel women's efforts beginning in 1870 when Christiane Elisabeth Perk (1833–1906) founded the General Association of Dutch Women, the first women's rights group in the country, together with its journal, *Our Calling* (*Onze roeping*). By the late 19th and early 20th centuries, Dutch women were joining their compatriots in Britain, the United States, and elsewhere in adopting militant tactics that included street parades and demonstrations to secure their right to the franchise. Perhaps most militant of all was Wilhelmina Elizabeth Drucker (1848–1925). The illegitimate daughter of a German-Jewish banker, she grew up poor and, as a self-educated women, she remained true to her background in turning to socialism as the best vehicle by which to win the vote. In 1889 she founded the Free Association of Women, the first women's socialist organization, and, four years later, she began producing its widely read journal *Evolution* (*Evolutie*).

Progress in obtaining female suffrage in the Netherlands suffered from the low priority given women's issue by the general public, the relatively small number of middle- and upper-class women who worked, and the concept of the dutiful, passive housewife that long characterized Dutch

Women suffragists from Zeeland dressed in traditional costume, c. 1918 (International Institute of Social History)

bourgeois culture. Gains were won gradually in other areas, including, under Pierson's cabinet, the legal right to seek paternity (1901) and the right of a married women to retain property in her own name (1901). Victory in the battle for rights to the ballot box came, as it did in Britain and the United States, only after the convulsions of World War I. In 1918 women were granted the right to run for elected office and Suzanna Groeneweg (1875–1940) of the Social Democratic Labor Party became the first woman member of parliament, where she served until 1937. Women won full voting rights in 1919.

The Arts Abound and the Sciences Surge

The work of Dutch artists, writers, and scientists reflected fully the currents of intellectual life coursing through Western society and the quickening pace of political and economic change in the country. The novel retained its position as the most popular form of literature earned at the end of the 18th century by writers such as Betje Wolf and Aagie Deken, whose novel-in-letters format proved so successful that it continued in use until the mid-19th century. Early 19th-century romanticism was foreshadowed in the Netherlands by a tranquil sentimentalism most prominently in evidence in the work of Rhijnvis Feith (1753–1824), a burgomaster of Zwolle, who wrote highly popular novels (*Julia; Ferdinand and Constantia*). Imitators of Feith later turned away from pure sentimentalism toward religious mysticism and pride in the country's medieval past, and both trends would remain popular among Dutch readers into the 20th century.

The poems of Anthoni Staring (1767–1840) and Hendrik Tollens (1780–1856) blend romanticism with rationalism in extolling Dutch moral virtues and praising triumphs over adversity. Tollens's patriotic verses gained lasting popularity after Waterloo, and the lines "Whosoe'er of Netherlands blood" were set to music to become one of the most beloved national songs. Willem Bilderdijk, the lawyer who earlier had drafted a Dutch version of the Napoléonic code and tutored Louis Bonaparte in Dutch, became a prolific writer. He penned romantic verses early in his career (*Mengelpoëzy,* 1799) before turning to works drawn from images of the past, including *Floris the Fifth* (*Floris de vijfde,* 1808), which he completed in only three days.

Romanticism's exemplary representative was Aernout Drost (1810–34), who, although he died young, produced a major work, *Hermingard of the Oaken Mounds* (*Hermingard van de eikenterpen,* 1832) which evokes love of God and virtue as conveyed in the historical setting of a battle between the Batavians and the Romans in 320 C.E. The novel greatly influenced Everhardus J. Potgieter (1808–75), one of the best-known authors of the mid-19th century. *The Rijksmuseum in Amsterdam* (*Het Rijksmuseum te Amsterdam,* 1844) recalls the glory of the Golden Age in pleading for a turning away from the decay that had set in during the 18th century. In 1837 Potgieter founded *The Guide* (*De gids*), which became the leading literary journal of the mid-19th century.

Many writers were practicing or former Calvinist ministers, and themes that stressed biblical values and conventional virtues of bourgeois domesticity figure prominently in their works. Nicolaas Beets (1814–1903) produced volumes of sermons and poems but is remembered for an entirely different work, his *Camera Obscura* (1839), humorous prose sketches of Dutch life that he wrote while a student and published under the pseudonym Hildebrand. Midcentury romanticists drew inspiration from far-off places, which for the Dutch meant the East Indies. Potgieter penned *Ditties of Bontekoe* (*Liedekens van Bontekoe,* 1840). At the same time, romanticism began to reflect emerging sentiments of social consciousness, a synthesis first and most famously represented in Eduard Douwes Dekker's (1820–87) influential book *Max Havelaar.* Other writers echoed Douwes Dekker's biting criticism of the comfortable middle-class smugness characteristic of much of Dutch literature, beginning with Conrad Busken Huet (1826–86). A critic who had worked for *The Guide,* Huet helped to inspire a movement of young writers who called themselves "Tachtigers" (Spirits of 1880), which gave new life and energy to Dutch literature. In 1888 they founded their own journal *The New Guide* (*De nieuwe gids*), whose contributors soon championed, first, naturalism (itself introduced to the Netherlands through Huet's familiarity with the writings of Honoré Balzac and Émile Zola) and, later, impressionism.

Emphasizing that style must match content, poets such as Jacques Perk (1860–81) and Marcellus Emants (1848–1923) employed language in unconventional rhythms to express intense, individual emotion. Louis Couperus (1863–1923) used naturalism to great effect in prose works such as *Of Old People the Things That Pass* (*Van oude menschen de dingen die voorbijgaan,* 1906), an outstanding study of the sordid undercurrents in Dutch colonial society. Dramatist Herman Heijermans (1864–1924), a committed socialist, called attention to the need to correct social injustices in plays depicting the plight of North Sea fishermen (*The Good Hope* [*Op hoop van zegen*], 1906) and coalminers (*Glück Auf,* 1911). In the 1890s impressionism emerged in poetry. Herman Gorter (1864–1927) penned a conversation among the poet, the spirit of May, and Balder, the ancient Germanic god of fertility, in his 200-line poem *May* (*Mei,* 1889). After *May,* Gorter turned to socialism, and he was joined by other Tachtigers, including Frederik van Eeden (1860–1932) and Henriette Roland Holst (1869–1952). Holst, who became a strident socialist, called herself and others of her generation "Negentigers" (Spirits of 1890) in seeking to join social consciousness as a chief aesthetic goal with the individualistic stresses of the Tachtigers, as expressed in perhaps her best-known collection of sonnets and verses *The Lady in the Forest* (*De vrouw in het woud,* 1912). Poet Albert Verwey (1865–1937) moved further afield in praising earthly beauty and divine, eternal life in verses that appeared in his journals *The Twentieth Century* (*De twintigste eeuw,* 1902) and *The Movement* (*De beweging,* 1905).

Liberals who played so prominent a role in governing in the 19th century looked askance on state support for the arts and the active intervention that marked King William's reign was not continued. Support came largely from private individuals and groups. Local governments did, however, back the establishment of public reading rooms and libraries, which appeared around 1900. Libraries had existed for centuries in many towns and villages but these had been open only to the middle classes. The masses across the socioeconomic spectrum gained access to these facilities for the first time, and the first reading rooms, which were nondenominational, were quickly followed by Catholic and Protestant counterparts.

Dutch pictorial artists followed general European trends. International reputations were earned by symbolist painter Jan Toorop (1858–1928) and postimpressionist Vincent van Gogh, whose most productive years were spent in France and for whom fame came only many years after his death. Artists of the Hague school introduced a daring, bold style to landscape painting in an effort to make viewers feel as if they were part of the picture in actually being outdoors. Representative painters included Hendrik Johannes (H. J.) Weissenbruch (1824–1903), who is noted for his town views, most famously those of Dordrecht in moonlight; Jozef Israëls (1824–1911), who specialized in solitary gloomy figures portrayed in dim light; and Willem Roelofs (1822–97), an astute painter of polder landscapes and light. They included the three Maris brothers—Jacob (1837–99), Matthijs (1839–1917), and Willem (1844–1910). Jacob concentrated largely on landscapes and Willem painted almost exclusively scenes of cattle grazing alongside waterways. Matthijs veered sharply away from realistic depictions toward more symbolic expressions in portraying objects in weird shapes. In

1877 he settled in a London slum where he developed an element of mysticism in his work that drew critical admiration. Hendrik Mesdag (1831–1915), a banker turned painter from Groningen, came to concentrate almost exclusively on panoramic seascapes, which he painted

Vincent van Gogh, Sunflowers *(1889). Oil on canvas, 95 × 73 cm* (Amsterdam, Van Gogh Museum [Vincent van Gogh Foundation])

159

VINCENT VAN GOGH

Arguably the Netherlands's and the world's best-known painter, Vincent van Gogh (March 30, 1853–July 29, 1890) did not produce the body of his work—some 900 paintings and 1,100 drawings—until the last 10 years of his life, during which he worked in complete obscurity. Born at Zundert, in North Brabant, the son of a Protestant minister, van Gogh learned to draw in middle school. He worked as an art dealer in The Hague and London and was then drawn to religion. He failed a three-month course at a Brussels missionary school, but, undeterred, he preached in Belgium's coal-mining district until dismissed by church authorities, appalled at his squalid living conditions.

Vincent van Gogh, Self-Portrait with Straw Hat *(1887). Oil on pasteboard 19 × 14 cm* (Amsterdam, Van Gogh Museum [Vincent van Gogh Foundation])

Following the suggestion of his younger brother Theo, van Gogh took up art work in earnest in 1880. His early work in the Netherlands (1880–85) features studies of miners and peasants (*The Potato Eaters,*

from a hotel room that he rented in Scheveningen. Born in Zaandam and a cousin of Vincent van Gogh, realist artist Anton Rudolf Mauve (1938–88) trained as an animal painter. His fashionable equestrian scenes at the seacoast, some painted in a silvery gray with touches of pink, became trademark images, while his paintings of flocks of sheep proved especially popular with American buyers. Masterpieces were given a first-rate place for display with creation of the Rijksmuseum in 1885.

In music, the Concertgebouw Orchestra, founded in 1888 in Amsterdam, earned a global reputation for high-quality musical per-

1885), and his canvasses are distinguished by the colors of the paints—dark greens and browns predominate—that are thickly applied. In 1886 Vincent moved to Paris, where Theo operated an art dealership, and there he met leading postimpressionist painters. In ill health and feeling himself a burden to Theo, on whom he depended entirely for financial support, he moved to Arles in 1888. The painter Paul Gauguin (1848–1903) joined him there for a brief, tension-filled period, during which van Gogh mutilated his left ear in the course of his first attack of dementia. During his time at Arles van Gogh painted his famous series of sunflowers and his portraits of his friend the postman Roulin and his family. Recurring illness confined him to hospitals, including the asylum of Saint-Rémy, where he painted *The Starry Night* (1889). Van Gogh's last three months were spent in Auvers-sur-Oise, near Paris, where he painted the sympathetic, eccentric Doctor Gachet, a physician and art collector who cared for him. Having failed to earn any income from his painting—he sold but one artwork in his lifetime—and conscious of his burden on Theo, now married and a father, van Gogh grew increasingly despondent. He shot himself on July 27, 1890, dying two days later in the arms of his brother.

An outstanding postimpressionist, van Gogh built on the techniques of the impressionists in using innovative brush strokes, interspersed with dotted or dashed brushmarks, applied in swirling or wavelike patterns that display color at once both intense and subtle. His work had a tremendous impact on 20th-century art and his paintings sell today for astronomical sums. His letters to Theo provide a revealing and moving narrative of his conflicts and aspirations. Many of his works are on display at the Van Gogh Museum in Amsterdam, which opened in 1973.

formances, beginning in 1895 under conductor Willem Mengelberg (1871–1951), who continued to direct until 1945.

In architecture, designs harkened back to neo-Gothic and Northern Renaissance styles, both of which inspired the Catholic architect Petrus J. H. Cuypers (1827–1921) in constructing Amsterdam's Rijksmuseum and Centraal Station. After 1900 adherents of a more conservative "Delft school" drew on older Byzantine and Romanesque models. Glass, steel, and concrete brought new building possibilities. Hendrik P. Berlage (1856–1934) garnered widespread attention. Abandoning neoclassicism, he turned to a more sober style in designing banks, the Amsterdam stock exchange, and the municipal museum in The Hague, buildings that foreshadow the arrival of functionalism. The Housing Act of 1901 made possible subsidized housing for the working class and gave architects an opportunity to showcase their talents. Berlage developed an ambitious scheme in Amsterdam South that employed use of brick, wood, and iron in decorative, distinctive shapes in designing windows, doors, and other architectural features. Known as the father of modern Dutch architecture, Berlage helped create a type of craft-based facade architecture dubbed, in 1916, the "Amsterdam School," and local variants appeared elsewhere in the country.

Enhanced educational training facilities in science bore fruit in a number of breakthroughs of international import. Dutch science excelled most especially in the study of the natural sciences. Nobel Prizes were earned by physicists Hendrik Lorentz (1853–1928) and Pieter Zeeman (1865–1943) for discovering the "Zeeman effect," in which a powerful magnetic field splits the spectrum of light (1902); Johannes D. van der Waals (1837–1923) for his equation describing the physical behavior of liquids and gases (1910); and Heike K. Onnes (1853–1926) for low temperature studies (1913). Jacobus H. van't Hoff (1852–1911) won the first prize in chemistry in 1901 for work on the laws of chemical dynamics. In 1900 Hugo de Vries (1848–1935), a botanist at the University of Amsterdam, was one among three scientists who rediscovered the laws of inheritance made public 35 years earlier by Austrian monk Gregor Mendel. De Vries later proposed his own anti-Darwinian mutation theory of evolution. Anatomist Eugène Dubois (1858–1940) won fame, if not immediate recognition, in discovering in 1891 in the East Indies *Pithecanthropus erectus* (Java Man), the first remains of early hominids found outside of Europe. Dubois was the first researcher to purposefully set out to unearth evidence of early man, and his finds were the first cited in support of Charles Darwin's theory of evolution.

Darwin's claim that species develop over time from a common source, with its implied claim—later made explicit by others—that man evolved from primitive species, not made in a moment by God in His image, added another proof to those who discounted theology's claim to absolute truth. Liberals placed their faith in progress and human perfectability—a faith seemingly evident in the technological advances that so increasingly impacted everyday life—and Marxist socialists despised religion, which distracted the working masses from pursuit of power. The new currents of thought began to effect a change in attitudes. By the turn of the 20th century, the tight grip that religion held in public belief began to lessen among growing segments of society. The trend would deepen in time.

A Small Country Rules a Large Empire

The Netherlands emerged from the Belgian debacle with no illusions about its place in the world. Aspirations to become a major global player were abandoned and the reality of its small size led the nation to adopt a foreign policy based on isolation and armed neutrality. Its link to tiny Luxembourg—the last remnant of the once united Netherlands—was severed in 1890 on the accession of Wilhelmina to the throne. The grand duchy, which required that a male descendant of the House of Orange-Nassau reign as the ducal head of state, switched its allegiance to the Walram line of that royal house. (A grand duchess did succeed subsequently, but the ties had long been broken.)

Centuries-old heirs to colonial possessions, the Dutch stayed out of the scrambling and squabbling for new imperial turf waged by their neighbors in the late 19th century. Even though it was ultimately the mutual jealousies of Britain, France, and Germany that preserved the Dutch overseas presence, the Netherlands moved to forestall any aggressive moves by these powers by consolidating its geographical hold on the East Indies, the great pearl of its transoceanic possessions. Throughout the 17th and 18th centuries the Dutch presence in the archipelago had been confined largely to plantations on the island of Java and a scattering of trading outposts elsewhere. Military campaigns were launched in the 1800s to suppress local autonomous rulers who threatened Dutch overlordship, to combat piracy rampant in East Indian waters, and to find and exploit raw materials in demand on world markets. The Java War, which began in July 1825, stemmed from efforts to prevent native princes from exploiting peasant labor by selling the latter's land to Europeans, Chinese, and Arabs. The princes balked at measures to stop the practice, and they waged war until March 1830, when Dutch forces under General Hendrik de Kock (1779–1845) defeated Prince Depo Negoro (1785–1855), who was captured and banished to the island of Macassar (now Ujung Pandang). A Royal Dutch Independent Army was created in 1832 composed of native troops commanded by European officers, and by 1845 the west coast of Sumatra had been pacified. On the northern tip of Sumatra the sultanate of Aceh comprised a considerable and resource-rich bit of unoccupied territory—in the 1820s it furnished more than half the world's supply of black pepper. In March 1873 the Dutch commenced hostilities to assert their control. They met fierce resistance and it took until 1903 to secure the surrender of Sultan Muhammad Daud Syan (r. 1874–1903). Local rulers on Bali also fiercely fought the Dutch. A drive to subdue the entire island, beginning in the 1840s with subjugation

Nicolaas Pieneman, The Submission of Prince Depo Negoro to General de Kock *(1830).* Oil on canvas, 77 × 100 cm (Collection Rijksmuseum Amsterdam)

of northern areas, proceeded slowly and bloodily until completed in 1910. Some local kings committed suicide, together with an estimated 4,000 followers, by marching themselves and their families in front of Dutch gunners in a final act of defiance. Direct Dutch rule was in place across the entire 3,000-mile length of the island chain by the early 20th century.

Dutch colonial policy in the newly conquered territories largely followed the dictates laid down by Christiaan Snouck Hurgronje (1857–1936), an Islamic scholar and principal adviser to the government between 1891 and 1904. Hurgronje counseled a policy of cooptation, a system of indirect rule in which the Dutch maintained supportive relationships with both local religious authorities among the largely Islamic population and local aristocrats (*priyayi*). The approach amounted to an extension of Dutch colonial practices in place for three centuries in Java. A strict separation was maintained between Europeans and the native peoples in a system (*partiklir sadjah*) under which whites enjoyed a privileged status in law and with whites-only social clubs and organizations.

Missionary activities met with only limited success. Islam was well entrenched on Java and Sumatra, having been introduced by Arabic traders as early as the 12th century. For 300 years under the Dutch East India Company, only Dutch Reformed ministers were allowed to operate, and Catholic efforts began in earnest only in the mid-19th century. Protestant missions made inroads on Sulawesi, Roman Catholic on Flores, and both faiths in the South Moluccas, where Christianity came to predominate. Proselytizing efforts were further hindered by the many different races and the existence of at least 60 separate languages spoken across the archipelago. Such diversity stymied efforts at education as well, a task made more difficult by the use of native languages, rather than Dutch, as the vehicles for instruction. Colonial authorities believed rule was made easier by maintaining linguistic fragmentation, as inculcation of a common tongue could promote greater unity among the population as well as provide access to Western ideas that could give rise to movements to undermine the regime.

A major portion of Dutch capital formation in the 19th century was financed by the wealth extracted from the far-flung empire, primarily from the East Indies. The Dutch exploited and exhausted their colonies, which they had come to rely on as important mainstays of their economy. Although the slave trade had been abolished in 1818 and slave ownership outlawed in the East Indies in 1858 and in the West Indies in 1863, the native inhabitants continued to toil under brutal working conditions, and the abundant wealth was bought at great cost. The Dutch East India Company's policy that forced peasants to cultivate only those crops currently in demand in Europe was followed by a similar practice, adopted by the Netherlands Trading Company in the early 1800s. This so-called culture system (*cultuurstelsel*)—put in place by Governor General Johannes van den Bosch (1780–1844) in 1830—mandated compulsory cultivation of export crops, mainly coffee but also tobacco, tea, pepper, cinnamon, sugar, and indigo. Under the supervision of rich native princes, the rural masses were compelled to grow more and more commercial crops, to the neglect of their own essential foodstuffs, and, to increase company profits, to do so at lower and lower wages.

Rising protests in the Netherlands and elsewhere in Europe, fueled in part by writers such as Douwes Dekker, who had lived in the Indies, led to an end to compulsory cultivation policies in the 1860s and to abandonment of the state monopoly on trade in 1870. In the course of the 19th century new products were introduced. Seeds from the cinchona tree, exploited to near extinction in its South American Andean

EDUARD DOUWES DEKKER (MULTATULI)

Eduard Douwes Dekker (March 2, 1820–February 19, 1887), better known by his pen name of Multatuli, was born in Amsterdam, the son of a ship captain. In a career in the civil administration in the Dutch East Indies that spanned 20 years (1838–58) he witnessed widespread abuses by colonial authorities. Threatened with dismissal after he began to protest, he resigned his appointment and returned to the Netherlands. He published his novel *Max Havelaar* in 1860 under the pseudonym Multatuli, which is derived from Latin and means "I have suffered much," in reference both to himself and, it is thought, to the victims of the oppression he saw. The book was read all over Europe and is credited with reforms subsequently enacted in colonial practices. In 2002 the Society of Dutch Literature pronounced Multatuli the greatest of all Dutch writers. Here is an excerpt from *Max Havelaar*:

> SAÏJAH's *mother died of a broken heart; and it was then that his father, in a moment of despondency, ran away from* LEBAK. . . . *He was flogged with rattan for leaving* LEBAK *without a pass, and brought back to* BADUR *by the police. There he was thrown into jail, because they took him to be mad (which would not have been beyond all comprehension) and because they were afraid that, in a fit of insanity, he might run amok or commit some other offence. But he was not a prisoner for long, as he died soon afterwards. What became of* SAÏJAH's *little brothers and sisters I do not know. The hut in which they lived at* BADUR *stood empty for a while, but soon collapsed, since it was only built of bamboo roofed with palm leaves. A little dust and dirt covered the spot which had seen much suffering. There are many such spots in* LEBAK.

Source: Multatuli, *Max Havelaar, Or, the Coffee Auctions of the Dutch Trading Company.* Translated by Roy Edwards (Amherst: University of Massachusetts Press, 1982), p. 259.

habitat, were imported by Dutch colonists, and quinine, derived from the bark of the tree grown on large plantations, was produced, helping to reduce fatalities from malaria both across Asia and worldwide among those fortunate enough to have access to the drug. Minister of Colonies Baron Willem Karl van Dedem (1839–95) proposed in 1891 that the East Indies's own interests should be considered in making policy. Greater rights to self-rule were granted in a series of laws in the early 20th century, notably a law instituting a People's Council in 1916. At first only an advisory body, by 1925 the People's Council possessed some legislative powers, thus breaking the grip the state bureaucracy held on governing. A system of schools for local elites, a program to promote village democracy, and a series of social welfare measures were enacted.

Crude oil and rubber exploration opened up important economic activities beginning in the late 19th century. For the first time, foreign investment was encouraged, chiefly to finance further rubber, tea, and tobacco cultivation. Founded in 1890, the Royal Dutch Petroleum Company developed oil fields, starting in Sumatra, that became of international importance. Under the direction of Henri Deterding (1866–1939), a dynamic young marketing director from Amsterdam who was hired in 1896, the company set up a vigorous sales organization and built its own tankers and bulk storage installations. Deterding succeeded as director general in 1902 and, in 1907, the firm entered into a partnership with Shell Transport and Trading Company, its British rival, to better battle the U.S.-owned Standard Oil Company, the major competitor of both. The full merger created the Royal Dutch Shell Group, two separate holding companies in which Royal Dutch held 60 percent of earnings and Shell 40 percent. With Deterding as its chief executive officer, the group expanded activities across the globe. Oil was also discovered after 1910 in the Caribbean Sea off the coast of Venezuela, and the company constructed refineries to market the increasingly essential raw material on Curaçao and Aruba.

The need to defend overseas territories made budget planners attentive to maintaining the country's naval strength throughout the 19th and early 20th centuries, but expenditures for the army were continually reduced, despite the costly war in Aceh. The nation's self-proclaimed neutrality led policy planners to discount the necessity for a strong military. There were also occasional deviations from the official policy, most notably during the Boer War (1898–1902) in South Africa, when Dutch sympathy for the Boers, their ancestral kin and linguistic cousins, led to support for them against the British, ranging from widespread sentiment to the sending of monies, advanced by a charity loan bank, and volunteers to fight. Queen Wilhelmina herself dispatched the battleship *Gelderland* to Mozambique in November 1899 to take Paul Kruger (1825–1904), president of the Transvaal Republic—one of the states the Boers had set up in the 1830s following their overland trek from the Cape of Good Hope to escape British overlordship—to

Europe in his quest for aid. In 1908 the *Gelderland* and a second battle-ship—the *Heemskerk*—were sent to the Caribbean in a show of force, with British and U.S. concurrence, to counter Venezuelan threats to Dutch possessions in the Leeward Islands.

Noninvolvement in international power politics did not preclude an active engagement in the world by Dutch charitable and corporate interests. Economic concessions for Dutch companies were obtained in China and the Netherlands South African Railway built the line from Pretoria to Lourenço Marques (present-day Maputo, Mozambique). Dutch experts lent advice in educational and civil service reforms enacted by several independent countries in South America and Asia, and Dutch missionaries of many denominations served worldwide.

Nor did neutrality imply an aloofness from diplomacy. At the turn of the 20th century the Netherlands led a drive to legislate limits on the conduct of war and to establish a system of international justice. Efforts to put a brake on the ever-mounting arms race led to a call by Russian czar Nicholas II (r. 1894–1918) for an international conference and the Netherlands offered to serve as host. Anxious to lend its prestige to moves for peace, the Dutch monarchy offered use of the royal palace of Huis ten Bosch (House in the Woods) as a venue for the negotiations. Tobias Asser (1838–1913) headed the Dutch delegations to the two international conferences, held in 1899 and 1907, respectively. A world-renowned expert in international law, he was awarded the 1911 Nobel Peace Prize for the central role he played in producing The Hague Conventions, a series of international laws to limit the indiscriminate use of weapons such as mustard gas and exploding shells and to put in place an international court of arbitration to settle disputes between nations amicably. Headquartered at the Peace Palace in The Hague and built with funds donated by Scots-American millionaire Andrew Carnegie (1835–1919), the Permanent Court of Arbitration (Hague Tribunal) opened in August 1913. The court was empowered to hear and settle cases brought by parties that included not only states but also national and international organizations, private enterprises, and even private individuals. It won for the Dutch considerable international prestige.

In the mid- and late 19th century, while the Netherlands turned away from engaging in international power politics, the neighboring great powers were vigorously competing to gain advantages in economic, territorial, and military might. The unification of Germany following the victory of German allied states in the Franco-Prussian War (1870–71) exemplified the ascendance of strong nationalist sentiments across

Often called the seat of international law, the Peace Palace at The Hague houses the International Court of Justice, the Hague Academy of International Law, and the Peace Palace Library. (AP Images)

Europe in states both new and old. Confident, ambitious, and impatient, the German Empire under its Hohenzollern kaiser Wilhelm II (1859–1941) set out to win its place as a powerful player on the world stage. By the turn of the 20th century, Germany had surpassed Great Britain in population and in many economic parameters.

The Netherlands maintained close trading relations with both nations. Britain served as an important export market for Dutch goods, especially agricultural products. Dutch ports, most prominently Rotterdam, handled much German traffic as transshipment places for continental commerce. After 1900 the pace of German-British competition quickened. Their rivalry began to focus more and more on building up their armed forces. Eyeing each other warily, they entered into an especially feverish naval shipbuilding race. The Netherlands looked on, watching both, keeping its distance but maintaining its vigilance.

8

NEUTRALITY, DEPRESSION, AND WORLD WAR (1914–1945)

Europe had not known war on a continental scale since 1815 and the shattering of the peace in August 1914 broke longtime trends in the affairs—and the minds—of men and women everywhere. Though the Netherlands was spared the carnage of World War I, shock waves from the conflict rocked the country. From 1914 to 1918 the armed forces remained on alert, trade patterns were disrupted, and economic shortages endured. Wedged geographically between the warring camps, the nation walked a precarious tightrope as a small nation anxious to remain impartial. Actions and reactions to the cataclysm taking place next door frayed the public's nerves, and the war left the country often at the mercy of events over which it had no control.

However, no interruption took place in trends toward social separatism based on confession and toward the organization of the economy along mass production lines, tendencies that deepened in the 1920s and 1930s. Advances in technology transformed society and culture, and modes and manners of life became faster, easier, and cheaper than they were a mere generation before. New ideological currents confronted established economic and political precepts. Communism appeared in 1920 to challenge socialism on the left while fascism, first introduced in 1922, lent a shrill and strident nationalism to the voices on the far right.

Boom times in the late 1920s gave way to the Great Depression in the 1930s, a decade made more dismal by the raucous rantings of Europe's fascist dictators, which found echoes on the edges of society in the Netherlands. The Dutch watched nervously from the sidelines as the decade progressed and Europe drifted toward war. When it came in September 1939 they reacted as they had in 1914. The nation, once again perched precariously between the same sets of belligerents, once again sought security in clinging tenaciously to its neutrality. The bombs that dropped without warning from the bright, blue skies on May 10, 1940, fell on a nation ill-prepared materially and mentally to deal with the reality of sudden war. A century and more of peace came to a crashing halt for five days that May, and the five years of hardship and horror that ensued would try institutions and individuals in profound and unprecedented ways.

Years of Testing, 1914–1918

By 1914 Europe resembled two armed camps. The Entente powers—Britain, France, and Russia—and the Central powers—Germany, Austria-Hungary, and Italy—stood aligned against each other, each striving to match and surpass any advantage the other side was perceived to have in the dual tools of international relations, diplomacy and weaponry. The assassination of Archduke Franz Ferdinand I (1863–1914), heir to the throne of Austria-Hungary, on June 28, 1914, set the alliance system in motion with a flurry of war declarations at the end of July. The Netherlands braced for an attack in mobilizing its armed forces speedily—on July 31, 1914, they were the first in western Europe to do so. The Germans set the Schlieffen plan in motion, invading neutral Belgium on August 4 in violation of the treaty of 1839, in a bid to encircle the French armies and quickly defeat France. The move led Britain to declare war. The German plan had originally included the southern Netherlands in the line of attack, but strategists drew back, deciding that a neutral Netherlands could better serve Germany in keeping open a conduit for trade. Unaware of German intentions, the Dutch public was thrown into a panic at the Belgian invasion. People hoarded money and food. Belgian refugees flooded southern portions of the country, fleeing before the advancing wave of German armies. The wave crested after the fall of Antwerp (October 9, 1914) when more than a million Belgians crossed into North Brabant and Zeeland. The numbers gradually decreased as the situation in Belgium stabilized, but about 100,000 remained in the country at war's end, which added to the strain on social services. Antwerp's fall also brought 30,000 defeated Belgian troops, who, under the Netherlands's obligation as a neutral, were interned and placed under the Dutch army's guard.

Invasion never came and the country settled down to four years of nervous neutrality. Vigilance and patience became the national watchwords adhered to by government and public alike. The country's

LEAKING THROUGH

In this editorial cartoon, from 1914–17, "Holland" holds his finger in the "neutrality dike" in trying to stop a leak caused by German contempt for the rights of neutrals. (Library of Congress, Prints and Photographs Division)

position as a virtual island between the belligerents mandated that it maintain a careful balance in word and deed so as not to give offense to the powers on either the Central or the Allied side. The woefully

173

inadequate conditions of the Dutch military made prudence even more essential. Some modernization had been made after 1900 but prewar pleas by advocates for increased defense spending were met by constant dithering and delay in the States General, so much so that a defense bill was not approved until 1913, and then for 12 million guilders only, not the 40 million originally allotted.

Though small and poorly equipped, the nation's forces were kept at the ready by the sacrifices of the Dutch public, who accepted shortages to allow essential resources to be diverted from civilian to military uses. Troops remained mobilized throughout the war, the army and navy manning the border defenses.

Dutch ships were subject to continual harassment by the navies of both sets of belligerents. Starting in 1914 vessels were stopped repeatedly on suspicion of carrying supplies to one or the other side. Seven merchant ships granted safe passage by the Germans through the English Channel from Britain were torpedoed by a U-boat on February 24, 1917, following Germany's declaration of unrestricted submarine warfare. In March 1918, the United States and Great Britain invoked the ancient right of angary, recognized in international law, to seize for their own use the shipping of a neutral, in commandeering 156 Dutch merchant vessels to transport troops. Germany countered with claims to be allowed to cross troops through south Limburg and to establish artillery batteries on Dutch soil. However, the Dutch were resolved to resist any attack; aware of the brutal occupation by the Germans in neighboring Belgium, they were acutely conscious of the fate that could await them. That fate was one the government and armed forces knew would likely ensue. Harboring no illusions about the conditions of his forces nor about the strategic straitjacket his country was in—surrounded by German armies on all the land borders—Dutch commander in chief Cornelis J. Snijders (1852–1939) informed the government that the infantry was ill-armed and the artillery was obsolete, possessing only a 10-day supply of shells on hand. The crisis subsided when the Germans dropped their demands.

Some war profiteers made fortunes, but the war severely affected the economy in general. The public hoarded silver coinage as a hedge during the uncertain times, forcing the government to issue small-denomination paper currency. After the steamship *Houtman* of the Dutch-owned Java-Australia line was stopped and searched by a German battleship on suspicion of carrying wheat to Britain only one day after hostilities commenced (August 5, 1914), the authorities succumbed to German pressure and agreed to stop the export of rice from the East Indies. Contraband regulations hit certain sectors hard, especially the margarine industry. The Allies blockaded the coast to extract promises that the Netherlands would not allow imports to proceed through to Germany, but the Dutch believed to give such assurances would compromise their neutrality. Only after the creation of the Netherlands Trust Company, a nongovernmental grouping of Dutch heads of industry set up to police procedures, would the Allies permit imports to resume. Even so, imports were continually blocked by both sides, creating havoc for the country's export trade, which relied on receipts earned from the sale of finished products using imported raw materials. Goods formerly imported, such as chemicals, specialized machinery, and porcelain, had to be manufactured domestically, thus furnishing some relief to the wartime doldrums in giving a boost to the nation's industrial independence. State monies funded creation of a domestic steel industry in 1918 with establishment of the Koninklijk Hoogoovens firm, established at IJmuiden to give the steelworks access to inland areas via the North Sea Canal.

Vegetables replaced wheat as the crop of choice, but the switch failed to make up for shortages caused by the drop in food imports. A system of food distribution was implemented in 1916 but shortfalls persisted. By 1917 the navy could no longer ensure safe passage of supplies from the Indies and bread rationing was introduced. Riots broke out.

With so much of daily life disturbed, the government met the crisis resolutely united. From 1913 to 1917 the liberals ruled unopposed, and, after the outbreak of war, all parties agreed to put aside their differences for the duration. The war gave an added impetus to resolving long-standing political issues, and liberals under Prime Minister Pieter W. A. Cort van der Linden (1846–1935), after their successful 1917 election, led the way in reaching the so-called pacification of 1917. Liberals on the left and religious conservatives on the right came together to approve settlement of the school conflict with the grant of state funds to confessional schools; creation of a cabinet post of education, arts, and sciences; and expansion of the franchise. A nationwide system of proportional representation replaced the winner-take-all district system, which ushered in a half century of elections that yielded relatively predictable party compositions in the Second Chamber.

Cort van der Linden led cabinets from 1913 to 1918, the last that were made up of members of all three liberal parties. The nation's attention lay elsewhere, remaining riveted on the conflict swirling around it. In October 1918, 40,000 refugees, largely from northern France, entered the country fleeing the retreating Germany armies, and the refugee camps would not be cleared until February 1919. For four years the guns roaring close by in Flanders could clearly be heard in southern Zeeland. And then they fell silent. Following the armistice (November 11, 1918), Dutch troops lined the roads in south Limburg and watched as columns of defeated German soldiers, granted permission, passed by on their way home.

Years of Anxiety, 1918–1939

A country that had stood on the sidelines could expect little goodwill from whichever side emerged victorious from a war that had produced unprecedented levels of death and destruction. Matters were little helped when probably the most famous Dutch name associated with the war, in Allied public opinion, was Mata Hari (1876–1917). Born Margaretha Geertruida Zelle in Leeuwarden, the exotic dancer and courtesan was arrested in Paris and shot by firing squad for alleged espionage. The outpouring of sympathy won by war-ravaged Belgium, defiant in resisting its violated neutrality, disinclined the victorious powers to treat the Netherlands with anything more than polite correctness. The Belgians drew on that goodwill in demanding from the Dutch parts of Zeeland Flanders and Dutch Limburg, the right to build a canal across North Brabant to link Antwerp with the Rhine, and the surrender of navigation rights on the Wielingen—the much trafficked southern estuary of the western Scheldt River.

The arrival in exile of the former German kaiser Wilhelm II complicated relations further when the Allies demanded that he be surrendered to stand trial for war crimes. The government refused and Queen Wilhelmina insisted that he be allowed to settle with his wife at the palace of Doorn, where he remained until his death in 1941. The government stalled for time, arguing the Belgian demands back and forth with Brussels until the mid-1920s, by which time, because interest among the former Allies had waned, the claims were quietly put aside.

The Netherlands tried to improve its international image in becoming a founding member of the League of Nations in 1920. The Permanent Court of International Justice, founded in 1922 as the judicial arm of the League of Nations, joined the Permanent Court of Arbitration in occupying premises at the Peace Palace in The Hague. Unlike the latter, only states could be parties to disputes brought before the tribunal, which was led by its first president, Judge Bernard C. J. Loder (1849–1935) of the Netherlands, from 1922 to 1924. Dutch diplomats signed

The Royal Palace on the Dam, Amsterdam, during the interwar years (Library of Congress, Prints and Photographs Division)

the Nine-Power Treaty of Washington in 1922, which regularized international relations in the Far East. The rise in international cooperative efforts matched the antimilitary mood at home, reflected in the election of a conservative government in 1918 that oversaw a reduction in armaments. Plans to expand the navy were dropped in 1923.

In the 1920s the economy recovered rapidly, stagnated, and recovered again. Wartime food shortages were replenished quickly when, in 1918, the government released the army's strategic stock of rations, and the vast supplies of foodstuffs and raw materials held up in the East Indies started flowing again. In 1923 a slowdown set in with the collapse of the German economy, which led to a stockpiling of transit goods that the Germans could not afford to purchase, and the need to buy imports from the United States led to a drawdown on the substantial reserves accumulated by the state bank during the war. Labor troubles erupted in strikes in the textile industries in 1923–24.

In the second half of the decade the boom experienced worldwide reverberated in the Netherlands. Britain replaced Germany as the country's chief trading partner. Reintroduction in 1925 of the gold standard, suspended before the war, led to a resumption of the nation's traditional role as an important international banker. By 1930 the proportion of the population employed in industry had reached almost 40 percent, while the numbers working in agriculture had dropped to approximately 20 percent. Light industries, including the production of chemicals, fertilizers, rayon, and the manufacture of electrical appliances, predominated over heavy industry, the Dutch lacking the raw materials, except for coal, needed to be competitive in the latter.

Manufacturers that had grown large domestically before the war now expanded internationally. Philips widened its markets across Europe, employing 20,000 workers by 1929. The butter and margarine firm of Jurgen Brothers and van den Burgh merged with Lever Brothers, a British soap manufacturer, to create Unilever in 1929, a new conglomerate whose interests grew to include seafoods. Demand for gasoline increased with the rapid spread of the motor car and by the end of the 1920s Royal Dutch Shell was the world's leading oil company, producing 11 percent of global crude oil supply and owning 10 percent of tanker tonnage.

The heightened attention to international developments induced by the war remained to affect immediate postwar politics. The Russian Revolution and the rise to power of Bolshevism stirred either hopes or fears in segments of Dutch society. Socialist leader Troelstra called on the government to resign in November 1918 and urged workers to win power by supporting Socialists at the ballot box. A citizens' guard was formed in some parts of the country where anxious residents sought to deflect threats to private property, but workers failed to rally in sufficient numbers and, in the end, revolutionary activism was confined to establishment, in 1918, of the Dutch Communist Party (Communistische Partij Nederland) by radicals of the now disbanded Social Democratic Party.

Liberals under Cort van der Linden brought an expansion of the franchise but they reaped no benefits in dropping from 37 to 20 seats in the Second Chamber in the 1918 elections. They reorganized and founded a Liberal State Party (Liberale Staats Partij) in 1921 while, for the first time, Catholics reaped large gains from Liberals' losses. And, for the first time, in 1918 a Catholic led the cabinet. Charles J. M. Ruys de Beerenbrouck (1873–1936) governed for 15 years (1918–33) in coalitions with the Protestant parties. Catholic and Protestant confessional parties would dominate governments into the 1960s by virtue of their vote-getting abilities, but governing principles would not markedly vary nor would they reflect a deviation from precepts widely accepted across the political spectrum. The liberal foundations laid in the 19th century, based on a belief in classic socioeconomic policies together with a growing acceptance of state regulatory intervention, would underpin governments up until the mid-20th century. In 1919 the government mandated the eight-hour workday and broadened unemployment benefits. Rudimentary health insurance and old age benefits laws were enacted.

The collapse of the U.S. stock market on October 24, 1929, produced little immediate effect. Prosperity prevailed until 1933 and unemployment remained low, thanks in part to a major public works project that entailed cutting off the Zuider Zee from the North Sea. Recognized since the 17th century as a flood danger, the great salt bay on which Amsterdam stood survived until the development of technical skills sufficiently advanced to permit its closure from the sea. Growing demands for an increase in both residential and agricultural land and for a freshwater source for summertime irrigation in Friesland and North Holland trumped opposition from fishermen in shoreline villages whose trade in herring, shrimp, eels, and oysters would fade once the waters of the rivers that drained the bay succeeded in expelling the salt. The massive project (1923–32) ended with completion of the 19.8-mile-long (32 km) enclosing dike (*Afsluitdijk*), which transformed the Zuider Zee into the IJsselmeer (IJssel Lake). Drainage of the enclosed waters began at the same time. The Wieringermeer polder (1927–30) in North Holland emerged as the first of four new polders planned. The first village here—Slootdorp—was founded in 1931 and intensive cultivation of the reclaimed land began in 1934.

The depression, when it did strike, hit hard. Dutch financiers took heavy losses on reconstruction loans to Germany and on investments in U.S. stocks, the cumulative effects of which began to be felt by the mid-1930s. Currency devaluations in trading neighbors and the United States brought about artificially high exchange rates for the guilder. At the same time the government stuck steadfastly to the gold standard, producing high prices for Dutch goods abroad and low prices at home. Prime minister in five successive governments (1925–26, 1935–37, 1937–39), Hendrikus Colijn (1869–1944), the leader of the Anti-Revolutionary Party, headed cabinets that injected state funds into the economy and sponsored high-profile projects. An industrial council set up by the government in 1933 aimed to assert its presence as a neutral broker to encourage conciliation between labor and management in drawing up collective bargaining contracts. A Labor Fund (Werkfonds) was created that distributed loan money to businesses to spur them to hire the unemployed, and female civil servants were forbidden to work unless they were a family's sole source of income. Construction of the luxury liner *New Amsterdam* gave jobs to those out of work and, at its launching in 1937, boosted national pride. All these measures, however, had but a limited effect. Unemployment jumped from 100,000 in 1933 to 476,000 in 1936.

Hard times spurred the growth, if not in size then in boldness, of political parties opposed to parliamentary politics. The Communists moved from antistate gestures—party members refused to rise to their feet when the queen opened the States General in 1932—to direct action. In early July 1934 street riots, prompted by reductions in unemployment benefits, erupted in Amsterdam's Jordaan district. A Red Front was proclaimed in "Red Amsterdam," and six people died and 30 were injured before police quelled the disturbances.

On the far right, fascism, which had appeared as early as 1922 in the wake of the accession to power of Benito Mussolini (1883–1945) in Italy, grew to include a number of small groups by the early 1930s, including the Black Front (Zwart Front) founded by Arnold Meijer (1905–65) in 1933 and the National Union (Nationale Unie), whose founder, Utrecht history professor F. C. Gerretson (1884–1958), resigned in disgust as German Nazism grew in influence. The German brand of fascism came to predominate in the largest fascist organization, the National Socialist Movement (Nationaal Socialistische Beweging, NSB), founded in 1931 by two civil servants, Anton A. Mussert (1894–1946) and Cornelis van Geelkerken (1901–76). Backed financially by the fortunes of a few wealthy members from the Indies, the party won almost 8 percent of the vote in provincial elections and eight parliamentary seats in national elections in 1935. Support fell away after 1937 when Mussert, in imitation of the Nazis whom he so admired, proclaimed racism and anti-Semitism to be the cornerstones of his policy. The NSB won a mere three seats in elections in 1939.

Recovery began in earnest after September 1936 when the government—the last in Europe to do so—took the country off the gold standard. The guilder was devalued by 22 percent and exports rebounded. A military buildup also aided recovery. By 1936, when Germany remilitarized the Rhineland, the Dutch could no longer ignore the rising tensions being ignited by the country next door. Long opposed by the Catholic and socialist parties, rearmament started from a woefully neglected base. The Naval Act of 1923 marked the start of a 10-year decline in military spending, culminating in 1933 when a commission recommended that the Dutch marines and the country's entire fleet of cruisers should be disbanded. Only one cruiser (*De Ruyter*) and five submarines were built during the entire period from 1929 to 1936. In the late 1930s, defense budgets rose precipitously—from 93 million guilders in 1937 to 261 million in 1939. The unemployed found work in defense plants. Having set world speed records for military aircraft, Fokker Industries switched to production of warplanes exclusively. War jitters mounted and, in 1939, the government, remembering 1914, started to lay in stocks of food.

Dutch Society, 1900–1939

The pillarization of Dutch society deepened after World War I. Liberals claimed that their organizations were national in scope, neutral, and apolitical, but, in fact, they formed one among four separate national networks that also included orthodox Protestants, Roman Catholics, and social democrats. The Dutch found it possible to live entirely within their own subculture. People voted for the political party, joined the trade union or employers' association, played on the sport's team, listened to the radio station, and participated in the avocational clubs of their own pillar. The divisions held except for education. The public schools served children from both neutral-liberal and social democratic households.

The pillars differed in ideologies, ways of life, and degree of cohesiveness. Catholics, who accounted for 35 percent of the country's 7 million people in 1920, were organized firmly around their church under the guidance of the hierarchy. The Catholic school system established at the primary and secondary levels in the 19th century was carried forward in 1923 with the founding of the Catholic University of Nijmegen (the name was changed to Radboud University Nijmegen in 2004). Roman Catholics stood for harmonious cooperation among the social groups and against what they viewed as the reason-based, godless liberal and socialist belief systems. They were not averse to social action and reform, however; prompted both by the papal encyclical *Quadragesimo Anno* (May 15, 1931), which reaffirmed the church's social role, and by the need to combat the effects of the depression, progressives would come to dominate political Catholicism by 1940.

In contrast to the Catholics, orthodox Protestants, approximately 40 percent of the population, experienced schisms that fractured the Reformed churches, first in 1922, and then in 1944. Protestants also splintered politically and a number of small parties won seats in parliament, including, most notably, the Political Reformed Party (Staatkundig Gereformeerde Partij, SGP). Founded in 1918, this orthodox Protestant party is still in existence, making it the oldest of the modern parties. Radically conservative in orientation, adherents advocate Bible-based government. Despite the divisions, many Protestant organizations, such as the trade union movement, recruited members from across the Protestant religious spectrum.

Ideology formed the core of the social democratic universe, and the SDAP, together with its trade union, the NVV, constituted the pillar's central institutions, all other organizations playing a secondary role. Having failed to win Christian workers to their cause, the socialists were compelled to abandon hopes of securing a majority in government and they turned to work actively within the parliamentary system for the benefit of their constituents. Communists and others on the far left denounced such compromising tactics as class treason, but, by the late 1930s, the socialists had become social democrats. They melded gradually into bourgeois society, even acknowledging the dual role played by both middle and working classes in their 1937 party platform. The SDAP's decision to participate in government, starting in 1939, bore fruit in social welfare legislation that broadened and deepened over time.

The liberal pillar was the weakest and most loosely organized, based on a commitment to few formal principles—the promotion of free trade the most prominent—and with no dense network of supporting organizations. Political heirs to the founders of the state, they suffered declining strength.

The liberal party (LU) garnered only about 15 percent of votes during the interwar period. The Catholic party (RKSP) could count on roughly 30 percent, the Protestant parties (CHU, ARP) about 25 percent, and the socialists (SDAP) about 25 percent.

Despite the pervasiveness of pillarization, a remarkable degree of cooperation characterized Dutch political life. None of the four pillars possessed a clear majority nor could they expect to win one; consequently, negotiating was essential if politicians and policymakers hoped to get anything done. Leading members of the pillars would discuss and debate contentious issues, usually behind closed doors, and a compromise would be hammered out. If one of the political players balked at a solution, lengthy delays and even a political crisis could ensue. Coalition-building was cultivated to the level of high art.

The leaders depended on the rank and file, whose backing they sought in order to retain their posts. And the rank and file, although splintered four ways, were acutely aware that, together, they formed a part of the historical Dutch nation. Pride in the values they believed the country stood for, as a peace-loving, morally high-minded society, transcended the subcultures.

The Dutch, as they grew more prosperous, became more socially, culturally, and politically literate. Mass-circulation journalism began in the 1890s, and the popular press arrived in 1900 with purchase of the Amsterdam daily *De Telegraaf* by H. C. M. Holdert (1870–1944), who transformed the paper into a vehicle for the general reader, and with the founding of *Het Volk*, the newspaper of the SDAP. Orthodox Protestants who resisted the trend to popular journalism read *De Standaard*, the organ of the Anti-Revolutionary Party, which was edited by Abraham Kuyper from 1872 to 1922. Catholics read *De Volkskrant*, founded in 1919. Liberal readers could choose between the *Nieuwe Rotterdamsche Courant* (f. 1844) and the *Algemeen Handelsblad* (f. 1828) of Amsterdam, two papers that merged after World War II to become, in 1970, the prestigious daily *NRC Handelsblad*.

During these years the Dutch became more closely linked spatially than ever before. The country's short distances and flat terrain made the bicycle, introduced in the late 19th century, ideally suited for, and immensely popular with, the public, and their presence everywhere soon became a hallmark of national life. Railways were electrified beginning in 1908 between Rotterdam and Scheveningen, and the system extended nationwide by 1927. The network was centralized and nationalized in 1937 with creation of the Netherlands Railways (Nederlandse Spoorwegen). Modern roadways began to be built to link the central cities in the 1920s, the decade that saw the first large-scale buying of motor cars. Aviation pioneer Anthony Fokker (1890–1939) began manufacturing airplanes in 1912. The firm built aircraft in Germany during World War I. Fokker returned to the Netherlands in 1919 and concentrated on construction of commercial craft. International airline service began on May 17, 1920, when newly founded Royal Dutch Airlines (Koninklijke Nederlandsche Luchtvaartmaatschappij, KLM) inaugurated its first service from Amsterdam's Schiphol airport to London. Connections to the Dutch East Indies began shortly thereafter. Schiphol, cited on the reclaimed Haarlemmermeer polder as Europe's lowest-altitude commercial airport, opened as

Soon after their invention, bicycles became a popular mode of transportation in the Netherlands, with its flat terrain and short distances. (The Netherlands Board of Tourism and Conventions)

Skating on the Diemermeer, c. 1910 (New York State Archives)

a military airbase in September 1916.

Transportation means for the masses were joined by developments in communications and recreation equally revolutionary. The barrel organs of the 19th century could still be heard, preserved after 1930 by philanthropists, but by then radio was the instrument listeners preferred. In 1919 the first music programs were transmitted from The Hague, and four broadcasting companies, each representing a pillar, were set up in 1924–25. The first Dutch motion picture was made in 1905 and the first cinema opened in 1910. Dutch-language films enjoyed national, though, because of the language barrier and the parochialism of much of the subject matter, not international popularity. However, documentary films by Dutch filmmakers, produced most prominently after 1931 by Polygoon and Orion-Profilti, earned worldwide plaudits.

Mass entertainment in sports had arrived, most spectacularly showcased in 1928 when Amsterdam hosted the Olympic Games. Soccer had first been imported from Britain in the 1870s as strictly a middle-class diversion but it became widely popular among all classes after 1914. Founded in 1889, the Dutch Football Association later split along the familiar confessional lines. Skating remained of central importance to national identity, and the Elfstedentocht (Eleven Towns' Tour) became the country's greatest sporting event following its inception in 1909. A marathon race that pits skaters gliding more than 100 miles (161 km) through 11 towns in Friesland, the event earned special significance because, since it depended on the safety of the ice, annual competitions could not be guaranteed.

Tourism flourished with the growth in income and leisure time and the arrival of faster means of communication. Although the health benefits of bathing in salty seawater were touted as early as the beginning of the 19th century, it was not until the turn of the 20th that lavish seaside resorts began to be built. Spas, arcades, and boardwalks could be found lining North Sea beaches by the 1920s.

The mass culture that began to emerge before 1914 and that surged during and after World War I shaped much of intellectual life. Historian

Johan Huizenga (1872–1945), a founder of cultural history, explicitly critiqued modern mass organizations through his aesthetic approach to the past. In his classic *Waning of the Middle Ages* (1919), he viewed the Renaissance as the death of the Middle Ages rather than the birth of the modern world. The profound impact made by expressionism in post–World War I Germany produced a much more muted effect in the Netherlands, a country spared the trials of modern warfare. The poets Hendrik Marsman (1899–1940), Dirk Coster (1887–1956), and Jan Jacob Slauerhoff (1898–1936) were influenced by expressionist themes, but Marsman and Coster soon moved on to stress spirituality while Slauerhoff intermingled expressionist views with strong subjectivism in his verses. Emotional idealism of any kind was eschewed by Charles du Perron (1899–1940) and Menno ter Braak (1902–40), who wrote in a spare style, more closely resembling heightened prose, in which form took precedence over any expression of personality. Novelist Ferdinand Bordewijk (1884–1965) delivered biting social commentary, including *Blocks* (*Blokkes,* 1931), a fantasy about revolt in a communist state, and *Grunting Beasts* (*Knorrende beesten,* 1933), a depiction of the rootlessness of modern industrial life. His later work delved into more personal themes. *Character* (*Karakter,* 1938) tells the story of a conflict between a father and his illegitimate son, and *Branch of Blossom* (*Bloesemtak,* 1955) details the triumph of peace and goodness over violence and hate. In his long career, novelist and poet Adrianus Roland Holst (1888–1976) returned often to the theme of the contrasting attractions offered by life on earth and after death (*The Song Outside the World* [*Het lied buiten de wereld*], 1919). Dutch architects exerted a profound influence on developments in the field. The craftsmanship characteristic of the "Amsterdam School" gave way in the 1920s to a "functional" architecture whose proponents stressed rationality and utility. Architects such as Mart Stam (1899–1986), J. B. van Logham (1881–1940), and others exemplified the New Building (Nieuwe Bouwen) movement of Dutch functionalism that saw the building "assembly-line style" of housing projects in large numbers for the masses. A movement inspired by postwar Dadaists emerged around the magazine *De Stijl* (*The style*), founded in 1917 by painter and designer Theo van Doesburg (1883–1931) and by painter Piet (originally Pieter) Mondrian (1872–1944), that sought to amalgamate all the existing elements of art and design into one coordinated whole characterized by simple, stark vertical and horizontal right angles and by primary colors. Mondrian and architect and furniture designer Gerrit Rietveld (1888–1964) would help to define modernism in creating internationally recognized concepts in architecture and

CANALS, CANALS

The canal (*gracht*) has always been an obvious transportation choice for a country sitting astride, and interlaced by, water. For centuries the canals of the Netherlands have drawn the admiration

Canal scene in Amsterdam (The Netherlands Board of Tourism and Conventions)

design. International stature in science was earned by two Dutchmen in particular during the interwar period. Willem Einthoven (1860–1927), a doctor and physiologist, invented the first practical electrocardiogram in 1903, a trailblazing device recognized by the award of the Nobel Prize to him in 1924. Also working in medicine, physician and pathologist Christiaan Eijkman (1858–1930) traveled to the Indies to study beri-beri and, by accident, determined that poor diet caused the debilitating disease. His research led to the discovery of vitamins, which earned for Eijkman the Nobel Prize in medicine or physiology in 1929.

War and Occupation, 1940–1945

Swift rearmament under way next door in Nazi Germany spurred the Dutch to launch their own military buildup, starting in 1936. They did so from a woefully depleted and dated base. The army, which numbered

186

of visitors, who have made them one of the country's most instantly recognizable features. The Czech writer Karl Čapek recorded the following impressions after a visit in the early 1930s.

> *The towns appear to be standing, not on the earth, but on their own reflections; these highly respectable streets appear to emerge from bottomless depths of dreams; the houses appear to be intended as houses and, at the same time, as reflections of houses.*
>
> *There are bustling grachts with boats, big and small, floating along them, and there are grachts overgrown with a green coating of water-weed; there are shabby grachts, which smell of swamp and fish, and high-class grachts which are privileged to reflect in full luster the frontages of patrician houses; there are holy grachts in which churches are mirrored, and dingy, lack-lustre canals in which not even the light of heaven is reflected. There are the grachts in Delft, in which red cottages are mirrored, and the grachts in Amsterdam, in which the black and white gables of tall buildings occupied by shipping firms view themselves, and the grachts of Utrecht, cut deep into the earth, and tiny, derelict grachtlets which look as if no human foot (shod with a boat) has ever stepped on them, and grachts, now filled in, of which only the name has been left.*

Source: Karel Čapek, *Letters from Holland*, translated by Paul Selver (London: Faber and Faber, 1933), pp. 23–24.

300,000 by 1940, relied on field artillery often more than 30 years old and on rifles some of which were of 19th-century vintage. The naval fleet included ships that dated from 1897. Hampered by a limited manufacturing capacity, the air force counted 120 planes by 1939, only 23 of which were of modern combat capability (largely the Fokker G.1).

It was hoped that strategy would make up for logistical deficiencies. Planners intended to carry out a defensive operation along the "Grebbe Line"—a series of fortifications running from the Grebbe River south through Baarn and Rhenen. Prime Minister Colijn assured British officials in 1937 that, with the "mere pressing of a button," the countryside could be inundated and the army drawn back behind the line to defend "Fortress Holland" north of the Waal and Maas rivers while the navy would thwart any invasion by sea.

Strict neutrality, announced by Queen Wilhelmina on August 28, 1939, remained official policy. The queen's last-minute appeal for peace,

The Oostplein in Rotterdam in 1946, showing the ground cleared in the wake of the 1940 bombing (Library of Congress, Prints and Photographs Division)

made with King Leopold III of the Belgians, met with no response, and the war that started September 1 found the country facing the same set of challenges encountered a quarter century before. The maintenance of neutrality in word and deed did not prevent the sinking by the belligerents of 11 ships on the high seas. German border violations occurred and reoccurred, most flagrantly on November 9, 1939, when German agents in Venlo carried out an operation that led to the capture of two British intelligence officers and the death of a Dutch liaison official.

Anxious to protect the Ruhr industrial zone, Germany laid plans to invade as early as March 1939. During the winter and spring of 1939–40, warnings of impending attack were not infrequent; even as late as the night of May 9, the Dutch military attaché at Berlin telephoned the War Department to advise: "Tomorrow at dawn, hold tight." When the dawn broke, however, the storm of war had already been unleashed. German planes had passed over the country during the night only to turn back over the North Sea to release their bombs on Dutch airfields beginning at 4:15 A.M. The attack came as a complete surprise. No declaration of war was ever made, the German government merely delivering a note hours later alleging Dutch collaboration with a British plan to invade the Ruhr.

Guided by information obtained earlier by extensive espionage activities, German forces—soldiers of the 18th Army, tanks of the 9th Panzer

Division, and planes of the 22nd Airborne Division—poured over the border. They moved swiftly through Limburg, capturing Maastricht. By 8 A.M. German shock troops had overpowered unalerted defenders and taken the Moerdijk bridge over the Rhine, which opened the way for troop concentrations to penetrate Fortress Holland. The country had not known invasion for 150 years, and confusion reigned among soldiers and civilians alike. The blitzkrieg proved so sudden that in some places daily routines were still to be seen. Milk, butter, and eggs were delivered on schedule between the wailing of air raid sirens. Rumors ran rife—German parachutists were spotted dressed in nuns' habits, the British and French were racing to the rescue. The main German thrust

QUEEN WILHELMINA'S PROCLAMATION FROM LONDON, MAY 15, 1940

The German invasion marked the most calamitous event to strike the country since the struggle for independence. Queen Wilhelmina's statement to her countrymen and women gave hope and inspiration and expressed determination to battle on.

When it became certain that we and our ministers would be unable to exercise freely the authority of the State, we took the harsh but imperative step of transferring our residence abroad for as long as would be necessary with the firm intention of returning to the Netherlands when possible.

The government is now in England. It wanted to prevent ever being placed in such a position that it would have to capitulate. By the steps which we have taken, the Netherlands remains a full member of the community of States and will be in a position to continue cooperation with its allies.

Our hearts go out to our compatriots in the fatherland who are experiencing difficult times.

The Netherlands will, by the grace of God, regain all territory. Do everything in your power for the good of the country, as we are doing. Long live the Fatherland!

Remember calamities in the past centuries and the repeated resurrection of our country. That will occur again.

Source: F. Gunther Eyck, *The Benelux Countries: An Historical Survey* (Princeton, N.J.: Van Nostrand, 1959), pp. 182–183.

reached and breached the Grebbe Line on May 11, the same day that the navy judged the situation hopeless and began sending ships across the North Sea to join the British fleet. On May 12 the remnants of the air force were all but destroyed. On May 13 Queen Wilhelmina and the royal family—and later the cabinet—fled The Hague for exile in Britain, her plans to sail for Zeeland Flanders cancelled because of the rapidity of the German advance.

Major fighting ceased on May 14. Encountering fierce resistance in Rotterdam, the German High Command ordered the city's destruction. Stuka dive bombers devastated the port, killing about 900 people, leaving about 70,000 homeless, and completely leveling about 1.9 square miles (2.6 square kilometers) of the urban center. Told a similar fate awaited Utrecht, Dutch commander in chief General Henri G. Winkelman (1876–1952) capitulated at Rijsoord outside Rotterdam on May 15. By then, their escape route blocked by fighting to the south, thousands had fled to IJmuiden, hoping to find means to flee to Britain. Only a few soldiers and civilians succeeded in leaving the port, which was partially blocked by sunken vessels. Troops in Zeeland fought on until May 19, surrendering after Middelburg was bombed. Some 2,000 fatalities had been incurred, but much of the navy escaped, together with a small number of air force and army personnel. The latter would form the Royal Dutch Brigade (Princess Irene Brigade), which would participate in the D-day landings of June 1944.

Prime Minister Dirk Jan de Geer (1870–1960) returned to the country in September 1940 in an attempt to effect a peace accord with Germany, which led to his disgrace, and the government-in-exile, now led by law professor Pieter Gerbrandy (1885–1961) of the Anti-Revolutionary Party, proved a deeply committed partner of the Allied coalition. Queen Wilhelmina never wavered in her resolve and, with most of the merchant fleet intact under British jurisdiction, the Netherlands brought valuable resources to the war effort.

The Dutch West Indies, under British and American control, supplied oil, and Dutch Guiana furnished bauxite. The fall of the East Indies to the Japanese in March 1942 proved a bitter blow, not only in loss of supplies of oil and rubber, but also in the destruction of the remaining Dutch navy. Most of the ships were torpedoed during the Battle of the Java Sea (February 27–28, 1942) when Rear Admiral Karel Doorman (1889–1942), in command of a combined Allied fleet, went down with his flagship *De Ruyter,* his supposed orders ("I am attacking, follow me!") immortalized in Dutch naval lore despite his more prosaic actual words ("All ships follow me"). Remnants of the Dutch army fled to the hills and jungles to conduct guerrilla operations and a few officials reached Australia, where they formed a government-in-exile ("the Brisbane Fifteen"), but more than 300,000 Dutch nationals endured three years of brutal treatment and forced labor in prisoner-of-war camps, where about a 10th of them perished.

Life in the occupied Netherlands changed little at first. The Germans were well-mannered. Appointed Reichskommissar of the Netherlands on May 29, 1940, the fanatic Austrian Nazi Arthur Seyss-Inquart (1891–1946) proclaimed that the country would be incorporated into the "New Europe" as *Westland* ("Land of the West"), but he declared that the occupying authorities would not impose their beliefs on the population.

Actions soon belied soothing words, however. Greatly esteemed by German racists for what they regarded as their Nordic racial purity, the Dutch were enjoined to actively assist the Nazi cause. Efforts were made to convert the Netherlands to National Socialism by reorganizing Dutch society. Demobilized soldiers were offered posts in the military police, and volunteers joined the Territorial Guard and the Home Guard set up by NSB leader Mussert, now enjoying official favor. About 10,000 would die fighting in the German army and, as members of the "Land of the West Brigade," in the Waffen-SS, the military arm of the German Nazi Party that operated in tandem with the German army (Wehrmacht). In June 1940 the Germans dissolved the States General, and they banned Orangist insignia and street names. In 1941 all political parties save the NSB were outlawed. New institutions that were national in scope such as the Dutch Labor Front for workers and the Landstand for farmers replaced the organizations aligned with each of the pillars. The Netherlands Union, created in the summer of 1940, aimed to transcend the old divisions and knit the country together in a new unity. The union was founded by a group of bureaucrats and academics and opened to all citizens. About 800,000 joined in the hope that it could serve as a non-Nazi organization with which the Germans might be able to work. Setting rather vague goals in calling for national cooperation, social justice, and religious freedom, including rights for Jews, the organizers displayed a degree of political naiveté in believing some degree of cooperation could be possible with a totalitarian state. The Germans simply disbanded it in 1941.

These measures gave rise to a growing unease, but in 1940–41 most people adopted a wait-and-see approach. Attitudes began to harden in opposition, however, as orders followed orders imposed on a people ill-disposed to being dictated to. By 1942 the Germans were engaging in outright theft. Radios were confiscated and bicycles commandeered.

QUEEN WILHELMINA

Queen Wilhelmina (Wilhelmina Helena Pauline Marie of Orange-Nassau) was born on August 31, 1890, the daughter of King William III and his second wife, Emma of Waldeck-Pyrmont. The king outlived his three sons by his first wife, and Princess Wilhelmina became queen—the first in Dutch history—on his death in 1890. Her mother served as regent until her 18th birthday, when she was invested in the Nieuwe Kerk in Amsterdam. She married Hendrik, duke of Mecklenburg-Schwerin, in 1901, and the marriage, which grew less warm over time, produced one child, Juliana, born on April 30, 1909. Strong-willed and intelligent, Wilhelmina spoke her mind forthrightly and, on occasion, acted forcefully, as when she ordered a Dutch warship to conduct Boer leader Paul Kruger to Europe, an act that

Queen Wilhelmina (Library of Congress, Prints and Photographs Division)

Industrial equipment, nonferrous metals, clothing, food supplies, railway rolling stock, and tramcars were carted off to Germany, all labeled as "loving gifts from Holland." The public drew hope and courage from knowing the battle went on. Beginning in the spring of 1942, they could hear almost nightly the drone of bombers passing overhead as Royal Air Force planes launched heavy night raids on German cities in the Ruhr. British and U.S. forces also occasionally attacked Dutch military targets, including the coal mines in Limburg, the Philips factories at Eindhoven, and the steel furnaces at Velsen.

Acts of resistance, at first few and largely symbolic, became more numerous and brazen, but they met with brutal reprisals. A nationwide work stoppage in April and May 1943 led to German troops firing into crowds of demonstrators and executing workers, killing more than won her widespread admiration. However, she never deviated from the tactfulness demanded of a constitutional monarch. A hands-on ruler during World War I, she visited the troops frequently and proved a tireless advocate for military funding. Wilhelmina endeared herself to her people in World War II when her broadcasts from exile in London brought hope and encouragement to her oppressed subjects. Knowledgeable, respected, and unwavering in her opposition to German and Japanese tyranny, she came close to losing her life in a bomb attack on her English residence. British prime minister Winston Churchill called her "the only real man" among the leaders of the governments-in-exile. Wilhelmina traveled the country after liberation to establish a closer rapport with the people. Burdened by the colonial war in the East Indies and suffering from a heart condition, she abdicated on September 4, 1948. Retiring to her palace of Het Loo, she made few public appearances, but she worked actively on behalf of the World Council of Churches to promote Christian ecumenism. She also set up a fund for cancer research. She died on November 28, 1962, and is buried in the Nieuwe Kerk in Delft. Wilhelmina's reign marks the real start of true affection among the Dutch for their royal family. The deep personal bond felt for Wilhelmina, her daughter Juliana, and her granddaughter Beatrix has stood firm despite war, exile, and scandal. Although they are among the world's richest monarchs, Dutch queens are admired for the bourgeois values they embody, values that were first exemplified by Wilhelmina, who, determined to display the "common touch," mingled among her subjects as comfortably on a bicycle as in a gilded state coach.

1,000. In retaliation, regulations required all men between 18 and 35 to register for work in Germany, and 148,000 laborers were transported in 1943. Sabotage, opposition, and delay led to a large-scale breakdown of the deportations in 1944. But the German reaction showed that covert operations were more effective, and, beginning in 1943, clandestine activities predominated.

Resistance (*verzet*) groups started as tiny, isolated bands as early as 1940, but the Netherlands was not an easy place in which to organize and carry out operations. Small, flat, with almost no forests or inaccessible areas, and densely packed with 9 million people, the country was crisscrossed by excellent communications networks. It was also effectively cut off from the rest of Europe—the land borders were heavily guarded and the coastal areas restricted to local residents. Only about

200 escapees managed to reach Britain by boat during the entire war. The Dutch, a people traditionally not given to fanaticism, had experience neither with foreign occupation nor with intelligence or underground work. German authorities could avail themselves of prewar official records, which were confiscated intact, and new identity cards for everyone over 15 years of age were issued. Controls on trains and in public places were frequent. Despite the obstacles, however, the effort to force a totalitarian dictatorship on the country drove the Dutch to launch a determined counterattack.

An underground press was the first to form. The best known was *Free Netherlands* (*Vrij Nederland*), launched on Queen Wilhelmina's 60th birthday on April 30, 1940, by editor Bernard IJzerdraad (1895–1941), who was also the leader of the Beggars' Group (Geuzenactie), perhaps the first organized band of saboteurs. Dutch patriots also read *Het Parool* (*The watchword*), a socialist journal, and *Je Maintiendrai* (*I will maintain*), an Orangist paper, and they listened to Radio Oranje, broadcast from London.

Early isolated and sporadic resistance acts having proved largely ineffective, a Dutch housewife was the first to see the need for creating broader networks. Using her connections to Protestant clergy and women's groups as a boardmember of the Union of Reformed Women's Associations, Helena Kuipers-Rietberg (1893–1944) set up the Nationwide Organization (Landelijke Organisatie, LO) at the end of 1942. By war's end, the LO had become the largest of the underground organizations, its 15,000 members looking after between 200,000 and 300,000 men and women, dubbed "divers" (*onderduikers*) and "cyclists" (*fietsers*), who went into hiding. Mrs. Kuipers-Rietberg paid with her life for her efforts, dying in Ravensbrück concentration camp in 1944.

Regrettably, much resistance work was compromised by effective German penetration of Dutch networks. IJzerdraad and 14 others were caught and executed on March 14, 1941. Captured radio operators sent to London messages drafted by the Germans, believing that the Allies would disregard them because they did not use their established security codes. Instead, the British ignored the absence of the codes. From March 1942 to November 1943 under an operation code-named by the Germans Northpole, the *Englandspiel* (England Game) led to the arrest of 57 Dutch agents dropped from Britain, 50 Royal Air Force crewmen, and about 400 members of the Dutch resistance. A total of about 22,500 members of the latter were killed during the five years from 1940 to 1945.

The early efforts of the LO were directed largely at saving Jews, especially children, who were placed with foster parents in the countryside. Many Jews were under no illusions about the fate that awaited them under Nazi occupation—200, including literary critic Menno ter Braak, committed suicide in May 1940. The Germans followed a policy of creeping persecution in instituting measures that progressively grew in severity. A Jewish Council was set up in Amsterdam in early spring 1941 by the Germans and given the task of implementing German orders. Following the introduction of identity cards stamped with the letter *J* (March 1, 1941); yellow Stars of David, with the word *Jew* (*Jood*) imprinted on them (May 2, 1941); and call-ups for forced labor (June 1942), Jews in considerable numbers began to go into hiding. Of the 20,000 who tried to disappear, about 60 percent were subsequently caught and arrested, betrayed by informers, careless gossip, or sheer bad luck. Their lives personified and immortalized by Anne Frank, they faced deportation and death in Nazi Germany's network of labor and extermination camps. When a Dutch Nazi was killed and then a German police patrol attacked by a small Jewish resistance group in Amsterdam in February 1941, 425 young Jewish men (all of whom later perished) were rounded up and deported in full view of the populace. Virtually the entire working population of the city, led by the dockworkers, staged a massive public protest on February 25 and 26, one of the few large antipogrom demonstrations ever held in European history. But the Dutch could do little against the organized might of the occupying forces. Police patrolled streets and shot at passers-by. The public slowly returned to work, but their actions had made an impact. The Germans no longer held any illusions about Dutch attitudes. Posters exhorting the populace to trust their occupiers disappeared.

The first transport train carrying Jews departed on July 14, 1942, the deportees having been informed by mail that they were to report for resettlement in eastern Europe. Call-ups through the post would continue in rural areas but, because few complied in the big cities, the Germans started rounding up Jews in night raids in urban neighbor-hoods. The police closed off whole streets, especially in Amsterdam, where most Jews had been confined in a virtual ghetto. Transports made up first of non-Dutch Jewish refugees and later of the native born, including Christian converts, departed—sometimes three a day from Amsterdam—for transit camps at Westerbork and Vught, where most remained for only a few weeks before being crammed into freight cars with 1,000 or 1,200 others and sent on to Poland and Germany. A Jewish community that had prospered for centuries in the tolerant, plu-ralistic climate of the Netherlands suffered almost complete annihila-tion. By liberation, 100,000 out of a prewar population of 140,000 had

ANNE FRANK

A nneliese Marie "Anne" Frank (June 12, 1929–February/March 1945) was born in Frankfurt am Main, Germany, the second daughter of Otto Heinrich Frank, a businessman, and Edith Höllander Frank. The Franks were Jewish and, after Adolf Hitler's accession to power in 1933, Otto Frank moved to Amsterdam when he received an offer to set up a company in the Netherlands.

Following the German occupation and the imposition of increasingly harsh anti-Jewish measures, the Franks went into hiding, beginning on July 6, 1942. Anne took along her diary—a gift for her 13th birthday—and from June 12, 1942, to August 1, 1944, she recorded the daily doings of her family and the four other occupants who together shared the *Achterhuis,* or "Secret Annex," a three-story space at the rear of an old building that housed her father's company at 263 Prinsengracht. Forbidden to move about during the day, Anne spent her time reading, studying, and writing in her diary, in which she detailed not only events as they happened but also her feelings, opinions, and ambitions.

On August 4, 1944, German security police stormed the building following a tip-off from an informer, who remains unidentified. Anne and the other occupants were deported on the last transport train from the Netherlands to Auschwitz. In October, Anne and her sister Margot were relocated to Bergen-Belsen. Ill from typhus and exhaustion, Anne perished sometime between the end of February and the middle of March 1945, several days after her sister's death and only

perished—the highest percentage of all western European countries, including Germany. Only 500 returned from Auschwitz.

By the time the last Jewish transport left in early September 1944, the Allies had arrived at the country's southern border. The Dutch waited in tense expectation of imminent liberation. An estimated 60,000 NSB members began to flee and, on September 5, 1944, the country erupted spontaneously in a "Mad Tuesday" (*Dolle Dinsdag*) demonstration in support of the Allies. U.S. troops reached Maastricht on September 17. Elements of the U.S. 82nd Airborne Division pushed on to the Waal River bridge at Nijmegen on September 20 as part of Operation Market Garden. Fording the river in canoes, raked by German gunfire, the Americans succeeded in taking the north end of the bridge in one of the boldest actions of the war, thus opening the way to Arnhem. But they three weeks before British troops liberated the camp.

Among the residents of the *Achterhuis,* only Otto Frank survived. He returned to Amsterdam after the war and retrieved Anne's diary. Remembering her oft-repeated wish to be an author, he secured publication of an edited version of her work in 1947. Subsequent editions included material deleted from the original book. *The Diary of Anne Frank* has become one of the world's most widely read books and has been translated into as many as 52 languages.

Anne Frank (Library of Congress, Prints and Photographs Division)

"I keep my ideals, because in spite of everything I believe people are really good at heart," she penned in her diary, and it is her youthful optimism and indomitable spirit that continue to inspire. Anne's tragic fate has come to symbolize the enormous loss to the world of the millions who perished in the Holocaust. Her legacy endures in her dairy, which stands as a testament to—and a warning against—the dangers of intolerance and racial violence.

arrived there too late, the British 1st Airborne Division having failed to secure a bridgehead over the lower Rhine on September 27 due to faulty execution of plans and poor weather, which hampered adequate reinforcement of men and supplies. The main British forces were cut off at the town of Oosterbeek, once a favorite summer residence of the Hague School painters. Forced to retreat back across the Rhine in the dark of night, the British suffered 8,000 casualties during the nine days of action.

The Germans subsequently intensified their requisitions of matériel, and they stepped up retribution for acts of resistance. At the start of Operation Market Garden on September 17, the Dutch government-in-exile asked the railway workers to assist the Allied efforts by launching a strike, and they did so. On September 30, a resistance group killed a

German officer and, in retaliation, Luftwaffe general Friedrich Christian Christiansen (1879–1972), commander of the armed forces in the Netherlands, ordered homes burned in the village of Putten and 590 male residents deported, of whom only 50 survived. The Dutch railway workers remained on strike and, in reprisal, under Operation Liese, the Germans prohibited movement of food to the Randstad from September to November. When shipments were resumed, supplies were meager.

Although the Allies were able to wrest control of the islands of Zeeland in hard fighting in October and November 1944, the great rivers to the north demarcated the border between occupied and liberated parts of the country for another six months. Until the waning days of the war, the struggle never slackened. From Wassenaar, the Germans launched their new V-1 and V-2 rockets at London and Antwerp. In late 1944 and early 1945 socioeconomic life shut down almost entirely in the northern Netherlands. The country had already been stripped bare of food supplies by the Germans, and the Allies refused all requests to airdrop shipments lest they fall into German hands. During the bitterly cold "hunger winter" (*hongerwinter*), people boiled wallpaper in an attempt to make an edible paste, they ate tulip bulbs, and they scoured the countryside for meager scraps. City dwellers trekked to rural areas carrying with them whatever wares they could with which to barter with farmers for food. In January 1945, Amsterdammers were dying at the rate of 500 a week. By spring Dutch urban dwellers were subsisting for weeks on two slices of bread, a few potatoes, and vegetables rotten from frost. Gas and electricity were cut off; in foraging for fuel, urban dwellers stripped the public parks of trees. Deaths from hunger, cold, typhoid, and diphtheria totaled more than 20,000.

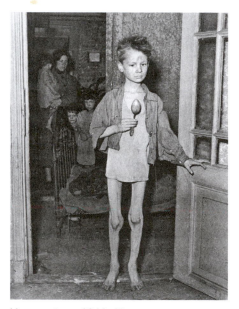

Hunger winter, 1944–45 (International Institute of Social History)

When it came, liberation arrived not from the west but from the east. In February 1945 under Operation Veritable, the First Canadian Army advanced through the Reichswald Forest east of Nijmegen. From western Germany, the British turned round and took Enschede on April 1, 1945, and two Canadian Army corps attacked fortifications along the IJssel River from the rear. British artillery began firing across the Meuse and Waal rivers on April 25. A cease-fire was subsequently declared. The Allies did not advance beyond the prewar Grebbe Line for fear of massive civilian casualties that would result from heavy fighting in the densely populated western part of the country.

The cease-fire facilitated provisioning the starving population in the still-occupied western cities, and a large-scale airlift of foodstuffs began. American B-17 Flying Fortresses and British Lancasters began dropping parcels on April 29 across the northern Netherlands, some crews even emptying their pockets to throw chocolate and cigarettes to the people below, many of whom waved back not just with their hands but with sheets, shirts, flags, and anything that would flap in the wind. By May 5 the country was completely free. German forces were disarmed and interned. Members of the NSB and other collaborators were rounded up—some beaten and abused—in front of crowds that jeered; the queen was greeted with joy wherever she appeared. From farmhouses, attics, and backrooms, those living in internal exile emerged—a little Jewish girl in The Hague stepping forward to hand a bouquet of flowers to the burgomaster, who promptly removed the yellow star she was still wearing to the cheers of the crowd. The costs of the few goods available soared as black market prices prevailed everywhere.

Relief and joy were tempered by a numbing shock at the toll exacted through five years of suffering unequaled in modern times. Bitterness at the Germans and Japanese would endure for decades and the memory of those fellow citizens who had cooperated with the nation's enemies would evoke anger and shame. The physical destruction mirrored the mental anguish. The infrastructure—of farm and factory, of dockyard, road, and railway—was depleted and destroyed. The end of the war on May 8, 1945, found all of central Rotterdam, except for the tower of the Church of St. Lawrence; all of the medieval center of Middelburg; and many of the beautiful centuries-old buildings of Arnhem, Nijmegen, Sluis, and Venlo in rubble. Retreating Germans flooded the Wieringermeer polder, the great dike at Westkapelle in Zeeland had been breached by bombing, and seawater covered the island of Walcheren and other areas in Zeeland. More than 205,000 Dutch men and women lay dead—the highest per capita death rate of the Nazi-occupied countries of western Europe.

9

RECONSTRUCTION AND REBIRTH AFTER WORLD WAR II (1945–2000)

I n 1945 the Netherlands lay prostrate. Never before in modern times had the nation experienced such massive destruction, with the spirit of the people, ravaged by famine, oppression, division, and death, seemingly as broken as the breached dikes that littered the landscape. In the late 1940s and into the 1950s more than a half million Dutch men and women left their war-torn homeland, most emigrating to English-speaking countries in North America, southern Africa, and the South Pacific.

Yet the Dutch rebounded quickly. A national will to make a new start fueled postwar reconstruction work and carried the country forward to produce decades of economic growth that brought unprecedented prosperity.

From 1946 to 1949 the country struggled to hold on to the East Indies. The loss of its Asian colonial empire following the grant of independence to the Republic of Indonesia in 1949 proved a bitter blow, but the impact was short-lived and failed to dampen the nation's drive toward a more comfortable, more secure environment both at home and abroad.

The country redirected its international energies toward the regional work of North Atlantic and European cooperation, joining enthusiastically in the Western alliance against the perceived threat of the Soviet Union and in each of the successive steps from common market to European Union that brought widespread and ever deeper integration of the member states' economies and societies. Farther afield, the Netherlands became a generous donor of humanitarian aid and assistance to developing countries and a reliable contributor to peacekeeping and conflict prevention efforts.

The nation itself became transformed. The welfare state emerged full-blown and, under the relentless push of modern culture, the confessional character of Dutch society trembled, then tumbled. The questioning of institutions, elites, and established patterns of thought and ways of doing things became commonplace. Secularism surged. Immigrants brought cultural change. Indeed, change became the order of the day, and advances in individual rights—for youth, women, gays, the elderly, and others—earned the country a reputation as one of the world's premier liberal places. At the same time, many traditional institutions remained intact; government retained its "consociational" character based on coalitions of political parties crafted by leaders well practiced in the art of compromise; the economy still depended on its customary sectors to thrive; and time-tested customs survived.

Reconstruction and "Breakthrough"

The Dutch plunged into the task of rebuilding the country with vigor and determination. They sought not only to restore the physical infra-structure but also to lay the foundation for a new social and political framework. Vast quantities of bread were imported from Sweden to bolster food stocks. Wartime damages were rapidly repaired. Roads, railroads, and the bridges over which they ran were back in service by the end of 1945, flooded polderlands were drained, and gaps in the dikes plugged and reinforced, all of it accomplished with financial assistance supplied most prominently by Marshall Plan aid. The plan (officially, the European Recovery Program), named for U.S. Secretary of State George C. Marshall (1880–1959), constituted the primary tool of the United States in rebuilding wartorn European allies and, in so doing, repelling the threat of communism. Under the program, the Netherlands received $1.128 million in assistance between 1947 and 1952. Reconstruction saw a boom in housing construction, with the state providing funding. Modernist blocks often four or more stories tall sprouted in Amsterdam and Rotterdam, precursors of even bigger blocks that appeared in the 1950s and 1960s. The nation's finances were reordered—the guilder was devalued and all money in circulation replaced.

The urge to avenge wartime suffering burned brightly in the immediate postwar years. The government submitted to the Allies suggestions for acquiring large neighboring sections of Germany as well as the grant of mining concessions, but an Allied decision in March 1949 awarded only some 70 square miles near Zevenaar (Gelderland) and Sittard (Limburg), most of which was returned to Germany years later. Authorities launched Operation Black Tulip, which called for the deportation of all holders of German passports in the Netherlands. Although such measures were never fully implemented, between 1946 and 1948 a total of 3,600 German nationals were duly ordered to leave the country.

Efforts to purge the population of Nazi collaborators (*zuivering*) proved much more difficult. Leading members of the NSB and other prominent German sympathizers were arrested, but, aside from a few show trials, which included those of Mussert and a handful of other collaborators (who were found guilty and executed), the government did little else, having encountered insurmountable complexities in trying to determine the degree of guilt of lower-level civil servants and others who might have cooperated with the enemy occupier.

Postwar cleanup and rebuilding were overseen by a government formed, following elections in June 1945, by new men on the political scene with new ideas. Under Willem Schermerhorn (1894–1977) as prime minister and Willem Drees (1886–1988) as minister of social affairs, the new government set out to fulfill the hopes expressed by the cabinet in exile during the war of overcoming the splintered society of the prewar years by establishing a "party of national unity" that would oversee a "breakthrough" (*doorbraak*) in political thinking. The new ministers had joined with others in founding the Dutch National Movement in 1945 and, under that group's forthright slogan of "Renewal and Reconstruction," the government worked to restore the country's trade-based economy, launch new industrial and public works projects, and implement social welfare measures. A new civil code for the country was drafted in 1947 by Eduard M. Meijers (1880–1954), a jurist and professor of law at Leiden University.

Oil had been discovered in Drenthe in 1943 in the course of a German-sponsored search for new fuel sources, and, by 1947, commercial quantities here supplied 12 percent of national needs. DAF Motors began building trucks, trailers, and buses in 1949. In 1958 a prototype automobile, featuring its trademark variomatic transmission, was presented to the public, who immediately placed orders for 4,000 vehicles. DAF survives today as a truck manufacturing company. True to their trading roots, Dutch long-distance haulers operated one of western Europe's largest postwar trucking industries, and the country's modern, multilane highway system constituted one of the Continent's densest by century's end. Plans were drafted for a vast industrial development project at the Botlek to the west of Rotterdam, whose subsequent completion would mark the start of Rotterdam's Europoort.

The flood of February 1953 (AP Images)

A "five-island" scheme to dam the Meuse River south of Rozenburg in South Holland to protect the area from salt seepage was implemented in 1950. Drainage of the IJsselmeer proceeded steadily throughout the postwar years. In 1953 alone, the year of a devastating North Sea storm, 119,999 acres (48,561 hectares) were wrested from the sea and made available for farming. In 1986 a new province—Flevoland—was created, reclamation having added some 19 percent to the country's arable land. The much-diminished lake is now a major freshwater reserve, serving as a source of recreation and drinking water. The most massive of all the projects—the Delta Works—would commence after inundations in 1953 made it imperative to end once and for all the recurring threat of North Sea flooding in Zeeland and parts of South Holland.

The nation turned an about-face in its foreign relations in abandoning its long-standing neutrality in favor of active participation in international organizations and nascent postwar alliances. The Netherlands became a founding member of the United Nations (UN), created in 1945 as a successor to the League of Nations. That same year the International Court of Justice (World Court) was established as the

DELTA WORKS

Studies on damming the Rhine-Meuse delta began in the 1930s but urgent action became essential after February 1, 1953, when a catastrophic North Sea storm broke dikes and sea walls in the Scheldt River delta in the southwest Netherlands, killing 1,835 people, drowning 10,000 animals, and leaving 70,000 homeless. To prevent such a tragedy from ever recurring, a large-scale flood defensive system called the Delta Works (Deltawerken), or the Delta plan, was drawn up and implemented. By 1958 the first project was operational—a storm barrier (38 ft. [11.5 m] high and 262 ft. [80 m] wide) across the IJssel River to protect the Randstad. In a series of stages, the islands in Zeeland were joined together by a series of giant causeways consisting of 13 dams, barrier walls, and raised dikes, culminating in the massive Eastern Scheldt storm surge barrier (Oosterscheldekering), inaugurated in October 1986, with 62 openings to allow saltwater through so as to maintain tidal flows while also preserving the river delta for wildlife and the fishing industry. The most recent construction was finished in 1997 with completion of the Maeslantkering, a storm surge barrier in the New Waterway (Nieuwe Waterweg) between the Hook of Holland (Hoek van Holland) and the town of Maasluis, and the Hartelkering,

(continues)

The Oosterscheldekering (Eastern Scheldt storm surge barrier), completed in 1986 between the islands of Schouwen-Duiveland and Noord-Beveland, is the largest of 13 Delta Works dams. (The Netherlands Board of Tourism and Conventions)

DELTA WORKS *(continued)*

a barrier on the Hartel canal near Spijkenisse built to protect the Europoort dock areas.

The Delta Works is one of the largest engineering and flood protection plans in the world. The project shortened the total coastline by 435 miles (700 km), reclaimed 6,100 acres (15,000 ha), improved the agricultural freshwater supply, made possible a better water balance for the area by allowing freshwater in and polluted or excess water out, led to creation of new nature reserves in the sheltered lakes formed behind the dams and barriers, and put in place road connections between the many islands and peninsulas of Zeeland, a province in which some towns and villages have been largely isolated for centuries.

The Delta Works is an ongoing project. Reinforcement of 249 miles (400 km) of dikes is underway, including dike revetment work along the Oosterschelde and Westerschelde waterways. The elevation of areas on the mainland is subsiding and global warming is causing sea levels to rise, necessitating that the dikes will eventually have to be made higher and wider.

primary judicial organ of the new world body, replacing the League's Permanent Court of International Justice, with its headquarters remaining at The Hague. The country joined its wartime western European allies as a partner in the Western European Union (1948) and, with the United States and Canada, the North Atlantic Treaty Organization (NATO) (1949). Links with Belgium were improved after a century of often frosty relations when, in 1944, the Dutch and Belgian governments-in-exile signed, together with Luxembourg, the Benelux accords, an agreement to create a customs union that took effect in 1947.

The new international activism derived not only from the realization that, in 1940, neutrality had failed but also from the need for European cooperation demanded by the United States as a condition for Marshall Plan aid and from fears of the incendiary danger posed by an aggressively communist Soviet Union. Dutch Communists won 10 percent of the vote in national elections in 1946 and the need to counteract the perceived threat they posed to Dutch bourgeois society prompted not only a determined stand in solidarity with the Western democracies but also increased domestic social welfare legislation to reduce the poverty that bred social unrest. The threats that were believed to exist from both within and without the country emerged just as the Netherlands faced a major challenge to its imperial holdings.

Loss of Empire

Starting from a weak base, Western-style nationalism in the Netherlands East Indies gained in intensity in the prewar years and advocates for independence joined local rulers, Islamic leaders, and communist agitators as sources of resistance to Dutch rule. The first mass political movement, Sarekat Islam, was started in 1911. Asia's first Communist Party was founded in 1920, and the oppression suffered under Dutch rule led to its rapid growth. In 1927 colonial authorities savagely suppressed a revolution launched by the party, which reduced its presence; however, during the same year a right-wing counterweight to the Communists appeared in the Indonesian Nationalist Party, founded by Sukarno (1901–70), a member of the small, educated native elite as a Dutch-trained, multilingual civil engineer from East Java. Dutch defeat and Japanese occupation in 1942 lifted the fortunes of the nationalists. On August 17, 1945, two days before Japan surrendered, the Republic of Indonesia was proclaimed by Sukarno, who had collaborated with the Japanese and, as a brilliant orator, had become a charismatic nationalist leader; and by Mohammad Hatta (1902–80), Sukarno's unassuming deputy.

During the war the Dutch government had devised postwar plans to create a royal commonwealth in which the Indonesians would be given equal status with the Dutch, but, when Dutch officials returned in 1945, they met armed resistance. The government refused to deal with Sukarno, whom it regarded as a traitor for having supported the Japanese. The next four years saw a hardening of positions as the Netherlands, reluctant to relinquish a colony on whose economic wealth it had long relied, sought to restore its authority by defeating an opposition bent on winning self-determination. Two Dutch "police actions" in 1947–48 met with little success as the war-ravaged country could not hope to procure the logistics and finances necessary to wage a full-scale military effort across the huge archipelago. A complex set of political solutions was proposed involving various federations and commonwealths in greater or lesser degrees of union with the Netherlands, but all of them foundered. The Dutch failed to grasp the extent of indigenous support for independence, and, when they lost the backing of their allies, especially the United States, they were compelled, in December 1949, to cede sovereignty to a federal Indonesian republic, which subsequently became a unitary state under Sukarno.

Most Dutch nationals and many Indo-Europeans were repatriated to the Netherlands. Large numbers of Moluccans (mostly Ambonese) joined them after a bid for independence by the inhabitants of the southern Moluccas island of Ambon (Amboina) was quashed by Indonesian forces in 1950. Many Moluccans had served as soldiers in the Royal Dutch Indian Army and they now fled to the Netherlands as refugees who harbored hopes of one day returning to their homeland with Dutch assistance.

The Netherlands suffered a diplomatic defeat in the loss of Indonesia that put the country in poor standing when, beginning in 1949, Indonesia demanded that the Dutch release their hold on Netherlands New Guinea (later known as West Irian or West Papua), the western half of the island that had remained under Dutch rule after 1945. After 1945 the territory saw much improvement, with new investments in timber, rubber, coconut, and cocoa production, and with standards of public health raised, notably in reducing malaria and tuberculosis. Unable to garner support in the United Nations, the Dutch government was obliged in 1962 to transfer the territory to Indonesia. Dutch New Guinea was placed under Indonesian administration in 1963 on the proviso that a UN-supervised plebiscite be held in 1969. The intervening years gave the Indonesians time to establish a significant administrative and military presence. On August 2, 1969, the plebiscite produced a unanimous vote in favor of Indonesian rule, but doubts about the genuineness of the sentiment have persisted given the primitiveness of the territory's inhabitants. The succeeding decades gave rise to indigenous efforts to secure independence, including the emergence of an armed guerrilla group, the Free Papua Movement.

The Netherlands's relations with its colonies in South America and the Caribbean evolved in a much more placid manner. Dutch Guiana (or Netherlands Guiana) had been an economic backwater since its acquisition in the 17th century. The hot, humid climate attracted few settlers and only the importation of slave labor from Africa and, later, indentured workers from India made possible the production of sugar, molasses, and rum on the large plantations, where the workers often suffered brutal treatment. The colony did not begin to pay its own way until the discovery of bauxite in the 1920s. Internal autonomy was granted in 1954, popular movements for independence began to gather momentum in the 1970s, and, after a complex series of negotiations, the country emerged as the Republic of Suriname in November 1975.

Though small and sparsely populated, the Netherlands Antilles—previously known as the Netherlands West Indies, the Dutch West Indies,

Territories of the Netherlands in the West Indies

Puerto Rico (U.S.)

Virgin Islands (U.S./U.K.)

Anguilla (U.K.)

DOMINICAN REPUBLIC

see inset

ANTIGUA & BARBUDA

ST. KITTS & NEVIS

Guadeloupe (FRANCE)

LESSER

DOMINICA

Caribbean Sea

ANTILLES

Martinique (FRANCE)

ST. LUCIA

Aruba (THE NETH.)

Bonaire (Neth. Antilles)

ST. VINCENT & THE GRENADINES

BARBADOS

GRENADA

Curaçao (Neth. Antilles)

TRINIDAD & TOBAGO

St. Martin (FRANCE)

Sint Maarten (Neth. Antilles)

Saba (Neth. Antilles)

Sint Eustatius (Neth. Antilles)

0   5 miles
0   5 km

ATLANTIC OCEAN

VENEZUELA

GUYANA

COLOMBIA

N

SURINAME

French Guiana (FRANCE)

BRAZIL

0   300 miles
0   300 km

© Infobase Publishing

or the Dutch Antilles—enjoyed more prosperity, thanks to their location. The islands of the Lesser Antilles lay at the crossing of international sea lanes. Situated in close proximity to the rich oil fields of Venezuela, Curaçao and Aruba featured deep sea harbors and offered stability just offshore of the oftentimes politically turbulent South American republic. Oil producers set up refineries on the islands, beginning in 1915 with Royal Dutch Shell on Curaçao and Shell–Standard Oil (Esso) on Aruba. The companies brought a degree of prosperity to the islands. The drop in refining after Venezuela began to build its own facilities following World War II led to high unemployment rates, reaching 23 percent in the mid-1960s and sparking social unrest. This led to some emigration to the Netherlands, though on a small scale (approximately 93,000 Antilleans in the Netherlands in 1996). The economic downturn was offset to some degree by a burgeoning postwar tourist trade, actively abetted by government monies, especially on Curaçao, Aruba, and Sint Maarten. Revenues from those who visit to enjoy the sun and surf are joined with earnings from shipbuilding and from calcium and phosphate production on Curaçao to provide financial support for the poorer islands of Bonaire, Saba, and Sint Eustatius. Ties with the Netherlands have never been severely strained due to the absence of a single, dominant racial group with a strong cultural identity, the use of Dutch as a common linguistic link, and the genuine affection felt by residents for the House of Orange.

Each island today has its own government that presides over domestic affairs. Aruba was separated from the Netherlands Antilles in 1986 and granted a "status apart" within the Kingdom of the Netherlands. The Netherlands Antilles was set to be dissolved following a vote by residents in Curaçao and Sint Maarten in 2005 for a change of relationship. They were due to become autonomous associated states under the Kingdom of the Netherlands, but deliberations in 2007 postponed final determination of their status until December 2008. In October 2006 Bonaire, Saba, and Sint Eustatius reached agreement to be incorporated directly into the Netherlands as special municipalities whose local governing arrangement will resemble municipalities in the home country, with a mayor, aldermen, and a municipal council.

Prosperity Prevails

The widespread belief that the loss of the East Indies would disastrously affect the Dutch economy proved illusory. After a brief downturn, growth resumed and then zoomed rapidly upward, powered by a postwar boom that expanded as the 1950s progressed. Gross national product swelled from 17.2 million guilders in 1950 to 32.9 million in 1958 and unemployment fell below 1 percent from 1960 to 1966. By 1990 the average number of hours worked per week had fallen to 34.3. They had stood at 52 in 1900.

Expansion was carried forward in part by the movement toward wider European cooperation, which the export-oriented Dutch embraced enthusiastically. A founding member of the European Coal and Steel Community (1952) and the European Economic Community (EEC)

(1957), the Netherlands benefited greatly from the progressive break-down of national barriers to capital, trade, and labor flows, and the country backed the admission of new members, notably of Great Britain in 1973, and the closer integration entailed in the progression from EEC to EC (European Community, 1967) to EU (European Union, 1992). The transit trade that had for so long nurtured the nation's wealth flour-ished, and Dutch shipping and truck traffic traversed the Continent's rivers and roads.

To handle the vast increases in trade and industry, dock and port facilities at Rotterdam, the largest port, spread, and the new Europoort complex led Europe in handling capacity. Major development projects transformed the landscape and added value to the nation's economic inventory. The rich polderlands of Flevoland added to agricultural wealth. The Delta Works protected southern parts of the country from flooding, and the highways built atop the massive dikes also brought improved road links between Rotterdam and Antwerp, Belgium.

During the 1950s rapid economic growth led commercial banks to expand both to serve large corporations and to attract sufficient sav-ings. They began to offer a wider array of services and, with the growth of private income, they set up branches to reach even the smallest communities. The introduction of personal loans contributed to the creation of the consumer society. At the same time, the banks began a process of concentration. In 1964 the Netherlands Trading Society merged with the Twentsche Bank to form the Algemene Bank Nederland (ABN). The process ended in the early 1970s with the formation of four general banks: ABN, AMRO-Bank, Postbank, and Rabobank. By the late 20th century, the onset of the international economy led the banks to set up substantial operations abroad in establishing branches and par-ticipating in international consortia. Deregulation of the banking and insurance industries resulted in creation of corporations combining the two services. By 1994 four large banks emerged: ABN AMRO Bank, Rabobank, ING, and Fortis. In September 2000 the Amsterdam Stock Exchange merged with the exchanges in Brussels and Paris to create Euronext, the first pan-European stock exchange.

Long-standing Dutch industrial giants experienced large-scale growth. Royal Dutch Shell, Unilever, and Philips became top-ranked multinational corporations, their expansion fueled by rising demands for oil and for consumer products that ranged from lighting fixtures to televisions to a host of others. In 1969 Philips began the manufacture of computers. In the 1980s the Royal Dutch Shell group expanded through acquisitions and launched large-scale offshore exploration projects while, in the 1990s, it entered new markets with huge oil and gas projects started in Russia and China. In 2005 the company was structurally reorganized, the partnership in place since 1907 between Royal Dutch and Shell Transport and Trading was dissolved, and one company created—Royal Dutch Shell plc—with its headquarters at The Hague.

The discovery of natural gas near the town of Slochteren in 1959 launched a major new industry. By the 1970s large amounts were being exported to West Germany, the Dutch having reestablished their traditional transit and export/import trade with their now economically surging neighbor to the east. A vast new island of natural gas was uncovered in the North Sea in 1975 along with small amounts of oil.

In 1975 an economic recession set in, spawned by an international oil crisis induced by Arab oil-producing countries, which had cut off all supplies to the United States and the Netherlands and increased prices by 70 percent to Western European countries in 1973 because of their support for Israel in the Yom Kippur War. The government succeeded in muting the full effects of the boycott by implementing rationing and by encouraging use of alternative transportation means—Prime Minister Johannes Marten "Joop" den Uyl (1919–87) set an example by cycling to work—but the ensuing worldwide recession bit deep, hitting hardest in labor-intensive industries, such as textiles, shipping, shipbuilding, and metallurgy. Coal deposits in Limburg became depleted and the last mine was closed in 1976. The Dutch State Mines, which had run operations, switched to production of chemicals. Capital-intensive production fared better while horticultural, vegetable, and dairy produce, which had accounted for much of the country's early contribution to the Benelux and EEC, remained central props of the export economy through the end of the century.

Unskilled laborers, recruited from Spain, Italy, and Portugal, trickled into the country in the late 1940s and 1950s and then arrived in droves from Morocco and Turkey during the boom times of the 1960s and early 1970s. The mid-1970s recession led to considerable unemployment among these groups, which continued despite the return of improved economic conditions in the 1980s. The economy remained strong in the 1990s with unemployment dropping below 2 percent late in the decade, and growth in gross domestic product averaged nearly 4 percent between 1998 and 2000, well above the European Union average. Social strains induced by unemployed so-called guest workers of non-Dutch ethnic origin combined with rising numbers of pensioners and fewer workers to produce severe pressures on the country's social services. The ratio of workers to welfare recipients shrank to one of the smallest in the world. Reforms in the 1980s and 1990s managed to reduce tax burdens and benefits payments without giving rise to wide-scale poverty or massive social protest. The essentials of the welfare state were maintained, but an intensive debate on the need for further change ensured that the issue would remain contentious.

Change Sweeps through Society

It was postwar prosperity that had launched the welfare system. Guaranteeing everyone a minimum income whether employed or not, the Netherlands had put in place after 1945 one of the world's model "cradle to grave" social welfare societies.

Social insurance programs are funded by premiums paid by both the employer and the employee. Coverage includes disability (Disability Benefits Act, 1967) and unemployment (Unemployment Benefits Act, 1949), both with benefits set originally at 80 percent of the last salary/wage the worker earned; sickness (Sickness Benefits Act, 1967), with benefits paid originally by the government equal to 70 percent of the last salary/wage earned; and health insurance (Health Insurance Act, 1966), with enrollment compulsory for everyone.

Social services are funded out of general tax revenues and include assistance benefits (National Assistance Act, 1965), which everyone with insufficient income to cover their cost of living in entitled to receive; old age pensions (General Old Age Pensions Act, 1957), set at minimum wage levels at age 65; survivor pensions (General Survivors Pension Act, 1996); children's benefits (General Children's Benefits Act, 1962); and insurance for medical costs not covered under the state health insurance program (General Act on Exceptional Medical Costs, 1967).

Trade and insurance unions, schools, and hospitals constitute the institutional framework of the system. Many of these agencies date from the time pillarization emerged in the late 19th and early 20th centuries, and they serve as the social partners of the government in administering programs. At the same time, the expansion of the state's social services also brought about a weakening of the old pillarized society. People could more easily cut ties to their subcultures because they were no longer materially dependent on them.

With reconstruction of the economy largely complete by the late 1960s, a more critical attitude toward traditional values and institutions gradually emerged under the impact of growing social discontent, which paralleled stirrings of protest then appearing throughout Western societies. Established habits of consensual compromise reached by social elites behind closed doors increasingly drew reproof, and those who had always opposed the confessional character of Dutch society began to win a wide hearing. Long-accepted customs were called into question. Demands grew for a more open society in which all citizens were given the opportunity to participate in public life.

Secularization

Movement toward greater democratization occurred in conjunction with trends toward secularization, which had been spreading progressively since the 19th century but which now intensified under the impact of mass consumerism and the emergence of a society in which the state, rather than the churches, served as the guardian of basic needs. Beginning in the 1960s, almost all religious denominations experienced radical changes in liturgy and organization. Traditional dogmas were reinterpreted to accommodate social action agendas, and ecumenism replaced separatism. Delegates from 147 Protestant churches met in Amsterdam in 1948 to create the World Council of Churches, the chief international Christian ecumenical organization. After 20 years of deliberations, the Dutch Reformed Church and the Reformed Churches announced their formal union in 1986.

Innovation rocked Roman Catholicism. Long loyal to Rome, the Catholic Church in the Netherlands was one of Europe's most conservative. Inspired and roused to action by the liturgical reforms launched by the Second Vatican Council (1962–65), Catholics under the leadership of Cardinal Bernardus Johannes Alfrink (1900–87) embraced change enthusiastically, which shook the foundations of their pillar. A pastoral council (1968–70) gave the laity an ample voice in ecclesiastical concerns, and Catholic strictures loosened as individual conscience took precedence in decision making on ethical and moral matters. By the 1990s the Dutch church had become Catholicism's most liberal. Viewed with suspicion by many Dutch Catholics for his conservative positions on such issues as birth control, priestly celibacy, and women's ordination, Pope John Paul II (1920–2005) met a chilly reception on his May 11–14, 1985, visit. The catcalls that greeted the papal processions, although they drew the displeasure of the Vatican, reflected the prominent place now occupied by the Dutch in the church's progressive wing.

Secularism undermined the religious character that had for so long distinguished so much of Dutch society. By 1990 almost half of the country's 15 million people were unaffiliated with any religious body. Church attendance dwindled steadily through the end of the century.

Protest Movements

The youth culture drove change forward. A rebellious subculture among the young that existed on the edges of society in the 1950s broke through in the 1960s to begin to shape the social culture in a significant way. Youth began to spend more and more time on the streets of the major cities and various gangs appeared in the late 1950s. Troublemakers (*nozens*), carrying out acts of public vandalism, clashed with police, notably when rowdies set fire to the municipal Christmas tree in The Hague on January 1, 1961, but purpose-driven intellectual and cultural opposition to mainstream society soon took precedence. Various strands of the emerging counterculture—anarchists, revolutionary socialists, pacifists—engaged in demonstrations, riots, strikes, and sit-ins against the established order. Activities mirrored those taking place elsewhere in the West, but by the end of the 1960s the Netherlands stood in the vanguard of protest.

Launched in 1965 by Roeland "Roel" van Duyn (1943–   ), a philosophy student at the University of Amsterdam, to protest capitalism and nuclear proliferation, the *provocateurs,* or *provo's,* won seats on the Amsterdam city council, and they drew international attention on March 10, 1966, when members threw smoke bombs in opposition to the marriage of Crown Princess Beatrix (1938–   ) and her German-born consort Claus von Amsberg (1926–2002) as the newlyweds rode in a gilded royal coach through the capital's streets. Amsberg had been a member of the Hitler Youth and served in the German army, and memories of the occupation were too fresh for many to acquiesce in a royal nuptial connection to the former enemy. Protesters chanted "I want my bicycle back" in reference to widescale confiscation of cycles by Germans during the war years. The act initiated a violent street battle with police and both symbolized and exemplified the major shift that now took place in attitudes and actions. Riots and public protests broke out, especially in Amsterdam. The term *provo's* gained rapid currency among the public.

Alternative became the catchword of the times—a willingness to experiment with different lifestyles and beliefs emerged. Their numbers more numerous than ever thanks to the postwar baby boom and the advent of jet air travel, youth from around the country and the world flocked to Amsterdam where a free-wheeling street life flourished. Throngs of the young, dubbed "asphalt youth" (*asfaltjeugd*), gathered in public squares and parks. Dressed in jeans and tattered jackets, hippies, flower people, gurus, and other assorted antiestablishment types arrived, many of them engaged in buying and selling drugs. Old buildings were converted into dormitories. Authorities tolerated their presence until concerns arose that they constituted a public health hazard and fears grew that the image they projected threatened business and tourism. In August 1970 police and Dutch marines cleared crowds from the most prominent gathering spot, the National Monument in Amsterdam's Dam Square, but it took two days of running battles to do so.

The *provo's* continued their protest activities, but in a more modified form and now under a new name. They called themselves *kabouters* (gnomes), a name derived from the dress they wore. Outfitted as garden gnomes, they advocated nonviolence and switched tactics in carrying out playful, humorous high jinks to attract attention to their goal, which they declared to be the creation of an "Orange Free State" to be set up side by side with the existing government, complete with its own alternative ministries. The *kabouters* captured five of 45 seats in municipal elections for the Amsterdam city council in June 1970. Having broken into the political system, they intended to use their position as a launching pad into national government, but, disillusioned by the political bickering on the council, van Duyn refused to stand as a candidate for the States General in national elections in April 1971 and, by 1972, the *kabouters* had faded from the scene. By the end of the 1970s the youth culture had largely subsided, but the country's reputation as a tolerant, progressive place spawned by this and other movements for social change that emerged in the course of the decade endured, and public demonstrations as a legitimate form of protest also remained, although the size and intensity of street actions lessened in the waning years of the century. In 1980 police used armored vehicles and tear gas to evict squatters (called *crackers* in Dutch) from properties in central Amsterdam, which they had occupied in protest against a severe shortage of affordable housing that ensued in the wake of the demolition of residential units to build a metro system, opera house, town hall complex, and hotels. Queen Beatrix's coronation that year was marred by continuing clashes, and unrest continued sporadically until sufficient housing was constructed to alleviate cramped conditions in the 1990s.

Women took up their protest actions of 50 years earlier. Gains came slowly at first. Anna de Waal (1906–81) was appointed the first female state secretary of education, arts, and sciences in 1953 and she was followed by Marga Klompé (1912–86) as the first minister of social services. Married women secured the legal right to conclude contracts, and the prohibition on their entering the civil service was lifted in 1957.

Inspired by their forebear, suffragette Wilhelmina Drucker, a group of radical activists nicknamed "Mad Mina" (Dolle Mina) appeared in 1970 and pressed for rights to workplace equality and to abortion. The latter right, proclaimed under the slogan "boss of your own belly," became a central political issue, and abortion was legalized, largely on demand, in 1983.

Women's claims led to a clamoring for further sexual liberation and, by the 1970s, the government had relaxed its strictures on what constituted pornography. Sex shops sprouted in Amsterdam, chiefly in the area off the Damstraat that had long been the traditional red light district, and then spread to other Dutch cities. Homosexuals organized to secure recognition of rights and, by century's end, the progress they made in social acceptance, notably in the churches and the armed forces, made the Netherlands a beacon and Amsterdam, in particular, a mecca of the international gay rights movement.

Pollution prevention and environmental protection were shown to be major concerns as early as 1971 with the creation of a Ministry of Health and Environment. Air pollution monitoring began in 1975, and lead-free gasoline, first introduced in 1987, was in use in 80 percent of vehicles a decade later. An Energy Regulation Tax, adopted in 1996, penalizes consumers who use more than stipulated amounts of electricity and natural gas and encourages the public to use and adopt energy-efficient appliances and practices. Funds garnered from the tax go to producers who supply energy from renewable resources, notably from wind and water. Manure control in a small country with a significant animal husbandry business and cleanup of pollutants in the country's major rivers, especially the Rhine, remain serious environmental problems.

Changes appeared everywhere. The Mammoth Act (1968) put in place uniform educational structures and financing arrangements in the midst of a huge upsurge in attendance at universities. The *provo's* initiated a campaign against marijuana prohibition and, by the 1970s, new laws lowered penalties for possession of soft drugs while Amsterdam earned a worldwide reputation as Europe's narcotics capital, harsh laws notwithstanding against use of hard drugs and international drug dealing. An extension of personal rights in the armed forces led to beards and long hair becoming commonplace. The police force was reorganized in 1993 when municipal departments were abolished and the country was divided into 25 regions, each with a corps, plus one corps to serve nationwide.

The influx of newcomers from non-Western cultures transformed the face of urban life and the cosmopolitanism that had characterized the country's major cities for centuries acquired a truly global allure. The nation's image as a place that gave to individuals wide latitude in tolerating differing beliefs and practices became set in the world's consciousness. The founder of Transcendental Meditation, Maharishi Mahesh Yogi (1917–) settled in the Netherlands in the early 1990s, epitomizing the country's newfound status as an international destination.

By the last quarter of the century no institution remained immune from scrutiny and censure. The House of Orange itself suffered a serious blow to its prestige in 1976 when Prince Bernhard (1911–2004), Queen Juliana's consort, was implicated in a bribery scandal with the Lockheed Corporation, a U.S. aircraft manufacturer. He resigned as inspector-general of the Dutch armed forces and relinquished his public functions.

Confronted by new attitudes and altered circumstances, organizations cut ties to their pillars and Dutch confessional society collapsed. The dense network of subcultural associations disappeared. The social democratic and Catholic trade unions merged to form the Federation of Dutch Trade Unions in 1975. The ability of the new medium of television to attract viewers of all political and religious persuasions began to loosen the grip the newspapers held on their pillarized audiences. At the same time the need to attract a larger readership to meet growing costs compelled the papers to adopt wider, less restricted viewpoints. The formerly nonconfrontational style of Dutch journalism gave way to hard-hitting investigative reporting, but also to sensationalistic, gossip-mongering writing that in the Netherlands, as elsewhere, sells well.

By century's end the growth in material wealth, educational attainment, technological sophistication, state intervention, and global involvement had produced the pervasive change that erased old patterns and altered old habits of thinking and acting. The effects were most clearly evident in the large cities—moral and social standards remained markedly more conservative in rural regions—and some pillarized organizations managed to survive, but the Dutch people no longer felt an unquestioning loyalty to traditional attitudes, values, and institutions.

The Modern Arts and Science Scene

Dutch culture mirrored the profound changes under way in society in the second half of the 20th century. The decline of the social pillars beginning in the 1960s led to a switch in government support of cultural activities based no longer on ensuring parity for each of the individual groups but on encouraging a wide array of individual expression within a national cultural framework. Quality and diversity became the new criteria on which state subsidies were distributed. In keeping with the tradition that value judgments on art and science should never be dictated by the state, the definition of quality is left to advisory committees, which make rulings on artists and institutions deemed worthy of support. In the past, artistic development was left mainly to private citizens and foundations, and state support had been given only on an occasional basis. Funds were now extended permanently. By the 1980s, cost concerns led to replacement of open-ended subsidies with fixed budget funding. A new Ministry of Education, Culture and Science was put in place in 1994 and the government began to offer financial incentives to cultural organizations in place of across-the-board funding. These organizations—theater companies, symphony orchestras, museums—were encouraged to become more financially independent, including seeking financial support from the private sector. In the midst of organizational developments, individual artists carried on, their work mirroring the society around them.

Literature

Early postwar novelists drew quite naturally on themes from a war that produced so cataclysmic an impact on the country. In *The Tears of the Acacias* (*De tranen der acacia's*, 1949), Willem F. Hermans (1921–   ) evokes the moral confusion arising from a wartime society in which it was not always easy to discern friend from foe. Likewise, in *Evenings* (*De avonden*, 1947), a book that has become a classic, Gerard Reve (1923–   ) depicts the boredom and emptiness of life when individuals are cut off from the world they knew. Reve's career reflects the changes that coursed through Dutch society. A writer on religious themes, Reve became the country's first celebrated gay writer; his later works, including *En route for the End* (*Op weg naar het einde*, 1963), dealt openly with homosexual sex. Marga Minco (1920–   ), a Jewish writer, wrote of the wartime persecution of Dutch Jews (*The Bitter Herb* [*Het bittere kruid*], 1957) and of the postwar disillusionment of those who survived (*An Empty House* [*Een leeg huis*], 1966).

Simon Vestdijk (1898–1971), a writer considered among the best in Dutch literature, published no less than 52 novels, poetry, essays on literature and music, and several works of philosophy in a career that spanned the period of the 1930s through the 1960s. Vestdijk, who was born in Harlingen and gave up medical school in favor of literature, wrote realistic novels, but his works always include subtle symbols and allusions to metaphysical problems as well. He considered *The Garden Where the Brass Band Played* (*De koperen tuin*, 1950), a coming-of-age story that takes a critical look at small-town life at the turn of the 20th century, to be his best work.

Other prose writers working in the second half of the 20th century include Hella Haase (1918–   ), who set her stories in a romanticized past (*A New Testament* [*Een nieuw testament*], 1966); Godfried Bomans (1913–74), who used humor to make a serious argument (*Daydreams* [*Mijmeringen*], 1968); Gerrit Krol (1934–   ), who draws on his computer programming background for his novels (*The Millimetered Head* [*Het gemillimeteerde hoofd*], 1967); and Jan Wolkers (1924–   ), whose collections of short stories have become popular in English translation. His *Turkish Delight* (*Turks fruit*, 1969) was made into a movie in 1973.

Cees Nooteboom (1933–   ) is an award-winning writer of fiction (*Rituals* [*Rituelen*], 1980), poetry (*The Black Poem* [*Het zwarte gedicht*], 1960), and travel (*Route to Santiago* [*De omweg naar Santiago*], 1992). Harry Mulisch (1927–   ) is a highly versatile writer in nonfiction (*Criminal Case 40/61, The Trial of Adolf Eichmann* [*De zaak 40/61*], 1962), and fiction (*The Discovery of Heaven* [*De ontdekking van de hemel*], 1992). Questions of morality figure prominently in his work, for which he poses no easy answers. Geert Mak's (1946–   ) narratives on Dutch history trumpet traditional themes and values and are popular best sellers.

Poets in the 1950s such as Remco Campert (1929–   ) argued for an open, experimental approach at the same time that language became the distinguishing feature of Dutch comic artistry. The immensely popular comic series *Tom Puss* (*Tom Poes*) and *Oliver B. Bumble* (*Olivier B. Bommel*) by Martin Toonder (1912–2005) appeared in newspapers from 1941 to 1986. Toonder exerted a great influence on the Dutch language in introducing new words and expressions.

Dutch authors are now seeing an increase in translations of their works as part of a trend that departs from the past, when only children's writers were widely available to non-Dutch-speaking audiences. Annie M. Schmidt (1911–95) wrote more than 60 books for children available in over a dozen languages, and illustrators Rien Poortvliet (1932–95) and Dick Bruna (1927–   ) have produced children's volumes whose stories in pictures require little dialogue. Poortvliet's work *Gnomes* won wide acclaim and became a cartoon series in the United States.

Art and Architecture

Dutch visual artists joined counterparts from Belgium and Denmark to form Cobra in 1948, a grouping whose members sought to defy traditional artistic categories and break the dominant position of Paris-based creators in Western art. Before the group disbanded in 1952, it included Corneille (Cornelis van Beverloo; 1922–   ), a Belgian-born painter and ceramicist whose work evolved from naturalism to cubism, and Karel Appel (1921–2006), a noted muralist and sculptor whose controversial abstract fresco *Questioning Children* in Amsterdam's city hall (1949) remained unveiled for 10 years. Graphic artist M. C. Escher (1898–1972) produced prints of almost mathematical precision whose repetitive images drawn from strange perspectives proved popular worldwide. Ger van Elk (1941–   ) is a conceptual artist whose impulse to create stems from the urge to explore the nature of the image and for whom therefore the message assumes greater importance than the material realization. His work has often been exhibited with that of conceptual photographer Jan Dibbets (1941–   ). Other, younger artists employ novel combinations of materials and instruments in their oeuvre. Michael Raedecker (1963–   ) uses his trademark technique of combining painting with embroidered and appliquéd elements in producing his landscapes, portraits, interiors, and still lifes. Arnhem-born visual artist Jennifer Tee (1973–   ) integrates video productions, photos, and text in presenting exhibitions throughout Europe and in the United States.

Dutch architects carried on their worldwide reputation for innovation and experimentation. New designers in the 1950s and 1960s, known as the Forum generation (after a magazine name), included Aldo van Eyck (1918–99) and J. B. Bakema (1914–81), and the modernist tradition of Dutch architecture endures, notably under the auspices of the Office of Metropolitan Architecture (OMA) and its director, Rem Koolhaas (1944–   ).

Film

Radio peaked in popularity in the immediate postwar years but was soon eclipsed by television. The first broadcast in the country appeared on October 2, 1951, and, by 1962, television had become an all-pervasive medium, with more than 2 million licensed sets. Noncommercial broadcasters did not appear until 1989 but they quickly carved an equal market share with the channels that had long been on the air. Quality news and documentary programs are presented, but television fare is drawn overwhelmingly from U.S. movies, miniseries, soap operas, and comedies, all aired in the original with Dutch subtitles, which facilitates the ability of viewers to acquire an in-depth fluency in the English language. The arrival of cable television late in the century with its profusion of channels loosened further whatever hold the pillars still had on Dutch communications.

After World War II, Dutch filmmakers sought to radically transform cinema production. A national cooperative for film production was set up and many commissions were secured from the government. The cinema union won a requirement that theater owners include a Dutch film in their fare once a month, although the small size of the industry—only about 10 to 15 films are currently produced each year—made this difficult to fulfill. Documentaries continued their prewar reputation for excellence and, after the 1960s, the freedom of expression that blossomed in the wider society was reflected in film production as well. Critical commentaries on racial prejudice, sexual freedom, Dutch colonialism, and human rights abuses appeared in films.

Although U.S. pictures dominate theater screens, Dutch artists have correspondingly secured a quality niche on the American scene. Actress Audrey Hepburn (1929–93), a Dutch baroness's daughter who lived in Amsterdam during the war, won early acclaim in achieving international stardom. Director Paul Verhoeven (1938–) and Dutch actors he has directed achieved signal success at home (*Soldier of Orange* [*Soldaat van Oranje*], 1977) and then undertook critically acclaimed work in the United States (*Basic Instinct,* 1992). Both he and Jan de Bont (1943–) with *Twister* (1996) and *The Haunting* (1999) have established respected reputations in Hollywood, as have actors such as Rutger Hauer (1946–), Jeroen Krabbé (1944–), and Johanna ter Steege (1961–). The Oscar for Best Foreign Film was won in 1986 by *De Aanslag* (*The assault*), based on the 1982 novel of the same name by Harry Mulisch and directed by Fons Rademakers (1920–); in 1998 by *Antonia* (*Antonia's Line*), directed by Marleen Gorris (1948–); and in 1998 by *Karakter* (*Character*), based on a novel by Ferdinand Bordewijk and directed by Mike van Diem (1959–).

Music

From 1950 to 1980 the number of symphony orchestras in the country grew from seven to 16. The already famed Concertgebouw Orchestra in Amsterdam probably remains the best known internationally. The orchestra travels worldwide, having made its first tour of the United States in 1954. The Netherlands Chamber Choir, the Netherlands Woodwind Ensemble, and the Rotterdam Philharmonic also garner international acclaim. Violinist André Rieu (1950–), born in Maastricht, travels the world in the 21st century bringing his festive classical concerts to enthusiastic audiences. Known as the "waltz king of Europe," he has produced more than 30 albums. Modern Dutch ballet dates from the mid-1950s. Sonia Gaskell (1904–74), a Russian émigré, took over direction of the New Dutch Ballet in 1954, and, in 1961, the Dutch National Ballet was created with the amalgamation of the New Dutch Ballet and the Amsterdam Ballet. The Netherlands Dance Theater, an offshoot of the National Ballet, is based in The Hague. Theater, dance, and music festivals are held annually, notably the Holland Music Festival in Utrecht; the Utrecht Film Festival, where all Dutch films produced in the preceding year are screened; and the North Sea Jazz Festival in The Hague, which is one of Europe's largest.

Sports

Soccer dominates the world of sports and the Dutch national team won the European championship in 1988, its best showing in international competition, although it achieved World Cup runner-up status in 1974 and 1978. Hooliganism by fans remains a problem, most especially at matches between rival national city teams. The death of an Ajax (Amsterdam) fan in a game against Feyenoord (Rotterdam) in 1997 led to a police crackdown on rowdyism, even announcing that crucial matches could be attended by fans of only one of the participating teams.

In Olympic and other international lineups, Dutch participants are particularly competitive in swimming, tennis, and speed skating, a sport that was invented in the Netherlands, possibly as early as the 13th century. Fanny Blankers-Koen (1918–2004) won four gold medals in the London Olympics of 1948 for running, helping to break down Dutch prejudices against women participating in sports and earning national and international fame. In 1999 the International Athletics Federation voted her the "Best Female Athlete of the Century." More recently, Richard Krajicek (1971–   ), who was born in The Hague of Czech parents, won the Wimbledon men's tennis title in 1996.

Science

Dutch scientists have won international renown, notably in the fields of physics and chemistry. Nobel Prizes in physics were earned by Frits Zerneke (1888–1960) in 1953 for his invention of the phase contrast microscope, which allows study of the internal cell structure without the need to stain (and thus kill) the cells; by Simon van der Meer (1925–   ) in 1984 for inventing the concept of stochastic cooling; and by Martinus J. C. Veltman (1931–   ) and Gerardus 't Hooft (1946–   ) in 1999 for discoveries in quantum mechanics. In chemistry, Paul J. Crutzen (1933–   ) won the prize in 1995 for his work on ozone

223

depletion. Jan Tinbergen (1903–94), an internationally recognized economist, developed a pioneering national macroeconomic model, first for the Netherlands and then for the United States and the United Kingdom. He won the Nobel Prize in 1969, and his younger brother Nikolaas (1907–88), an ethnologist and ornithologist, won the prize in physiology or medicine in 1973 for study of individual and social behavior patterns in animals. His work reflects a long tradition carried on by others as well, including Frans de Waal (1948–   ), in research on animal behavior, especially regarding the great apes, that has won international esteem. The Amsterdam zoo, one of Europe's earliest (1838), has played an important role in facilitating and sponsoring research. Astronomer Jan Hendrik Oort (1900–92) devoted most of his long career to trailblazing investigation into the makeup and dynamics of the Milky Way galaxy. He determined that the Earth's solar system did not occupy the center of the Milky Way, as was long believed, but rather the galaxy's outer edges. In the 1950s Oort helped to develop radio astronomy, which revolutionized study of the structure of the Milky Way.

Old Political Patterns Are Shattered

Just as Dutch society changed profoundly over the course of succeeding decades after 1945, politics too moved from traditional to novel configurations. The confessional divisions in Dutch politics had remained largely intact in the immediate postwar years despite the hoped-for "breakthrough" to new ways of thinking. The Social Democratic Labor Party and the Freethinking Democratic League, together with socially conscious members of other political parties, came together to form a new Labor Party (Partij van de Arbeid, PvdA) in 1946, but the well-entrenched, pillarized parties retained their allegiances and, within a few years, the PvdA became just another social democratic party. Catholics reordered their political vehicle in creating the Catholic People's Party (Katholieke Volks Partij, KVP). Despite the urge to swerve away from established formulas, a hardening of attitudes surprisingly occurred in 1954 when the Catholic Church forbade its members from associating with the PvdA or with the parties of the neutral pillar. The directive was roundly condemned by many as anachronistic, which did at least give evidence of the potential for real reform. Reform came in institutional rearrangements. In 1956 the Second Chamber was enlarged to 150 seats from 100, a number that had not changed since the late 19th century.

Throughout the first six decades of the 20th century electoral contests produced reliably predictable results, with the three large confessional parties—the Anti-Revolutionary Party, the Christian Historical Union, and the Catholic People's Party—forming coalitions and typically gaining or losing one or two seats. Broad coalitions led by PvdA leader Willem Drees, supported by socialists and Catholics, ruled through most of the 1950s. By the 1960s, however, the changes that were stirring society in general began to ripple through politics. Gains and losses ranging from five to 10 seats became more common, and the major parties saw their combined share of the vote decline from one-half to one-third from 1963 to 1972. Antiestablishment parties that would come to play an important role later in the century first appeared in the late 1950s with the founding of the right-wing populist Farmers' Party (Boeren Partij). Formed when police had forcefully confiscated farms from occupants unable to pay their taxes, the party won seats in 1963, but internal splits and struggles led to its dissolution by the 1970s.

Splintering of political parties, although it had occurred since the introduction of proportional representation in the 1920s, now began to promote the depillarization of the system. The PvdA government fell in 1958, and the succeeding years out of power led to a breakaway by members in 1962. The Pacifist Socialists (PSP) emerged as the first of the new parties in espousing a far left agenda. It was followed by the Democratic Political Party of 1966 (Politieke Partij Democraten 1966, D66) formed by 44 young "new men," 25 of whom had never previously been members of a political party. Founded by journalist Hans van Mierlo (1931–   ) and Amsterdam municipal councilor Hans Gruijters (1931–2006), the progressive, social liberal party sought to break the grip of the confessional parties and usher in genuine democratic reforms. Wheeling and dealing among the parties under proportional representation produced cabinets that differed little from one another and D66 members sought to end this decades-old formula by calling for the direct national election of the prime minister, a district-based electoral system, and the introduction of popular referenda. They failed to achieve these aims, but, as a party of youth, they did manage to survive, although support has fluctuated wildly. The mid-1970s saw a drastic drop in support, the party reviving only under a vigorous new leader, Jan Terlouw (1931–   ), who launched a membership drive and broadened the party program to include issues beyond the central call for democratic reform. The D66 first participated in government in 1973–77 in the cabinet of PvdA leader Joop den Uyl. In 1981 the party dropped the "1966" from its name, calling itself

Democrats 66 to keep the brand recognition but remove a reference to a no longer modern year.

Splits broke out among the confessional parties as well. Three members of the Catholic People's Party left in 1968 to form the left-leaning Political Radical Party (Politieke Partij Radikalen, PPR). Coalition-building proved more and more arduous as the number of parties proliferated. The trend culminated in the 1973 cabinet, which took many months of bargaining to assemble and, in the end, amounted to a cumbersome grouping of Catholics, Anti-Revolutionaries, Labor, PPR, and D66. The Christian Historicals declined to participate in such a cobbled-together affair. In remaining aloof, they forced the other denominational parties, all of them suffering from declining support, to think seriously of a closer alliance. Catholics, Anti-Revolutionaries, and Christian Historicals soon joined together in the Christian Democratic Appeal (Christen Democratisch Appèl, CDA), with the word *appeal* used to describe the first step in forming a party. The trio put forward a united list of candidates in 1973, and they won the elections of 1977 under the Catholic leader Andreas van Agt (1931–), who headed three successive governments until 1982. The parties formally merged in 1980 and the CDA title was retained. A party that is not based on the creed of any one church, the CDA restricts its religious pronouncements to general statements in support of the Christian gospel. The party views itself as philosophically positioned between the PvdA on the left and the VVD on the right. Because it pursues a largely centrist agenda, it held about one-third of the seats in the States General in the 1980s and early 1990s. Following the retirement of its popular leader, Prime Minister Rudolph ("Ruud") Lubbers (1939–), in 1994 it fell back below 25 percent of seats.

The PvdA had emerged in the 1970s as the major power player. A social democratic party, it formed the centerpiece of coalition governments from 1973 to 1977 under party leader Joop den Uyl, an idealistic but polarizing politician who sought to radically reform government, society, and the economy. A staunch believer that government action could transform society, he met with growing criticism over budget deficits created in the course of making that effort, and with mounting friction in cabinets that were riddled with personal and ideological conflicts. The PvdA managed to win a third of the seats in the 1980s, but, after 1994, it, like the CDA, saw support drop to less than a quarter of all votes.

Formed after World War II by an amalgamation of prewar liberal parties, the socially liberal and economically conservative People's Party for Freedom and Democracy (Volkspartij voor Vrijheid en Democratie, VVD) garnered a fairly constant 20 percent of seats from the 1970s to the 1990s. Small orthodox Protestant parties secured stable support, but they held very few seats. On the left, the Communists never matched their peak performance in the late 1940s and their meager share shrank further following the collapse of communism in Europe in 1989. Most of the Communists merged with several tiny leftist parties, including the PPR, in the late 1980s to create GreenLeft (GroenLinks), a party with an agenda focused on environmental and pacifist issues. Rump Communists formed the New Communist Party (Nieuwe Communistische Partij) in 1992, whose vote tallies total only in the hundreds and show declining support with each election.

The distinguishing feature of Dutch politics at the turn of the 21st century is the explosion in the number of parties that has occurred in recent years. Groups come and go, some merge with others and some disappear entirely. The proliferation of parties in the wake of the drastic decline of the confessional parties, the end of compulsory voting in 1970, and the lowering of the voting age to 18 in 1972 have all contributed to the unpredictable character of Dutch electoral politics. Voter swings that produce wide gains and losses are now possible, a scenario that stands in marked contrast to the stable, staid political world that prevailed before 1970.

The Dutch Peace Movement: Hollanditis

Neutrality, pacifism, and antimilitarism had played prominent roles in Dutch foreign and defense policies in the past, but, after 1945, the Netherlands disavowed such precepts in opting to join the Western alliance in the wake of the rise of international communism. In 1957 the government of Prime Minister Willem Drees approved placement of U.S. nuclear weapons in the country without even a parliamentary debate. However, social changes in the 1960s and 1970s brought a renewal of old attitudes in public opinion, if not in official policy. Opposition to the Vietnam War sparked public protests, which escalated in intensity following the decision by NATO in 1979 to base 48 Pershing II missiles in the Netherlands. The center-right government of Andreas van Agt (1931–) agreed to do so, but the ensuing public clamor against the move compelled the incoming government under Ruud Lubbers in 1982 to offer compromise proposals that stopped short of actual installation. The peace movement mushroomed with massive street protests, which prompted U.S. historian Walter Laqueur

Students in Amsterdam protest the Vietnam War in 1966, when the city began to emerge as a mecca for international youth. (AP Images)

(1921–) to give a name to the phenomenon: Hollanditis. Lubbers subsequently secured approval for deployment, and the issue became moot in 1987 with the conclusion of the Intermediate-Range Nuclear Forces Treaty between the United States and the Soviet Union, which held that all ground-launched intermediate and shorter-range nuclear missiles held by the two powers in Europe were to be eliminated over the three-year period ending in May 1991.

After 1985 the peace movement waned, but a growing commitment to international peacekeeping emerged. Dutch military forces contributed to UN peacekeeping operations in Lebanon and the Golan Heights, which are ongoing. In the 1990s, experts participated in monitoring the destruction of weapons of mass destruction in Iraq, detecting land mines in Angola and Cambodia, and training local police forces in Albania and Bosnia-Herzegovina.

A force of 400 Dutch peacekeepers (DutchBat) serving with the United Nations Protection Force (UNPROFOR) in Srebrenica, Bosnia-Herzegovina, failed to prevent the seizure by Serbian units of a safe-haven zone for Bosnian Muslims in July 1995. The troops, outfitted with light arms, offered no resistance to penetration of the enclave by Serbs, who massacred an estimated 8,000 Muslim males on July 11, the largest mass murder carried out in Europe since the end of World War II. Reports affirmed that Dutch troops fraternized with the Serbs. Dutch commander Thomas Karremans (1948–) was filmed drinking a toast with war crimes suspect and Serb general Radko Mladić. Defenders of the Dutch attest that the soldiers felt abandoned by their command headquarters in Sarajevo, had limited food and supplies, and, as virtual and even actual hostages of the Serb troops, could have done little to prevent the killings. The incident led to widespread censure of the Dutch force both in the Netherlands and worldwide.

The fall-out from Srebrenica caused the military's reputation to suffer and a drop-off in recruits ensued at a time when the armed forces could ill afford a reduction in ranks. The draft had been ended after the end of the cold war and the military budget slashed in the early 1990s by almost 30 percent. Naval and air force strength had remained stable, but ground forces had fallen by almost half, from 66,200 men and women in 1986 to 33,735 by 1998.

The continuing criticism sparked rising demands that those responsible be called to account, leading to a growing loss of confidence in the government. Several weeks before scheduled elections in May 2002, Prime Minister Wim Kok and his cabinet stepped down, acknowledging the failure of the Dutch mission to resist—even if it could not have prevented—the massacre at Srebrenica.

10

THE NETHERLANDS IN THE TWENTY-FIRST CENTURY: THE TRIUMPHS AND TRIALS OF A TOLERANT SOCIETY

By the close of the 20th century the Dutch no longer felt an unquestioned sense of belonging to a major religion, political party, or ideological group. The toppling of the pillars in the last quarter century produced a pronounced shift away from implicit acceptance of the authority of church, state, employer, interest group, political party, school, and even family, and toward personal independence. Moral standards, long a central characteristic of Dutch bourgeois society, remained preeminently important, although now as defined and practiced by the individual.

Social manners are much more informal today and sexual taboos have been largely discarded. By century's end the birth rate had dropped dramatically, and the large families once so typical of Catholic and orthodox Protestant homes have almost disappeared. A two-children family has become the norm. Once considered disgraceful, divorce is common and many Dutch now live together outside marriage.

Whatever changes have transpired in Dutch society, a centuries-old involvement in world affairs remains. Geography dictates, as it always has, that the Dutch play an active role as global traders and financiers. The Netherlands holds a prominent place in the work of diplomacy—former foreign minister Jaap de Hoop Scheffer (1948–) became secretary-general of NATO in 2004—and takes center stage in international legal affairs. The Hague serves as the seat for the world's four major international tribunals. The International Criminal Tribunal for the Former Yugoslavia, set up in 1993, acts as a UN ad hoc tribunal to try individuals accused of committing crimes during the wars in the former Balkan nation. It aims to complete trials by 2008 and appeals by 2010. Joining the Permanent Court of Arbitration and the International Court of Justice, the International Criminal Court, established in 2002, serves as a permanent tribunal for the prosecution of individuals accused of genocide, war crimes, and crimes against humanity.

The second coalition government led by Jan Pieter Balkenende (1956–) supported the war launched by U.S. and U.K. forces against Saddam Hussein's regime in Iraq in March 2003. The government sent 1,100 troops in June 2003 to assist in restoring security in the southern province of Al-Muthanna and to train some 2,800 Iraqi security officers. The contingent was withdrawn some 20 months later, having suffered two fatalities.

The start of the 21st century saw the Netherlands taking an increasingly active stance in international environmental efforts, a move dictated by growing evidence of the steady rise in global temperatures occasioned by the release of ever-greater amounts of greenhouse gases into the earth's atmosphere. Predictions that future sea levels could rise by alarming degrees, given the dire consequences such an outcome would have for the country, have elicited calls for action. As such, the nation supports internationally agreed limits on emissions of heat-trapping gases, and its commitment to active involvement was given institutional expression in 2000 when the meetings of the sixth Conference of Parties to the UN Framework Convention on Climate Change were held at The Hague. The conference was called to resolve issues that remained outstanding following enactment of the Kyoto Protocol (December 1997), which assigns to signatory countries mandatory emissions limitations by 2012 and which the Netherlands supports. The Hague conference failed to resolve disagreements between and among the European Union members, the United States, and developing countries over setting target dates, among other issues.

Not content to wait on international developments, the country is taking measures to meet the potential threat. Dike repairs and prevention of beach erosion are ongoing, and it is acknowledged that, at some future date, storm surge barriers will have to be raised. A host of innovative plans to counter rising seas are proffered, including a proposal to literally make land from water in creating virtual floating cities, namely, buildings erected on pylons that can float on water.

Attention to global affairs continues as an enduring hallmark of Dutch national life while, at the same time, distinctly more critical viewpoints among the public have emerged. In national and regional affairs, institutions and the attitudes that sustained them, which had come to be widely accepted throughout society in the second half of the 20th century, came under growing scrutiny. The start of the third millennium saw the Dutch taking a more discriminating look at the welfare state, now well entrenched, and the European Union, now well advanced in both form and function.

Just as the by now widely acknowledged liberal character of society deepened with adoption of legislation that made the country an international trend-setter, the issue of immigration has challenged that character description. A rise in ethnic tensions, brought on by a new influx of non-Western newcomers, the outbreak of anti-Western international terrorism, and the shock of political assassination, has led the Dutch, in the face of threats both domestic and foreign, to ponder how best to preserve values such as tolerance, compassion, and compromise in which they have for so long taken so much pride.

A Global Pace-Setter of Social Change

The Netherlands's reputation as one of the world's most progressive societies, which emerged in the 1970s in conjunction with ongoing societal shifts, moved forward after 2000 with passage of legislation making the country a world pioneer in controversial sociocultural issues.

Famous for its tolerance of homosexuality, the Netherlands became the first country in the world to recognize same-sex marriage when, on April 1, 2001, four couples—three male and one female—exchanged vows at Amsterdam's city hall. The new law capped a 15-year campaign during which recognition of equal rights for gays and lesbians garnered growing public acceptance. Same-sex couples also secured the right to adopt children of Dutch nationality.

Official recognition of a more permissive society found further expression in the government's legalizing brothels in 2000. The government sought, by doing so, to make it easier to tax and regulate the prostitution carried on in Amsterdam's red light district, which has been in existence since the 17th century and has long been tolerated by officials to such a degree that it has become one of the city's famed tourist sites. To combat the crime spawned by the brothels, the city passed a law in 2003 to deny or revoke licenses of operators whose premises were suspected of engaging in money laundering and other illegal financial activities. In November 2006 the city shut down 101 of the 350 existing prostitution "windows," where scantily dressed women beckon tourists as they once did sailors, as part of an ongoing campaign to crack down on petty crime, including human trafficking and drug dealing.

In 1976 the government legalized the sale of soft drugs in coffee-houses, of which there are about 700 in the country, half of them in Amsterdam. Large-scale dealing, production, and import and export of marijuana and hashish are still prosecuted, but the government has adopted a policy of nonenforcement (*gedoogbeleid*) on sales to individuals over 18 for personal use. Foreign drug tourists have become major buyers and, because of stricter drug policies in neighboring countries and the fact that absence of border controls makes detection virtually impossible, the government has lowered the per-purchase amount of soft drugs that can be sold to an individual per each purchase from 30 grams (1 oz.) to five grams (.18 oz.); however, those in possession of the larger amount are not prosecuted.

The country's maritime geography makes it an important transit point for drugs entering Europe. It is a major producer and exporter of amphetamines, and consumption of illicit hard drugs remains a problem, which the government combats by employing both an active narcotics trafficking interdiction effort and an extensive demand reduction program that reaches about 90 percent of the country's approximately 26,000 hard drug users. The number of hard drug addicts has stabilized in recent years, and the Netherlands has the lowest number of drug-related deaths in Europe.

On April 1, 2002, the Termination of Life on Request and Assisted Suicide (Review Procedures) Act took effect; it legalized euthanasia and physician-assisted suicide under carefully prescribed criteria. The law stipulates that requests must be voluntarily made by patients over the age of 12 who are fully cognizant of the action contemplated and who, based on doctor consultations, are suffering unbearable pain from incurable disease. Supported by wide margins of Dutch society, the law codified procedures practiced for 30 years and it represents one of the world's most precedent-setting measures.

Opposition to these steps has come largely from the churches. However, even the once formidable Christian congregations count many adherents who support the positions of the majority social libertarian Dutch.

Welfare State under Debate

By the third quarter of the 20th century the Netherlands had put in place one of the world's most advanced welfare states. Social security, old age, unemployment, disability, and health insurance became very nearly universal in scope, financed from both public and private monies. Generous, egalitarian social and economic programs grew both from steady prosperity and from the willingness of all parties to cooperate in policymaking.

By the 1980s, however, the country began to realize that, following two decades of ballooning premiums and payments, the welfare state was proving too expensive. By that decade expenditures for social insurance, social services, and pension outlays and insurance accounted for approximately one-third of gross national product. Calls for change came in the wake of budget deficits brought on by the failure of revenues from taxes and social insurance premiums to sufficiently fund programs. The ruling coalition of the Christian Democratic Appeal (CDA) and People's Party for Freedom and Democracy (VVD), in control from 1982 to 1994 under Prime Minister Ruud Lubbers, instituted a "no-nonsense" commitment to reducing the role of the state in the socioeconomy. Calling for "more market, less government," Lubbers's center-right coalitions—in power for the longest period in modern Dutch history—uncoupled benefits and civil service salaries from wage rises in the private sector, cut civil service salaries, and reduced sickness, unemployment, and disability benefits from 80 percent of the last salary/wage earned to 70 percent.

The attitude of compromise that had built the welfare state also underlay reforming efforts. In the 1980s growing deficits and an unemployment figure that had grown to more than 600,000 required major economic reform, a call advanced most especially by the Central Planning Bureau, created in 1976 to provide economic advice and which now issued an appeal for wage restraint. The so-called polder model began to emerge following the Wassenaar Accords of 1982, under which the government, unions, and employers reached agreement on economic revitalization, which included policies of full employment and budget cuts as part of an effort to strengthen export earnings. Deregulation, decentralization, and privatization became watchwords of the government. Large-scale state subsidies to unprofitable businesses were stopped. Government deficits were reduced by almost half, dropping from 11 percent of national income in 1983 to 6.5 percent in 1986.

Based on the same spirit of consensus-building that had heretofore characterized the society of the pillars, the model was perfected when center-left "purple" coalition governments were crafted for eight years beginning in 1994 between the two traditional antagonists in Dutch politics, the "red" social democratic PvdA, under its leader Willem ("Wim") Kok (1938–), and the "blue" free-market–favoring VVD, which achieved the best electoral results in its history in 1994 (winning 28 seats). The ruling coalition included the D66 with 24 seats. That party had evolved in the 1990s into a grouping that included two ideological currents—radical democrats and progressive liberals—and it viewed itself as the glue that held the coalition between the PvdA on the left and the VVD on the right together. The exclusion of the CDA marked the first time since 1918 that no Christian party participated in the government.

The polder model's formula of compromise reached through consultations is credited for rapid economic growth in the 1990s. Under the purple coalition's motto of "work, work, work," employment shot up, and the model drew considerable international attention to the Dutch "economic miracle." However, steady progress gave way to a severe boom-and-bust cycle after 2000, with growth falling from 7 percent in 2000 to only 2 percent in 2003. A drop in revenues combined with worries about growing global competition, an aging population, and overly generous benefits programs led to spending cuts and calls for further welfare reform.

The Christian Democrats won the 2002 elections and a coalition was put in place led by Jan Peter Balkenende, a former city councilor in Amstelveen and professor at the Free University of Amsterdam. The government moved to make a break with the polder model. Costly early retirement programs were abolished, work benefits scaled back, tax cuts put in place, and the health care system, for which co-payments for services were introduced in 1997, opened to private insurers, who could now compete with the public system in service provision.

These changes, together with imposition of wage restraints, proved too much for the unions, which, increasingly convinced that the public sector had been neglected, balked at further bargaining. Widespread strikes broke out in 2004, including 200,000 protesters who gathered in Amsterdam in October. Ongoing reform will prove necessary given that international competition will grow, putting pressure on businesses operating in a high-tax, high-wage country like the Netherlands. In addition, the number of part-time, temporary, and independent workers is rising, which will require adjustments to social security, and the aging of the population will produce strains in the form of soaring costs met by insufficient revenues.

While agreement is general that higher labor participation, in both numbers of workers and hours worked, is essential, the question of whether the country can continue to afford expensive welfare programs evokes lively debate. Lower taxes will produce more jobs but also fewer funds for welfare, leading to greater income inequality; this would depart from the universal character of the system, long a source of pride to the egalitarian-minded Dutch. A recent innovative reform involves adoption of an individual life-cycle savings scheme (*levensloopregeling*) under which workers can place a percentage of their gross wages in savings accounts, to be drawn down for purposes that amount to unpaid leave, including child, elderly, and sickness care, schooling, or early retirement.

Civil servants demonstrate in Museum Square, Amsterdam, on June 9, 2005, to protest declining social benefits and wages. (AP Images)

A Closer Investigation of European Integration

The Netherlands has been a pioneer and a staunch advocate of greater European cooperation. The country was a founding member of all the organizations created after World War II to knit Europe's nations more closely together. The city of Maastricht served as the site for negotiating, and for signing on February 1, 1992, the Maastricht Treaty (formally the Treaty on European Union), which led to creation of the European Union (EU) and its common currency, the euro, that became the unit of exchange on January 1, 2002.

A small country with an economy geared overwhelmingly to exports, the Netherlands has benefited immensely from access to Europe-wide markets. Three-quarters of exports go to other member-states and the country is the EU's second-largest agricultural exporter after France.

While the Dutch remain committed to regional integration, out of both conviction and necessity, the growth in power of what are perceived to be unelected and unaccountable Brussels-based bureaucrats out of touch with the country has led to a much more critical examination of continental cooperation. In a referendum on June 1, 2005, 61.6 percent of voters rejected a proposed constitution for Europe. The Dutch negative vote, coming just days after French voters also turned down the document, led to a call by the European Council for a period of reflection before moving ahead.

Debate is ongoing about the future path of the EU. Opinions revolve around issues that include fears of loss of national identity and sovereignty and of insufficient democratic checks on EU institutions. The exodus of industry to lower-cost locales—electronics giant Philips now produces light bulbs in Poland, where labor costs are lower—and the influx of low-wage workers from new member-states occasioned by the free movement of capital, labor, services, and industry also remain worrisome concerns.

Cultural Clash and Anti-Immigrant Backlash

No issue in recent years has proved more troubling than that of accommodation of newcomers. The presence of large numbers of immigrants from non-Western countries and the problems encountered in their assimilation into the larger society has sparked an intense debate that goes to the heart of who the Dutch believe themselves to be as a people.

A nation that has always derived great pride in being a place that has welcomed and sheltered the displaced and persecuted, the Netherlands, however, never confronted large influxes of arrivals from non-Western lands until after World War II. Those who came from former Dutch colonies posed few problems, although they were not universally welcomed and assimilation took place only slowly. Activists of South Moluccan origin, frustrated over poor living conditions and the failure of the Dutch government to support their goal of an independent homeland in their South Asian islands, waged a terrorist campaign in the mid-1970s that included train hijackings and hostage takings. Roundly condemned for their actions, which included the murder of several hostages, they met immediate suppression, and tensions soon subsided. Well-educated Surinamese settled in the country before 1975, and poorer immigrants totaling almost a third of Suriname's population arrived after the country's independence; although far from complete in the latter case, assimilation has proven successful.

Workers who came from southern Europe in the late 1940s and 1950s have largely returned home. Such is not the case with immigrants from North Africa and Turkey, who began arriving in the mid-1960s in search of better economic opportunities. Their numbers reached a peak in 1970–71 and they continued to enter the country throughout the succeeding decade. Filling primarily menial labor jobs, they remained aloof from the larger society, many of them failing to learn Dutch while maintaining the customs and practicing the Islamic faith of their homelands. They were "guest workers" who were supposed to stay temporarily and so they were not regarded as immigrants. However, they did not return home; rather, they brought their families to the Netherlands to join them. By the early 1980s the government finally recognized that guest workers had turned into immigrants. Disdain grew among some elements of the native population who viewed the new immigrants as culturally exclusive, resented the drain they were perceived to be on the country's social services, and began to believe they took jobs away from the ethnic Dutch, despite minority unemployment rates equaling approximately one-quarter of their population. Instances of theft, drug dealing, and street violence, fueled by pervasive unemployment and poverty, grew in immigrant areas, which added to public anxiety. At the same time, the rise of a militant anti-Western Islam and acts of international terrorism committed on its behalf have led to growing fears that the children of Muslim immigrants, now young adults, pose a potential threat to the nation's secular, democratic traditions. The Dutch have always assumed that immigrants will assimilate into their society, and, because previous modern-day arrivals all spoke Dutch and came from former colonies, their expectations were largely met. They failed to understand why these newcomers, who came of their own choice, did not readily adapt to Dutch habits and customs.

As early as 1994 voters in opinion polls named the problem of the integration of minorities as the nation's most urgent political issue. By the end of the decade anti-immigrant sentiment had coalesced around Pim Fortuyn (1948–2002). A charismatic, openly gay politician, Fortuyn joined the Livable Netherlands (Leefbaar Nederland) Party in 2001, one of a number of independent political parties that began to emerge in the 1990s. Created in 1999 by former radio producer Jan Nagel (1939–) and singer, songwriter, and radio host Henk Westbroek (1952–), the party saw itself as an antiestablishment force, appealing to independents in calling for a reduction in bureaucratization, greater democratization in public life through such tools as increased referendums, and stricter policies on asylum seekers. Calling Islam "a backward culture," Fortuyn advocated stringent restrictions on immigration, including an end to admission of Muslims, and he garnered growing support, taking

PIM FORTUYN

Wilhelmus Simon Petrus, "Pim," Fortuyn (February 19, 1948–May 6, 2002) was born in Velsen, North Holland, the son of a traveling salesman and a doting mother. He studied sociology, earned a doctorate, and taught at the University of Groningen and Erasmus University. An active public speaker and prolific writer of books and newspaper editorials, he gravitated toward politics. Formerly a communist and a member of the social democratic PvdA, Fortuyn joined the Livable Netherlands (Leefbaar Nederland) Party in 2001. He championed Dutch nationalism over a European identity and called on immigrants to conform to Dutch customs and traditions, but it was his controversial views on Islam, expressed in a series of newspaper interviews, that swiftly drew national attention. He told the *Rotterdams Dagblad* that: "I am . . . in favor of a cold war with Islam. I see Islam as an extraordinary threat, as a hostile religion." He called for closing the border to Muslims if legally possible.

Labeled a far right extremist by mainstream politicians and media, Fortuyn was ejected from his party. He founded his own party, List Pim Fortuyn, in February 2002. The party won a third of the seats in local elections in Rotterdam in March.

Running as a candidate in the May 2002 national elections for the Second Chamber, he was assassinated nine days before the vote in Hilversum by Volkert van der Graaf, an animal-rights activist who viewed Fortuyn as a right-wing extremist. The most sensational political murder since the lynching of the de Witt brothers in 1672, Fortuyn's death elevated him to superstar status. Tens of thousands gathered

with him many of Livable Netherlands's supporters when he formed his own party, List Pim Fortuyn (Lijst Pim Fortuyn, LPF) on February 11, 2002. His assassination on May 6, 2002, by an angry opponent who viewed him as a threat, produced a spontaneous outburst of grief and anger and shocked the country in making starkly real long-simmering sentiments of cultural unease.

Fortuyn's LPF party went on to win 26 seats in the May elections, and the party formed part of the first governing coalition led by Jan Peter Balkenende and his CDA party in July. Squabbling within the LPF led to the coalition's breakup after only 86 days, however, and new elections were called. Other political parties scrambled to adopt some of the LPF's policies with a view to attracting voters, but in the elections held for his funeral. Lionized as a political martyr, his LPF party made an unprecedented debut in parliament, winning 26 seats.

Political support of the party has dropped off, but Fortuyn remains a compelling icon, whose contradictory character continues to fascinate. An openly gay man who boasted of having sex with Moroccan boys, he never abandoned the Roman Catholicism of his birth. A staunch supporter of modern-day liberal values, he evoked nostalgia for simpler times, when the country faced no threats from foreigners or from pan-European and global interests. A flamboyant figure who stood in marked contrast to the popular image of the sober, bourgeois, consensus-

Pim Fortuyn (AP Images)

seeking Dutch politician, Fortuyn shook up the complacent political scene. He reflected, in both his person and his policies, the complex, contrasting realities of today's society. A television poll in November 2004 rated him the greatest individual in Dutch history.

on January 22, 2003, the traditional parties recovered strength. The LPF dropped to eight seats and the Labor Party (PvdA) jumped from 23 to 42. A coalition—the second led by Balkenende—took office on May 27, 2003, composed of the CDA, which remained the largest party, the VVD, and the Democrats '66 (D66).

The first political assassination in modern Dutch history (the events of World War II excepted), Pim Fortuyn's death was followed in November 2004 by the murder in Amsterdam of filmmaker Theo van Gogh (1947–2004), great-grandnephew of the artist. Van Gogh was shot by Mohammed Bouyeri, the son of Moroccan immigrants, for making a movie with Dutch politician Ayaan Hirsi Ali (1967–   ) that "insulted the prophet Muhammad." The killing led to shock waves anew and, with it, the Netherlands joined the company of other Western countries that have experienced violent attacks by adherents of a militant Islam.

Amid official recriminations over the failure of civil authorities to prevent the murder, all major political parties called for more restrictive controls on immigration. The government has tightened citizenship requirements, and, in January 2006, parliament approved passage of legislation mandating that newcomers take examinations to test their knowledge of Dutch and of the history, culture, and political institutions of the country. Those who fail do not gain admittance. The Netherlands is the first country in Europe to establish such admissions tests. The government has also banned the wearing of full-face helmets and masks and full-length veils, such as the tentlike Muslim burqa, in public places, and it has ordered the detention of asylum seekers while their applications for entry to the country are reviewed.

Many moderate Muslims find themselves caught in the middle. They have urged their coreligionists to adapt to Dutch social and cultural mores, but their calls, while meeting vehement opposition from radical Islamicists, have not always been welcomed by the general public, segments of whom regard them with suspicion. Moroccan-born politician and deputy mayor of Amsterdam Ahmed Aboutaleb (1961–) has urged Muslims to either adopt Dutch ways of life or leave the country. Shortly after van Gogh's murder, it was revealed that he had been placed on a death list by the same extremist cell whose member Bouyeri had targeted van Gogh. Aboutaleb, along with Dutch politicians including Mayor Job Cohen of Amsterdam (1947–) and right-wing populist Geert Wilders (1963–), now move about accompanied by bodyguards, an entirely new phenomenon in the Netherlands.

Balkenende's third coalition continued the policies pursued by earlier governments in carrying out civil service reform, toughening immigration laws, and putting in place historically large public spending cuts. Issues of socioeconomic reform together with immigration framed the debate during the campaign for parliamentary elections held on November 22, 2006. The elections were necessitated by the departure of the D66 members from the ruling coalition on June 30, 2006. Prime Minister Balkenende immediately submitted his resignation, announced early elections, and set up a minority cabinet, which he headed, made up of the CDA and VVD parties.

The government broke up because of a political upheaval engendered by controversial author, filmmaker, and politician Hirsi Ali. Somali-born Hirsi Ali acquired asylum in the Netherlands in 1992 and subse-

Muslim men praying on Dam Square, Amsterdam, on February 11, 2006, in a demonstration against publication in a Danish newspaper of cartoons depicting the prophet Muhammad (AP Images)

quently secured citizenship. An outspoken critic of Islam, she wrote the script for *Submission,* a low-budget film directed by van Gogh, and a note pinned to his body warning her of death threats prompted her to go into hiding. Still, she managed to serve in parliament as a VVD member from January 2003 to June 2006. Admitting that she entered the country under a false name and date of birth, she resigned from parliament and signed a letter of regret that she subsequently said had been coerced from her by Minister for Immigration Rita Verdonk (1955–   ) of the VVD, the party that has taken the lead in tightening immigration laws. The prime minister's waffling on whether or not Hirsi Ali retained her Dutch citizenship sparked the cabinet crisis.

The elections saw the CDA retain its position as the largest party in the Second Chamber in gaining 41 seats, but the center of power shifted from right-leaning to left and center-left parties. The VVD and D66 lost seats, as did the PvdA, the largest opposition party in the outgoing parliament. The biggest winner was the Socialist Party (Socialistische Partij, SP). Founded in 1971 as a Maoist party, it has emerged, together with GreenLeft, as a major left-wing party in the wake of the move in the 1990s by the social democratic PvdA toward the political center.

A conservative-leaning trend in politics has emerged with the appearance of several new parties. They include the ChristianUnion (ChristenUnie, CU), founded in 2002. An orthodox Protestant party in the tradition of Dutch confessional groupings, it espouses a conservative stance on ethical issues and a center-left position on social, economic, and environmental matters. The conservative Party for Freedom (Partij voor de Vrijheid, PVV) won nine seats in the 2006 elections. Founded in 2004, the new party is largely the personal vehicle of Geert Wilders, who broke with the VVD in opposition to the latter's support for negotiations to consider admission of Turkey to the EU. A populist in the image of Fortuyn, Wilders calls for immigrant restrictions and advocates for the rights of the individual, which he says have been neglected by elitist, left-leaning politicians. A new group with an entirely new focus appeared with the Party of the Animals (Partij voor de Dieren, PvdD), which won two seats. Only recently formed, the party is the first in the world to win parliamentary seats with a program centered primarily on promotion of animal rights. Another two seats were garnered by the orthodox Protestant ultra-right Reformed Political Party (SGP). In 2005 a district court in The Hague threatened to cut off state subsidies to the party because it refused to admit women to membership. The party has

	Election Results for the Second Chamber in 2003 and 2006			
	2003 Number of Seats	Vote Percentage	2006 Number of Seats	Vote Percentage
CDA	44	28.6	41	26.5
PvdA	42	27.3	33	21.2
SP	9	6.3	25	16.6
VVD	28	17.9	22	14.6
PVV	–	–	9	5.9
LPF	8	5.7	–	–
GL	8	5.1	7	4.6
CU	3	2.1	6	4.0
D66	6	4.1	3	2.0
PvdD	–	–	2	1.8
SGP	2	1.6	2	1.6

appealed the decision, but in June 2006, under its leader Bas van der Vlies (1942–   ), the SGP lifted the ban on women.

Following the elections considerable attention was given to a report issued by a citizens watch group that revealed widespread security flaws in computer voting machines. New security measures were put in place mandating installation of new, improved machines, which some municipalities will use in future elections. Other localities, including Amsterdam, will switch to the traditional pen and red pencil manner of marking ballots.

Protracted negotiations lasting three months led to installation by Queen Beatrix on February 22, 2007, of a fourth Balkenende cabinet in which the CDA, the PvdA, and the Christian Union parties succeeded in crafting a coalition government. Although the PvdA did not participate in the previous government and although it lost support in the election, the party embodied the overall swing leftward revealed in the election results at the same time that its move in recent years toward the center made it a workable coalition partner with the CDA, the largest party. The Christian Union, the other coalition member, shares these two parties' left-of-center positions on social, economic, and environmental concerns.

The issues that dominated the 2006 elections will continue to shape the political discourse. Economic reform and immigration both necessitate a reexamination of cherished social values. High levels of guaranteed economic and social security, long perceived as a mainstay of the modern state, now require a reassessment in view of the realities of global competition and interdependence. Accustomed to believing that multiculturalism flourishes in the Netherlands in an environment of tolerance, secularism, and pluralism, the Dutch have begun to question to what extent their society can accommodate those living among them who do not share such values. Diligent, industrious, and enterprising, the Dutch have been cultivating these values ever since they first began to wrest their land from the ocean's threat. At the same time, battling the sea compelled them, by necessity, to seek consensus and to come together in cooperative efforts to sustain life in their low-lying homeland. Later, that same unity of purpose brought them victory in their war of independence. And yet that struggle was waged to restore and ensure respect for the rights of each of the individual—and very different—provinces. The preservation of the "particular" while working to uphold the "general" is a theme that runs throughout Dutch history, seen in the rise of the pillars and the concurrent need for compromise. In the same way, the Dutch today take pride in the values and beliefs they share as citizens of the Netherlands while, at the same time, they give to the individual a wide latitude—some would say the widest in the world—to believe differently and to act independently.

Contrasts are a hallmark of Dutch history and paradoxes abound. The nation was a republic and yet it honored a family of princes. It styled itself the "United" Provinces but there were few central institutions and no national bureaucracy. Provinces and municipalities jealously guarded their privileges and traditions, while geography dictated they open themselves to the world. A steady stream of human traffic—visitors and refugees arriving, explorers and merchants departing—turned Dutch cities into cosmopolitan crossroads.

Old and new coexist comfortably here. Computer and cable television screens flicker inside 17th-century townhouses. Speedboats and yachts jostle flat-bottomed barges and weathered fishing smacks on the water-riven landscape. The ringing of cell phones mingles with the jingling of bicycle bells on cycling lanes and paths.

Yesterday's world leaders in creating and shaping practices and principles that define Western society—democracy, capitalism, freedoms of creed and expression—the Dutch today pioneer innovative social policies, control multinational economic wealth, and cooperate fully in international humanitarian, environmental, and peace-keeping endeavors. One constant abides across the ages. The Dutch were, and they remain, important global actors. They show that great nations are not defined by physical size, that, indeed, a people relatively few in number inhabiting a small place can play a great role on the world's stage.

Appendix 1

RULERS OF THE NETHERLANDS

The United Provinces – Stadholders of the House of Orange-Nassau in Holland and Zeeland*

1572–84	William of Orange ("the Silent")
1585–1625	Maurits
1625–47	Frederick Henry
1647–50	William II
1650–72	*First Stadholderless Period*
1672–1702	William III (last of the house in the direct line)
1702–47	*Second Stadholderless Period*
1747–51	William IV
1751–95	William V
1795–1806	Batavian Republic
1806–10	Louis Napoleon, king of Holland
1810–15	French Empire

*The same stadholder in Holland and Zeeland usually (but not always) held the post also in Utrecht, Overijssel, and Gelderland. The same was true in Drenthe and Groningen, but to a lesser extent.

The Kingdom of the Netherlands

House of Orange-Nassau

1815–40	William I (abdicated; d. 1843)
1840–49	William II
1849–90	William IV
1890–1948	Wilhelmina (abdicated; d. 1962)*
1948–80	Juliana (abdicated; d. 2003)
1980–	Beatrix

*Emma of Waldeck-Pyrmont, Wilhelmina's mother, served as regent 1890–98

Prime Ministers of the Netherlands, 1945–

Willem Schermerhorn	1945–46	VDB, PvdA
Louis Beel	1946–48	KVP
Willem Drees	1948–58	PvdA
Louis Beel	1958–59	KVP
Jan de Quay	1959–63	KVP
Victor Marijnen	1963–65	KVP
Joseph Cals	1965–66	KVP
Jelle Zijlstra	1966–67	ARP
Petrus ("Piet") de Jong	1967–71	KVP
Maarten Biesheuvel	1971–73	ARP
Johannes ("Joop") den Uyl	1973–77	PvdA
Andreas ("Dries") van Agt	1977–82	CDA
Rudolph ("Ruud") Lubbers	1982–94	CDA
Willem ("Wim") Kok	1994–2002	PvdA
Jan Peter Balkenende	2002–	CDA

ARP	Anti-Revolutionary Party
CDA	Christian Democratic Appeal
KVP	Catholic People's Party
PvdA	Labor Party
VDB	Freethinking Democratic League

APPENDIX 2

BASIC FACTS ABOUT THE NETHERLANDS

Official Name
Kingdom of the Netherlands (Koninkrijk der Nederlanden)

Government
The Netherlands is a constitutional monarchy (since 1815) and parliamentary democracy (since 1848). The monarch is head of state and the prime minister is head of the government. Parliament is divided between a Second Chamber (lower house), the more important body, and a First Chamber (upper house). The Second Chamber consists of 150 members elected under proportional representation every four years, but governments rarely serve the full term. The First Chamber consists of 75 members, one-third of whom are elected by provincial assemblies every two years. The First Chamber can only accept or reject laws.

The Netherlands is a multiparty system, with coalition governments the norm. Major political parties include the Labor Party (PvdA), Christian Democratic Appeal (CDA), Democrats '66 (D66), People's Party for Freedom and Democracy (VVD), GreenLeft, Socialist Party (SP), and List Pim Fortuyn.

Coalitions are formed on the basis of two stages:

1. Information. An *informateur,* usually a veteran politician not active on the current political scene, is appointed by the monarch after consulting with the chairpersons of the parliamentary parties in the Second Chamber. He or she investigates possible coalition combinations.

2. Formation. A *formateur,* appointed by the monarch, conducts negotiations among the parties that have expressed a willingness to participate in a cabinet. The *formateur* in traditionally the leader of the largest political party taking part in the discussions and, thus, the prospective prime minister.

A civil law system is practiced. There are 19 district courts, 5 courts of appeal, 2 other appeals bodies (Central Appeals Tribunal and Trade and Industry Appeals Tribunal), and 1 Supreme Court. Courts base their decisions on government laws, case law, local customs and conventions, and international treaties.

Political Divisions

Provinces
Twelve provinces plus the Netherlands Antilles and Aruba.

Capital
Amsterdam; The Hague is the seat of government.

Geography

Area
The Netherlands covers an area of 16,033 square miles (41,526 sq km), including 419 square miles (1,085 sq km) of land reclaimed from the IJsselmeer.

Boundaries
The Netherlands is bounded on the north and west by the North Sea, on the south by Belgium, and on the east by Germany.

Topography
The Netherlands is low-lying, with almost half the surface less than 3.3 feet (1 m) above sea level, and flat. Much of the west and southwest lie below sea level, protected from flooding by dunes along the North Sea coast and along the rivers by dikes. An elaborate system of dunes and dikes (Delta Works) is in place along the coasts of the southwest islands. The entire province of Flevoland consists of reclaimed land. The great rivers—Rhine, Waal, Maas—drain much of western Europe's hinterland and bisect the country's center. The Scheldt River detaches the mainland part of Zeeland (Dutch Flanders) from the rest of the

country. Traveling west to east, coastal flatlands and marshes give way to sandy plains and heathlands. Low ridges and rolling hills are found to the south and east where they rise gradually to 1,000 feet (300 m) in the extreme southeast.

Climate
Despite its northern latitude, the Netherlands has a maritime climate tempered by the North Sea and predominant southwesterly winds that give it cool summers and mild winters. The average temperature in January is 35 degrees Fahrenheit (2 degrees Celsius) and in July 63 degrees Fahrenheit (7 degrees Celsius). Cloudy to partly cloudy days predominate and rainfall averages between 700 and 800 millimeters with highest amounts along the coast. Snow and ice occur, but they are not assured every year.

Highest Elevation
The Vaalserberg, at 1,053 feet (321 m), in the extreme southeast corner of the country.

Demographics

Population
The population of the Netherlands is 16,357,000 (est. 2007). It is the 23rd most densely populated country in the world, with about 393 inhabitants per square kilometer (1,023 sq. mi.). Many of the 22 countries with a higher density are tiny microstates, and of countries with larger territories and populations, only Bangladesh, South Korea, and Taiwan are more densely populated. Growth in population has declined steadily with the rising standard of living during the last half century and is stagnant (0.57 percent, 2004 est.) today, the result of a below-maintenance-level birthrate, a growing death rate, and a higher emigration than immigration rate. Life expectancy at birth is 78.28 years. The Dutch are physically the tallest people in the world, with an average height of 6 feet (1.83 m) for adult males and 5 feet 7 inches (1.70 m) for adult females. There is universal literacy. The Dutch are ethnically homogeneous (80.8 percent Dutch) but about 12 percent come from diverse origins, and they include: Indonesian (Indo-European, Indo-Dutch, and Moluccan, 2.4 percent), German (2.4 percent), Turkish (2.2 percent), Surinamese (2.0 percent), Moroccan (1.9 percent), Indian (1.5 percent), and Antillean and Aruban (0.8 percent).

Major Cities

Amsterdam is the largest city, with a population of 743,027 (est. 2006), Amsterdam, Rotterdam, The Hague, and Utrecht are the four largest cities. Although each has less than 1 million inhabitants, they all lie in close proximity and, when taken together, they form the Randstad ("rim city"), with more than 7.5 million residents. About 90 percent of the Dutch live in cities.

Language

Dutch is spoken by almost everyone in the Netherlands. Frisian, along with Dutch, is an official language in the province of Friesland. Limburgisch is recognized as a minority language in the province of Limburg. Low Saxon dialects (e.g., Gronings) are spoken in northern and eastern areas. The Dutch are among the world's most multilingual people. It is estimated that about 85 percent of the population possess at least a basic knowledge of English; 55–60 percent of German; and 35 percent of French.

Religion

Approximately 34 percent of the Dutch profess themselves to be Roman Catholics, 20 percent Protestant (predominantly Dutch Reformed), and 8 percent "other religions." Most Catholics live in the southern provinces and most Protestants in the northern. About 42 percent declare themselves as unaffiliated with any church. There are about 920,000 Muslims and 30,000 to 40,000 Jews.

Economy

Gross Domestic Product

Total: $625,271 billion (2004 est.) (16th in the world).
Per capita: $38,618 (2005 est.) (10th in the world).

Currency

Euro (€) since January 1, 2002, which replaced the Dutch guilder.

Agricultural Products

Food processing, fishing, potatoes, sugar beets, dairy products (milk, butter, margarine), vegetables, fresh cut flowers and plants, flower bulbs. The Netherlands ranks third in the world in the value of agricultural exports, behind the United States and France.

Industrial Activity

Petroleum refining, chemicals, electrical machinery and equipment, metal and engineering products, microelectronics.

Trade

More than two-thirds of gross domestic product is derived from merchandise trade. The chief trading partners are Germany, Belgium, the United Kingdom, France, and the United States. In 2005 exports amounted to approximately $365.1 billion and imports to $326.6 billion. The largest foreign investors are the United States (18.5 percent), United Kingdom (14.1 percent), Germany (12 percent), and Belgium (10.1 percent).

Media

Newspapers

The largest newspapers are *De Telegraaf* (Amsterdam; conservative); *Algemeen Dagblad* (Rotterdam; moderate Protestant); *De Volkskrant* (Amsterdam; left-of-center, Catholic); *NRC-Handelsblad* (Rotterdam; liberal, business-oriented); *Trouw* (Amsterdam; left-of-center, nondenominational).

APPENDIX 3

CHRONOLOGY

From Early Settlements to Frankish Rule

c. 5300–1550 B.C.E.	Neolithic period; first farmers
c. 1400–750 B.C.E.	Bronze Age
c. 750–57 B.C.E.	Iron Age
57 B.C.E.	Julius Caesar begins conquest of Belgian tribes
12 B.C.E.	Frisians fall under Roman dominion
28 C.E.	Frisian revolt against Rome
48	Utrecht founded as a Roman castellum
68–69	Batavians revolt against Rome
c. 256	Frankish tribes invade
c. 406	Germanic peoples arrive in large numbers
c. 455	Roman rule ends
c. 500–600	Franks converted to Christianity
561	Low Countries south of the Rhine become Austrasia, a Frankish subkingdom
c. 678–785	Frisians converted to Christianity
800	Charlemagne crowned emperor; his territories include all of the Netherlands
834–36	Dorestad devastated by recurrent Viking raids
843	Frankish Empire divided; Netherlands becomes part of Middle Kingdom under Lothair I
882–885	Vikings rule in the Rhine delta
916	Dirk I becomes first count of Holland
959	Netherlands becomes part of Duchy of Lower Lotharingia

Political Strife and the Rise of Urban Life

c. 1075–1100	Holland, Gelderland, Groningen, and Frisia emerge as autonomous counties
c. 1100	Amsterdam founded

1200s	Town charters granted across the Netherlands
1231	Emperor Frederick II recognizes de facto independence of local rulers
1296	Murder of Floris V, count of Holland and Zeeland
1306	Amsterdam granted municipal charter
1349–50	Black Death
1421, November 18–19	St. Elizabeth's Day flood
1432	Holland and Zeeland pass to House of Burgundy
1464	First meeting of the States General at Bruges
1473	Charles the Bold conquers Gelderland
1477	Holland and Zeeland pass to House of Habsburg; Mary of Burgundy grants the Great Privilege
c. 1500	Modern Dutch language gradually begins to emerge

Wars of Religion and Emancipation

1515	Charles V reigns; purchase of lordship of Friesland
1528	Lordship of bishops of Utrecht transferred to Habsburgs
1531	Administrative and legal reforms of Charles V; Lutheranism proscribed
1543	Habsburgs acquire Gelderland
1550s	Doctrines of John Calvin spread widely
1555	Charles V retires, succeeded by his son Philip II
1562	League of noblemen present petition to Margaret of Parma asking for respect for local privileges and an end to religious persecution
1566	Iconoclastic Fury: churches ransacked
1567	Duke of Alva arrives
1568	Beginning of Dutch Revolt (Eighty Years' War)
1572	Sea beggars capture Briel and other towns; William of Orange appointed by provinces as stadholder of Holland, Zeeland, and Utrecht
1574	Spanish siege of Leiden lifted
1579, January 23	Union of Utrecht formed
1581	Act of Abjuration severs obedience to Philip II
1584, July 10	William of Orange assassinated
1585	Amsterdam begins to replace Antwerp as the commercial metropolis of northern Europe

1585–1625	Maurits of Nassau stadholder of Holland, Zeeland, Utrecht, Gelderland, and Overijssel
1590–97	Spanish driven from northern Netherlands
1595–97	First Dutch voyage to the East Indies
1602	Dutch East India Company is formed
1609	Start of Twelve Years' Truce; de facto independence of Dutch Republic

Resplendent Republic

1619	Synod of Dort; Oldenbarnevelt is executed
1621	Dutch West India Company is formed
1624	New Amsterdam (New York) is founded
1625–47	Frederick Henry stadholder of Holland, Zeeland, Utrecht, Gelderland, and Overijssel
1628	Admiral Piet Hein captures the Spanish silver fleet
1630–54	Dutch occupy Brazil
1632	Recapture of Maastricht
1642	Voyage of Abel Tasman to Australia and New Zealand
1647–50	William II stadholder of Holland, Zeeland, Utrecht, Gelderland, and Overijssel
1648	Treaty of Münster; de jure recognition of Dutch Republic's independence
1650–72	First stadholderless period in all provinces but Friesland and Groningen
1652–54	First Anglo-Dutch War
1652	Dutch land at the Cape of Good Hope
1662	Dutch driven from Taiwan (Formosa)
1664	New Netherland falls to the English
1665–67	Second Anglo-Dutch War
1672	Johan de Witt is executed
1672–74	Third Anglo-Dutch War
1672–1702	William III stadholder of Holland, Zeeland, Utrecht, Gelderland, and Overijssel
1688–1702	William III rules England with his wife Mary following the Glorious Revolution

Dynamo in Decline

| 1702–47 | Second stadholderless period in all provinces but Friesland |

1713	Treaty of Utrecht signed with France
1715	Third Barrier Treaty with Austria
1747	French invasion; stadholderate is restored and made hereditary
1747–51	William IV (William Friso) stadholder of all provinces
1751–95	William V stadholder of all provinces
1780–84	Fourth Anglo-Dutch War
1780–87	Period of the Patriots
1782	*Sara Burgerhart,* first Dutch novel, is published
1787	Prussians invade and restore William V to full power
1795	French invade; Batavian Republic proclaimed

From Republic to Kingdom to Empire

1806	Louis Bonaparte proclaimed king of Holland
1809	Civil and penal codes enacted
1810	Kingdom of Holland is annexed to French Empire
1815	Battle of Waterloo; Belgium is united with the Netherlands in a joint kingdom under King William I
1830	Belgian revolution
1830–31	Sporadic hostilities with the Belgians
1839	Belgian independence recognized; first railway opens

Building the Modern Nation-State

1840	King William I abdicates
1840–49	King William II reigns
1848	William II accepts democratic constitution; liberals rule under Johan Rudolf Thorbecke
1853	Roman Catholic hierarchy is restored; protests lead to fall of liberal government
1858	Slavery abolished in Dutch East Indies
1863	Slavery abolished in Dutch West Indies
1866	First trade unions formed
1876	Opening of the North Sea Canal between Amsterdam and IJmuiden
1878–84	Political parties emerge

1895	First factory safety act
1899	Permanent Court of Arbitration founded at The Hague
1901	First compulsory education act
1903	Railway strike

Neutrality, Depression, and World War

1914–18	World War I; the Netherlands remains neutral
1917	Universal manhood suffrage; proportional representation introduced; financial equality for nondenominational public primary and secondary schools and religious schools
1918	Communist Party founded
1919	Female suffrage granted
1920	The Netherlands joins the League of Nations
1928	Olympic Games held in Amsterdam
1932	Enclosing dike completed
1933–39	Great Depression
1940	May 10: The Netherlands invaded by Nazi Germany; May 13: Government goes into exile in Britain
1941	February strike over Nazi anti-Jewish measures
1942	Deportations of Jews, forced laborers, and others begin
1944–45	Hunger winter

Reconstruction and Rebirth after World War II

1945	Liberation; International Court of Justice established at The Hague; the Netherlands joins the United Nations (UN)
1947	Counterinsurgency campaign begins in the Dutch East Indies
1948	Benelux treaties enter into force
1948–80	Queen Juliana reigns
1949	Indonesia is granted independence; the Netherlands joins the North Atlantic Treaty Organization (NATO)
1953	Floods devastate southwest coastal areas; Delta Works begins

1957	The Netherlands signs the Treaty of Rome as a founding member of Euratom and the European Economic Community
1962	Benelux agreements on cross-border cooperation in judicial and criminal matters
1962–67	Welfare state put in place
1966	Public protests at Princess Beatrix's marriage to a German launches a period of widespread demonstrations
1967	Princess Beatrix gives birth to Willem-Alexander, the first male heir to the throne since Prince Alexander (1851–84), son of King William III
1975	Suriname is granted independence
1980	Queen Juliana retires and Beatrix succeeds to the throne
1982	Wassenaar Accords launch major changes in government financing and the social security system
1986	Flevoland becomes the 12th province
1992	The Netherlands signs the Maastricht Treaty creating the European Union
1994	"Purple" coalition governments come to power that include left-leaning (PvdA) and right-leaning (VVD) parties
1995	Major floods in the Netherlands; Dutch peacekeepers fail to resist penetration of UN safe haven at Srebrenica, Bosnia-Herzegovina, by Serbs, leading to massacre of Muslim men and boys
1999	Beemster polder named to UNESCO's World Heritage site list

The Netherlands in the Twenty-First Century: The Triumphs and Trials of a Tolerant Society

2000	Euthanasia legalized
2001	Same-sex weddings begin
2002	The euro replaced the guilder as the official currency; Pim Fortuyn is assassinated; Christian Democrats under Jan Peter Balkenende replace Labor Party as leading party in government.

2003	KLM Royal Dutch Airlines and Air France merge to form Air France–KLM; Dutch troops sent to Iraq; avian flu outbreak compels government to destroy 30.7 million birds
2004	Filmmaker Theo van Gogh is murdered
2006	Immigration regulations are tightened; Christian Democrats under Jan Peter Balkenende remain largest parliamentary party, but in November elections center and center-left parties replace right-leaning parties in the coalition government
2007	Balkenende forms fourth government with a coalition of CDA, PvdA, and Christian Union parties

Appendix 4

Bibliography

Anon. *A Description of Holland; or, The Present State of the United Provinces. Wherein Is Contained a Particular Account of the Hague, and all the Principal Cities and Towns of the Republic . . . of the Manner and Customs of the Dutch, Their Constitution, etc. etc.* London: n.p., 1743.

Barbour, Violet. *Capitalism in Amsterdam in the Seventeenth Century.* Baltimore: Johns Hopkins University Press, 1950.

Barlow's Journal of His Life at Sea in King's Ships, East and West Indiamen and Other Merchantmen from 1659 to 1703. Edited by Basil Lubbock. 2 vols. London: n. p.

Boswell, James. *Boswell in Holland, 1763–1764, Including His Correspondence with Belle de Zuylen (or Zélide).* Edited by Frederick A. Pottle. New York: McGraw Hill, 1952.

Boxer, C. R., trans. and ed. *The Journal of Maarten Harpertszoon Tromp, Anno 1639.* Cambridge: Cambridge University Press, 1930.

Čapek, Karel. *Letters from Holland.* Translated by Paul Selver. London: Faber and Faber, 1933.

Carr, William. *An Accurate Description of the United Netherlands.* London: n.p., 1691.

Dash, Mike. *Tulipomania: The Story of the World's Most Coveted Flower and the Extraordinary Passions It Aroused.* New York: Crown Publishers, 1999.

Drees, W. *Herinneringen en opvattingen.* Naarden, Netherlands: Strengholt, 1983.

Ellis, G. *History of the Late Revolution in the Dutch Republic.* London: n.p., 1789.

Eyck, F. Gunther. *The Benelux Countries: An Historical Survey.* Princeton, N.J.: Van Nostrand, 1959.

Frank, Anne. *The Diary of a Young Girl: The Definitive Edition.* Edited by Otto H. Frank and Mirjam Pressler. Translated by Susan Masotty. New York: Doubleday, 1995.

Gordon, Pryse Lockhart. *Belgium and Holland: With a Sketch of the Revolution in the Year 1830*. London: Smith, Elder, 1834.

Grattan, Thomas Colley. *Holland: The History of the Netherlands*. New York: Peter Fenelon Collier, 1899.

Haley, K. H. D. *The Dutch in the Seventeenth Century*. London: Thames and Hudson, 1972.

Hickey, William. *Memoirs of William Hickey, 1749–1809*. Edited by Albert Spencer. 4 vols. New York: Knopf, 1923–25.

Hirschfeld, Hans Max. *Herinneringen uit de jaren 1933–1939*. Amsterdam: Elsevier, 1959.

Howell, James. *Epistolae Ho-Elianae. Familiar Letters Domestic and Foreign*. Aberdeen: F. Douglass and W. Murray, 1753.

Jacobs, Aletta. *Memories: My Life as an International Leader in Health, Suffrage and Peace*. Translated by Annie Wright. New York: Feminist Press of the City of New York, 1996.

James, J. Franklin, ed. *Narratives of New Netherland, 1609–1664*. New York: C. Scribner's Sons, 1909.

Kossman, E. H. *De lage landen, 1780–1980: Anderhalve eeuw Nederland en België*. 2 vols. Amsterdam: Elsevier, 1986.

Meijer, R. P. *Literature of the Low Countries*. Assen, Netherlands: Van Gorcum, 1971.

Montias, John M., and John Loughman. *Private and Public Spaces: Works of Art in Seventeenth-Century Dutch Houses*. Zwolle: Waanders B. V., 2001.

Multatuli. *Max Havelaar, Or, the Coffee Auctions of the Dutch Trading Company*. Translated by Roy Edwards. Amherst: University of Massachusetts Press, 1982.

Mundy, Peter. *The Travels of Peter Mundy, 1597–1667*. Edited by John Keast. Redruth, England: Dyllansow Truran, 1984.

Onslow, Burrish. *Batavia Illustrata: Or, a View of the Policy and Commerce of the United Provinces, Particularly of Holland, with an Enquiry into the Alliances of the States General with the Emperor, France, Spain, and Great Britain*. London: n.p., 1728.

Parival, Jean de. *Les délices de la Holland: En deux parties*. Amsterdam: Chez Henri Wetstein, 1697.

Pannekoek, Anton. *Herinneringen uit de arbeidersbeweging*. Amsterdam: Van Gennep, 1982.

Quack, Hendrik P. G. *Herinneringen uit de levensjaren*. Nijmegen: Socialistische Uitgeverij, 1977.

Spinoza, Benedictus de. *Tractatus Theologico-politicus: A Theological and Political Treatise, Showing under a Series of Heads That Freedom of Thought and of Discussion May Not Only Be Granted with Safety to Religion and the Peace of the State, but Cannot Be Denied without Danger to Both the Public Peace and True Piety.* Translated by Robert Willis. London: Trübner and Co., 1868.

Stokes, Anton Phelps. *Church and State in the United States.* Vol. 1. New York: Harper and Brothers, 1950.

Temple, William Sir. *Observations upon the United Provinces of the Netherlands.* Edited by Sir George Clark. Oxford: Clarendon Press, 1972.

Thomas à Kempis. *The Imitation of Christ.* Translated by Edgar Daplyn. New York: Sheed and Ward, 1950.

Thunberg, Carl Pieter. *Travels in Europe, Africa and Asia. Performed between the Years 1770 and 1779.* 4 vols. London: n.p., 1795.

Veryard, Ellis. *An Account of Divers Choice Remarks Taken in a Journey through the Low Countries, France, Italy and Part of Spain.* London: n.p., 1701.

Zunthor, Paul. *Daily Life in Rembrandt's Holland.* Translated by Simon W. Taylor. London: Weidenfeld and Nicolson, 1962.

Appendix 5

Suggested Reading

General Works

Abdeweg, Rudy, and Galen A. Irwin. *Dutch Government and Politics.* New York: St. Martin's Press, 1993.

Arblaster, Paul. *A History of the Low Countries.* Basingstoke, England: Palgrave Macmillan, 2006.

Barzini, Luigi. *The Europeans.* New York: Simon and Schuster, 1983.

Beek, Leo. *Dutch Pioneers of Science.* Assen, Netherlands: Van Gorcum, 1985.

Blei, Karel. *The Netherlands Reformed Church, 1571–2005.* Translated by Allan J. Janssen. Grand Rapids, Mich.: W. B. Eerdmans, 2006.

Blom, J. C. H., and E. Lamberts, eds. *History of the Low Countries.* Translated by C. Kennedy. Oxford: Oxford University Press, 1999.

Boxer, C. R. *Dutch Merchants and Mariners in Asia, 1602–1795.* London: Variorum Reprints, 1988.

Cotterell, Geoffrey. *Amsterdam: The Life of a City.* Boston: Little, Brown and Company, 1972.

Davids, Karel, ed. *The Dutch Republic in European Perspective.* Cambridge: Cambridge University Press, 1996.

Devoldere, Luc. *The Low Countries: Arts and Society in Flanders and the Netherlands.* Rekkem, Belgium: Stichting Ons Erfdeel, 2004.

Donaldson, Bruce C. *Dutch: A Linguistic History of Holland and Belgium.* Leiden: Martinus Nijhoff, 1983.

Emmer, P. C. *The Dutch in the Atlantic Economy, 1580–1880: Trade, Slavery and Emancipation.* London: Ashgate, 1998.

Fokkema, Douwe Wessel, and Frans Grijzenhout, eds. *Dutch Culture in a European Perspective.* Vol. 5. *Accounting for the Past: 1650–2000.* Basingstoke, England: Palgrave Macmillan, 2005.

Fourest, Henry-Pierre. *Delftware.* London: Thames and Hudson, 1980.

Gaastra, Femme S. *The Dutch East India Company: Expansion and Decline.* Zutphen, Netherlands: Walburg Pers, 2003.

Geyl, Pieter. *History of the Dutch-Speaking Peoples, 1555–1648.* London: Phoenix Press, 2001.

Goedegebuure, Jaap. *Contemporary Fiction of the Low Countries.* Rekkem, Belgium: Stichting Ons Erfdeel, 1993.

Harinck, George, and Hans Krabbendam, eds. *Amsterdam–New York: Transatlantic Identities and Urban Identities since 1653.* Amsterdam: VU Uitgeverij, 2005.

Horst, Han van der. *The Low Sky: Understanding the Dutch.* The Hague: Nuffic, 1996.

Huussen, Arend H., Jr. *Historical Dictionary of the Netherlands.* Lanham, Md.: Scarecrow Press, 1998.

Israel, Jonathan I. *The Dutch Republic: Its Rise, Greatness and Fall, 1477–1806.* Oxford: Clarendon Press, 1995.

Jacobs, E. M. *In Pursuit of Pepper and Tea: The Story of the Dutch East India Company.* Zutphen, Netherlands: Walburg Pers, 1991.

Kistemaker, Renée. *Amsterdam: The Golden Age, 1275–1795.* Translated by Paul Foulkes. New York: Abbeville Press, 1983.

Lucas, Henry S. *Netherlanders in America: Dutch Immigration to the United States and Canada, 1789–1950.* Grand Rapids, Mich.: W. B. Eerdmans, 1989.

Mak, Geert. *Amsterdam: A Brief Life of the City.* Translated by Phillip Bom. London: Harvill Press, 1999.

Meijer, Reinder. *Literature of the Low Countries: A Short History of Dutch Literature in the Netherlands and Belgium.* The Hague: Martinus Nijhoff, 1978.

Moore, Bob, and Henk van Nierop. *Twentieth-Century Mass Society in Britain and the Netherlands.* Oxford: Berg Publishers, 2006.

Muller, Sheila D. *Dutch Art: An Encyclopedia.* New York: Garland, 1997.

Netherlands Ministry of Foreign Affairs. *A Concise History of the Netherlands.* URL: http://www.history-netherlands.nl. Accessed March 24, 2007.

Oostindie, Gert. *Paradise Overseas. The Dutch Caribbean: Colonialism and Its Transatlantic Legacies.* Oxford: Macmillan Caribbean, 2005.

Postma, Johannes Menne. *The Dutch in the Atlantic Slave Trade, 1600–1815.* Cambridge: Cambridge University Press, 1990.

Price, J. L. *Dutch Society, 1588–1713.* New York: Longman, 2000.

Rowen, Herbert H. *The Princes of Orange: The Stadholders in the Dutch Republic.* Cambridge: Cambridge University Press, 1988.

Shetter, William Z. *The Pillars of Society: Six Centuries of Civilization in the Netherlands*. 2d rev. ed. Utrecht: Netherlands Centrum Buitenlanders, 1997.

Slive, Seymour. *Dutch Painting 1600–1800*. New Haven, Conn.: Yale University Press, 1995.

Smit, Pamela, and J. W. Smit. *The Netherlands: A Chronology and Fact Book*. Dobbs Ferry, N.Y.: Oceana, 1973.

Steenbrink, Karel A. *Dutch Colonialism and Indonesian Islam: Contacts and Conflicts, 1596–1950*. Amsterdam: Rodopi, 1993.

Taylor, Jean. *The Social World of Batavia: European and Eurasian in Dutch Asia*. Madison: University of Wisconsin Press, 1983.

t'Hart, Marjolein, Joost Jonker, and Jan Luiten van Zanden, eds. *A Financial History of the Netherlands*. Cambridge: Cambridge University Press, 1997.

Threlfall, Tim. *Piet Mondrian: His Life's Work and Evolution, 1872 to 1944*. New York: Garland, 1988.

Vandenbosch, Amry J. *Dutch Foreign Policy since 1815: A Study in Small Power Politics*. The Hague: Martinus Nijhoff, 1959.

Van Nierop, Henk F. K. *The Nobility of Holland: From Knights to Regents, 1500–1650*. Cambridge: Cambridge University Press, 1993.

Van Zanden, J. L. *The Rise and Decline of Holland's Economy*. Manchester: Manchester University Press, 1993.

Vreis, Jan de, and Ad ven der Woude. *The First Modern Economy: Success, Failure, and Perseverance of the Dutch Economy, 1500–1815*. Cambridge: Cambridge University Press, 1997.

Vries, Johan de. *The Netherlands Economy in the Twentieth Century: An Examination of the Most Characteristic Features in the Period 1900–1970*. Assen, Netherlands: Van Gorcum, 1978.

Weil, Gordon L. *The Benelux Nations: The Politics of Small-Country Democracies*. New York: Holt, Rinehart and Winston, 1970.

Wels, C. B. *Aloofness and Neutrality: Studies on Dutch Foreign Relations and Policy-Making Institutions*. Utrecht: H and S, 1982.

Wesseling, H. L. *Imperialism and Colonialism: Essays on the History of European Expansion*. Westport, Conn.: Greenwood Press, 1997.

White, Colin, and Laurie Boucke. *The Undutchables. An Observation of the Netherlands: Its Culture and Its Inhabitants*. 3rd ed. Montrose, Calif.: White Boucke Publishing, 1993.

Wolf, Manfred, ed. *Amsterdam*. San Francisco: Whereabouts Press, 2001.

Yarak, Larry W. *Asante and the Dutch, 1744–1873*. Oxford: Clarendon Press, 1990.

From Early Settlements to Frankish Rule (Prehistory–c. 1000)

Drinkwater, John F. *Roman Gaul: The Three Provinces, 58 B.C.–A.D. 260.* London: Croom Helm, 1983.

Hodder, Ian. *The Domestication of Europe: Structure and Contingency in Neolithic Societies.* Cambridge: Cambridge University Press, 1990.

Kooijmans, L. P. Louwe, P. W. van den Broeke, H. Fokkens, and A. L. van Gijn. *The Prehistory of the Netherlands.* 2 vols. Amsterdam: Amsterdam University Press, 2005.

Lambert, Audrey. M. *The Making of the Dutch Landscape: An Historical Geography of the Netherlands.* New York: Seminar Press, 1971.

Molen, J. van der, and B. van Dijck. "The Evolution of the Dutch and Belgian Coasts and the Role of Sand Supply from the North Sea." *Global and Planetary Change* 27 (2000): 223–244.

Tacitus. *Great Books of the Western World.* Vol. 15. Chicago: Encyclopedia Britannica, 1952.

Wrightman, Edith Mary. *Gallia Belgica.* London: B. T. Batsford, 1985.

Zvelebil, Marek, ed. *Hunters in Transition: Mesolithic Societies of Temperate Eurasia and Their Transition to Farming.* Cambridge: Cambridge University Press, 1986.

Political Strife and the Rise of Urban Life (c. 1000–1515)

Colledge, E., ed. *Reynard the Fox and Other Medieval Netherlands Secular Literature.* Translated by Adriaan J. Barnouw. Leiden: A. W. Sijthoff, 1967.

Nijsten, Gerard. *In the Shadow of Burgundy: The Court of Guelders in the Late Middle Ages.* Translated by Tanis Guest. Cambridge: Cambridge University Press, 2004.

Oostrom, Frits Pieter van. *Court and Culture: Dutch Literature, 1350–1450.* Translated by Arnold Pomerans. Berkeley: University of California Press, 1992.

Prevenier, Walter, and Wim Blockmans. *The Burgundian Netherlands.* Cambridge: Cambridge University Press, 1986.

Verhulst, Adriaan. *The Rise of Cities in Northwest Europe.* Cambridge: Cambridge University Press, 1999.

Zijl, Theodore van. *Geert Groote: Ascetic and Reformer (1340–1384).* Washington, D.C.: Catholic University of America Press, 1963.

Wars of Religion and Emancipation (1515–1609)

Anonymous. *The Dutch Revolt: A Chronicle of the First Ten Years by an Anonymous Nun of s'Hertogenbosch*. Translated and annotated by Paul Arblaster. Oxford: Oxford University Press, 2001.

Duke, Alastair C. *Reformation and Revolt in the Low Countries*. London: Hambleton Press, 1990.

Gelderen, Martin van. *The Political Thought of the Dutch Revolt, 1555–1590*. Cambridge: Cambridge University Press, 1992.

Hall, Gordon L. *William, Father of the Netherlands*. New York: Rand McNally, 1969.

Jardine, Lisa. *The Awful End of Prince William the Silent: The First Assassination of a Head of State with a Handgun*. London: HarperCollins, 2005.

Keeney, William E. *The Development of Dutch Anabaptist Thought and Practice from 1539–1564*. Nieuwkoop, Netherlands: B. de Graaf, 1968.

Molen, R. L. de. *The Spirituality of Erasmus of Rotterdam*. Nieuwkoop, Netherlands: De Graaf, 1987.

Oosterhoff, F. G. *Leicester and the Netherlands, 1586–1587*. Utrecht: HES, 1988.

Parker, Geoffrey. *The Dutch Revolt*. Rev. ed. New York: Penguin, 2002.

Robb, Nesca A. *William of Orange*. 2 vols. London: Heinemann, 1962, 1966.

te Brake, Wayne Ph. *Regents and Rebels*. Cambridge, Mass.: Harvard University Press, 1989.

Tracy, James D. *Holland under Habsburg Rule, 1506–1566: The Formation of a Body Politic*. Berkeley: University of California Press, 1990.

Van Gelderen, Martin. *The Political Thought of the Dutch Revolt, 1555–1590*. Cambridge: Cambridge University Press, 1992.

Voolstra, Sjouka. *Menno Simons: His Image and Message*. North Newton, Kans.: Bethel College, 1996.

Wee, Herman van der. *The Low Countries in the Early Modern World*. Translated by Lizabeth Fackelman. Aldershot, England: Variorum, 1993.

Resplendent Republic (1609–1702)

Anthonisz, Richard G. *The Dutch in Ceylon*. New Delhi: Asian Educational Services, 2003.

Bangs, Carl D. *Arminius: A Study in the Dutch Reformation*. Grand Rapids, Mich.: F. Asbury Press, 1985.

Bogaert, Harmen Meyndertsz van den. *A Journey into Mohawk and Oneida Country, 1634–1635*. Translated and edited by Charles T. Gehring and William A. Starna. Syracuse, N.Y.: Syracuse University Press, 1988.

Boxer, Charles Ralph. *The Dutch in Brazil, 1624–54*. Oxford: Clarendon Press, 1957.

Brown, Christopher. *Scenes of Everyday Life: Dutch Genre Painting of the Seventeenth Century*. London: Faber and Faber, 1984.

Bruijn, Jaap R. *The Dutch Navy of the Seventeenth and Eighteenth Centuries*. Columbia: University of South Carolina Press, 1993.

Dash, Mike. *Tulipomania: The Story of the World's Most Coveted Flower and the Extraordinary Passions It Aroused*. New York: Crown Publishers, 1999.

———. *Batavia's Graveyard: The True Story of the Mad Heretic Who Led History's Bloodiest Mutiny*. London: Weidenfeld and Nicolson, 2002.

Davids, Karel, and Jan Lucassen. *A Miracle Mirrored: The Dutch Republic in European Perspective*. Cambridge: Cambridge University Press, 1995.

De Vries, Jan. *The Dutch Rural Economy in the Golden Age*. New Haven, Conn.: Yale University Press, 1974.

Gellinek, Christian. *Hugo Grotius*. Boston: Twayne, 1983.

Geyl, Pieter. *The Netherlands in the Seventeenth Century*. Vol.1. New York: Barnes and Noble, 1964.

Goodfriend, Joyce D., ed. *Revisiting New Netherland: Perspectives on Early Dutch America*. Leiden: Brill, 2005.

Goslinga, Cornelis Ch. *The Dutch in the Caribbean and on the Wild Coast, 1580–1680*. Assen, Netherlands: Van Gorcum, 1971.

Hainsworth, David R. *The Anglo-Dutch Naval Wars 1652–1674*. Stroud, Gloucestershire, England: Sutton, 1998.

Harline, C. E. *Pamphlets, Printing, and Political Culture in the Early Dutch Republic*. The Hague: Martinus Nijhoff, 1987.

Hsia, R. Po-Chia, and Henk van Nierop, eds. *Calvinism and Religious Toleration in the Dutch Golden Age*. Cambridge: Cambridge University Press, 2002.

Israel, Jonathan I. *The Dutch Republic and the Hispanic World*. Oxford: Clarendon, 1982.

Juet, Robert. *Juet's Journal. The Voyage of the Half Moon from 4 April to 7 November 1609*. Edited by Robert M. Lunny. Newark: New Jersey Historical Society, 1959.

Massarella, Derek. *A World Elsewhere: Europe's Encounter with Japan in the Sixteenth and Seventeenth Centuries*. New Haven, Conn.: Yale University Press.

Mee, Charles L. *Rembrandt's Portrait: A Biography.* New York: Simon and Schuster, 1988.

Mulder, W. Z. *Hollanders in Hirado, 1597–1641.* Haarlem, Netherlands: Fibula/Van Dishoeck, 1985.

Nash, John M. *The Age of Rembrandt and Vermeer: Dutch Painting in the Seventeenth Century.* New York: Holt, Rinehart and Winston, 1972.

North, Michael. *Art and Commerce in the Dutch Golden Age.* New Haven, Conn.: Yale University Press, 1997.

Ouwinga, Marin Thomas. "The Dutch Contribution to the European Knowledge of Africa in the Seventeenth Century, 1595–1725." M.A. thesis. Indiana University, 1975.

Price, J. L. *The Dutch Republic in the Seventeenth Century.* New York: St. Martin's Press, 1998.

Raven Hart, R., ed. *Cape of Good Hope, 1652–1702: The First Fifty Years of Dutch Colonisation as Seen by Callers.* 2 vols. Cape Town: Balkema, 1979.

Rink, Oliver A. *Holland on the Hudson: An Economic and Social History of Dutch New York.* Ithaca, N.Y.: Cornell University Press, 1986.

Rothschild, Nan A. *Colonial Encounters in a Native American Landscape: The Spanish and Dutch in North America.* Washington, D.C.: Smithsonian Books, 2003.

Schama, Simon. *The Embarrassment of Riches: An Interpretation of Dutch Culture in the Golden Age.* New York: Alfred A. Knopf, 1987.

———. *Rembrandt's Eyes.* New York: Alfred A. Knopf, 1999.

Schilder, Günter. *Australia Unveiled: The Share of the Dutch Navigators in the Discovery of Australia.* Translated by Olaf Richter. Amsterdam: Theatrum Orbis Terrarun, 1976.

Shomette, Donald. *Raid on America: The Dutch Naval Campaign in 1672–1674.* Columbia: University of South Carolina Press, 1988.

Shorto, Russell. *The Island at the Center of the World: The Epic Story of Dutch Manhattan and the Forgotten Colony That Shaped America.* New York: Doubleday, 2004.

Slot, B. J. *Abel Tasman and the Discovery of New Zealand.* Amsterdam: Cramwinckel, 1992.

Snelders, Stephen. *The Devil's Anarchy: The Sea Robberies of the Most Famous Pirate Claes G. Compaen, and the Very Remarkable Travels of Jan Erasmus Reyning, Buccaneer.* Brooklyn, N.Y.: Automedia, 2005.

Sonnino, Paul. *Louis XIV and the Origins of the Dutch War.* Cambridge: Cambridge University Press, 1988.

Steadman, Philip. *Vermeer's Camera: Uncovering the Truth behind the Masterpieces.* Oxford: Oxford University Press, 2001.

Svetlana, Alpers. *The Art of Describing: Dutch Art in the Seventeenth Century.* Chicago: University of Chicago Press, 1983.
Van Deursen, Arie Theodorus. *Plain Lives in the Golden Age: Popular Culture, Religion, and Society in Seventeenth-Century Holland.* Cambridge: Cambridge University Press, 1991.
Verbeek, Theo. *Descartes and the Dutch; Early Reactions to Cartesian Philosophy, 1637–1650.* Carbondale: Southern Illinois University Press, 1992.
Vere, Francis. *Salt in Their Blood: The Lives of the Famous Dutch Admirals.* London: Cassell, 1955.
Yount, Lisa. *Antoni van Leeuwenhoek: First to See Microscope's Life.* Springfield, N.J.: Enslow Publishers, 1992.
Zee, Henri, and Barbara van der Zee. *A Sweet and Alien Land: The Story of Dutch New York.* New York: Viking Press, 1978.

Dynamo in Decline (1702–1780)

Anderson, Matthew S. *The War of the Austrian Succession, 1740–1748.* London: Longman, 1995.
Dunthorne, H. *The Maritime Powers, 1721–1740: A Study of Anglo-Dutch Relations in the Age of Walpole.* New York: Garland, 1986.
Goslinga, Cornelis C. *The Dutch in the Caribbean and the Guianas, 1680–1791.* Assen, Netherlands: Van Gorcum, 1985.
Jacob, Margaret C., and Wijnand W. Mijnhardt, eds. *The Dutch Republic in the Eighteenth Century: Decline, Enlightenment, and Revolution.* Ithaca, N.Y.: Cornell University Press, 1992.
Schulte Nordholt, J. W. *The Dutch Republic and American Independence.* Translated by H. H. Rowen. Chapel Hill: University of North Carolina Press, 1982.

From Republic to Empire to Kingdom (1780–1839)

Kloek, Joost, and Wijnand W. Mijnhardt, eds. *Dutch Culture in a European Perspective.* Vol. 2. *1800: Blueprints for a National Community.* Basingstoke, England: Palgrave Macmillan, 2004.
Michman, Jozeph. *The History of Dutch Jewry during the Emancipation Period, 1787–1814: Gothic Turrets on a Corinthian Building.* Amsterdam: Amsterdam University Press, 1995.
Plemp van Duiveland, Leonard Jan. *William Frederick, King of the Netherlands.* Amsterdam: Nederlandsche Handel-Maatschaapij, 1949.
Schama, Simon. *Patriots and Liberators: Revolution in the Netherlands, 1780–1813.* New York: Alfred A. Knopf, 1977.

Building the Modern Nation-State (1839–1914)

Bank, Jan, and Maartine van Buurman, eds. *Dutch Culture in a European Perspective.* Vol. 3. *1900: The Age of Bourgeois Culture.* Basingstoke, England: Palgrave Macmillan, 2004.

Bouma, Hendrik. *Secession, Doleantie, and Union 1834–1892.* Translated by Theodore Plantinga. Pella, Iowa: Inheritance Publications, 1995.

Elson, Robert E. *Village Java under the Cultivation System, 1830–1870.* Sydney: Asian Studies Association of Australia, 1994.

Gogh, Vincent van. *The Letters of Vincent van Gogh to His Brother Theo and Others, 1872–1890.* London: Constable, 2003.

Jackman, Sidney W., and Hella Haasse, eds. *A Stranger in The Hague: The Letters of Queen Sophie of the Netherlands to Lady Malet, 1842–1877.* Durham, N.C.: Duke University Press, 1989.

Jacobs, Aletta. *Memoirs: My Life as an International Leader in Health, Suffrage, and Peace.* Edited by Harriet Feinberg. Translated by Annie Wright. New York: Feminist Press, 1996.

Mokyr, J. *Industrialization in the Low Countries, 1795–1850.* New Haven, Conn.: Yale University Press, 1976.

Multatuli. *Max Havelaar, Or, The Coffee Auctions of the Dutch Trading Company.* Translated by Roy Edwards. Amherst: University of Massachusetts Press, 1982.

Thomson, Belinda. *Van Gogh.* Chicago: Art Institute of Chicago, 2001.

Whitely, Linda. *Van Gogh: Life and Works.* London: Cassell, 2000.

Wintle, Michael J. *Pillars of Piety: Religion in the Netherlands in the Nineteenth Century, 1813–1901.* Hull, England: University Press, 1987.

Neutrality, Depression, and World War (1914–1945)

Anne Frank Remembered. Culver City, Calif. Columbia Tri-Star Home Video, 1996.

De Jons, Louis. *The Netherlands and Nazi Germany.* Cambridge, Mass.: Harvard University Press, 1990.

Frank, Anne. *The Diary of a Young Girl: The Definitive Edition.* Edited by Otto H. Frank and Mirjam Pressler. Translated by Susan Masotty. New York: Doubleday, 1995.

Fuykschot, Cornelia. *Hunger in Holland: Life during the Nazi Occupation.* Amherst, N.Y.: Prometheus Books, 1995.

Giskes, H. J. *London Calling Northpole.* London: William Kimber, 1953.

Gouda, Frances. *Dutch Culture Overseas: Colonial Practice in the Netherlands Indies, 1900–1942.* Amsterdam: Amsterdam University Press, 1995.

Hibbert, Christopher. *The Battle of Arnhem*. London: B. T. Batsford, 1962.

Koskimaki, George E. *Hell's Highway: Chronicle of the 101st Airborne Division in the Holland Campaign, September–November 1944*. Havertown, Pa.: Casemate, 2003.

Moore, Bob. *Victims and Survivors: The Nazi Persecution of the Jews in the Netherlands, 1940–1945*. London: Arnold, 1997.

Ryan, Cornelius. *A Bridge Too Far*. London: Hamish Hamilton, 1974.

Tuyll van Scrooskerken, Hubert P. van. *The Netherlands and World War I: Espionage, Diplomacy and Survival*. Leiden: Brill, 2001.

van der Zee, Henri A. *The Hunger Winter: Occupied Holland 1944–45*. London: J. Norman and Hobhouse, 1982.

Womack, Torn. *The Dutch Naval Air Force against Japan: The Defense of the Netherlands East Indies, 1941–1942*. Jefferson, N.C.: McFarland, 2006.

Reconstruction and Rebirth after World War II (1945–2000)

Amersfoort, Hans van. *Immigration and Formation of Minority Groups: The Dutch Experience, 1945–1875*. Translated by R. Lyng. Cambridge: Cambridge University Press, 1982.

Cox, Robert H. *The Development of the Dutch Welfare State: From Workers' Insurance to Universal Entitlement*. Pittsburgh: University of Pittsburgh Press, 1993.

Dutt, Ashok K., and Frank J. Costa, eds. *Public Planning in the Netherlands: Perspectives and Change since the Second World War*. Oxford: Oxford University Press, 1985.

Elteren, Mel van. *Imaging America: Dutch Youth and Its Sense of Place*. Tilburg, Netherlands: Tilburg University Press, 1994.

Grimal, Henri. *Decolonization: The British, French, Dutch, and Belgian Empires, 1919–1963*. Translated by Stephen De Vos. Boulder, Colo.: Westview, 1978.

Hartog, Jan de. *The Little Ark*. New York: Harper and Brothers, 1953.

Klandermans, Bert, and Nonna Mayer, eds. *Extreme Right Activists in Europe: Through the Magnifying Glass*. London: Routledge, 2006.

Kroes, Rob. *Soldiers and Students: A Study of Right- and Left-Wing Radicals*. London: Routledge and Kegan Paul, 1975.

Megens, Ine. *American Aid to NATO Allies in the 1950s: The Dutch Case*. Amsterdam: Thesis Publishers, 1994.

Oostindie, Gert. *Decolonising the Caribbean: Dutch Policies in a Comparative Perspective*. Amsterdam: Amsterdam University Press, 2003.

Penders, Christian L. M. *The West New Guinea Debacle: Dutch Decolonization and Indonesia, 1945–1962.* Honolulu: University of Hawai'i Press, 2002.

Schendelen, M. P. C. M. van, ed. *Consociationalism, Pillarization and Conflict-Management in the Low Countries.* Meppel, Netherlands: Boom, 1984.

Schuyt, Klees, and Ed Taverne, eds. *Dutch Culture in a European Perspective.* Vol. 4. *1950: Prosperity and Welfare.* Basingstoke, England: Palgrave Macmillan, 2004.

Visser, Jelle. *A Dutch Miracle: Job Growth, Welfare Reform and Corporatism in the Netherlands.* Amsterdam: Amsterdam University Press, 1997.

Walters, Menno, and Peter Coffer, eds. *The Netherlands and EC Membership Evaluated.* London: Pinter, 1990.

The Netherlands in the Twenty-first Century: The Triumphs and Trials of a Tolerant Society

Buruma, Ian. *Murder in Amsterdam: The Death of Theo van Gogh and the Limits of Tolerance.* New York: Penguin Press, 2006.

Delsen, Lei. *Exit Polder Model? Socioeconomic Change in the Netherlands.* Westport, Conn.: Praeger, 2002.

Hirsi Ali, Ayaan. *The Caged Virgin: An Emancipation Proclamation for Women and Islam.* New York: Free Press, 2006.

INDEX

Note: **Boldface** page numbers indicate primary discussion of a topic. Page numbers in *italic* indicate illustrations. The letters *c, m,* and *t* indicate chronology, maps, and tables, respectively.